True Stories
of the SBS

Other books by Robin Hunter

TRUE STORIES OF THE SAS
TRUE STORIES OF THE
FOREIGN LEGION

TRUE STORIES
OF THE SBS

A history of Canoe Raiding
and Underwater Warfare

ROBIN HUNTER

First published in Great Britain by
Virgin Publishing
Thames Wharf Studios
Rainville Road
London W6 9HT

A catalogue record for this book is available from the
British Library.

ISBN 0 7535 0267 4

Typeset by T.W. Typesetting, Plymouth, Devon
Printed and bound in Great Britain by
Mackays of Chatham PLC

CONTENTS

Acknowledgements
Introduction: A Small Adventure with the SBS   1

1   What is the SBS?   7
2   The Folboat Section, 1941–42   20
3   Enter the Frogmen, 1941–43   39
4   SBS Equipment, Techniques and Training   52
5   2 SBS and 101 Troop in North Africa, 1942–43   70
6   Enter the Royal Marines, 1942   86
7   Operation *Frankton*, The Cockleshell Heroes, December 1942   94
8   The Fate of *Frankton*, 1942–43   108
9   SBS and SSRF, Western Europe, 1942–43   121
10   Chariot Operations, 1942–44   133
11   The End of the *Tirpitz*, September 1943   143
12   The SBS in the Aegean, 1942–43   153
13   The SBS in the Dodecanese, Greece and Italy, 1943–45   165
14   D-Day and After, 1944–45   187
15   Canoes and X-craft in the Far East, 1945   200
16   The SBS in the Post-War World, 1945–91   220

Select Bibliography   246

DEDICATION

The veterans of the SBS have requested that
their accounts are dedicated to the men of the
Submarine Service, Royal Navy, who took
great risks, carrying them to their tasks, and to
bring them home again

ACKNOWLEDGEMENTS

A great many men helped with this book and my thanks go therefore to: Lieutenant Colonel Godfrey Courtney of the Army Commandos; Stan Weatherall of 101 Troop, 6 Commando and the Small Scale Raiding Force; Ken Richardson of 40 Commando; Jim Booth of COPP; in Australia to Mike Nibbs, editor of *Strike Swiftly*, the journal of the Australian Commandos, for permission to use extracts from contributions to that excellent Special Forces magazine; Captain Tony Newing RM, editor of the *Globe and Laurel*, the journal of the Royal Marines, for all his help, contacts and access to his archives; in the USA, to Matthew Kaye of the US Scouts and Raiders; the SEALS, Camp McDill, Tampa, Florida.

Thanks also to Major General Julian Thompson CB OBE; Colonel Mike Storrie RM, former CO of the Royal Marines base at Poole, Dorset; Lieutenant Colonel Peter 'Pug' Davis DSC RM, commander of the first post-war SBS unit, for a great deal of help and advice and for rounding up a houseful of former SBS men, in order that I might 'tell a good tale and get my facts right' – I have tried and I hope I have succeeded; Matthew Little of the Royal Marines Museum, Eastney, Portsmouth; the Royal Marines Historical Society; the Submarine Museum, Gosport, Hampshire; the National Army Museum and the Imperial War Museum, London; Terry Brown of 42

Commando, and some of our old SBS mates, like 'Mac' Hine and 'Mick' Byrne, for good times in the RMFVR and on the Devizes to Westminster Canoe Race.

Finally, my thanks to a number of gentlemen in the SBS and SAS who gave me a great deal of help without giving away any secrets – 'No names, no pack drill', as we used to say in the dear old days before everyone went mysterious, but I don't want to leave them out. This is their story, and I hope they enjoy it.

Robin Hunter
Wiltshire, 1998.

INTRODUCTION
A SMALL ADVENTURE
WITH THE SBS

I did not serve in the SBS. In the 1950s and 1960s I served in the 3rd Commando Brigade, Royal Marines, and then in the Commando wing of what was then the RMFVR and is now the Royal Marines Reserve. In both units I met up with SBS people for, unlike the SAS Regiment, which recruits from the army at large, the SBS is drawn exclusively from the ranks of the Royal Marines and SBS personnel circulate in and out of the SBS – the Special Boat Service – to more regular posts and employment elsewhere in the Corps. The SBS have a definite and clearly defined role in support of Commando operations and it was quite normal for a Commando troop and an SBS team to work together on operations or in training, a practice that led me to the event I am about to describe, an event I have included because it illustrates that even in peacetime SBS training is not without risk.

This incident took place in the chilly winter seas off the south coast of England some thirty years ago, when I was young and good-looking and not over-burdened with caution. A joint SBS–Commando training exercise was in prospect, organised for his troop by my 'oppo', Sergeant Terry Brown, and, along with Corporal Derek 'Lou' Lucas, another willing lunatic, I had been asked to act as the enemy, or to be exact, the target, for the

Saturday-morning ambush. Lou and I duly drove down to Sussex in my car and then went up and down a road near Lewes, waiting to be ambushed by Terry Brown and his intrepid band of green-bereted warriors, who had reached this spot by paddling overnight down the local river, under the guidance of the SBS, and were supposed to be lying in wait.

Getting ambushed took some time, for the tripwire they had brought to trigger a device beside the road turned out to be too short. As Lou and I – always anxious to be helpful – drove past the appointed spot time and time again, Terry and his blokes were lurking behind the hedge, hastily removing their boot laces in order to extend the wire. They eventually succeeded and we drove into the ambush. There was a satisfying bang; Lou and I were duly overwhelmed and we all retired to the pub, well satisfied with the operation so far. Phase One of the weekend's exercise had been successfully completed.

Phase Two was a night canoe 'raid' on the shipping in Newhaven harbour where the SBS were to paddle about in the dark, marking ships, and we were to try to detect them. As far as I can remember this went all right. We prowled the quays – and heard nothing – and the SBS got their ration of excitement when a cross-Channel ferry suddenly sprang to life and surged out of the harbour exit, scattering their canoes as it swept past. We wrapped it up sometime after midnight, brewed a pot of tea, lay about telling lies for a couple of hours and slept on the floor of the local TA centre. Then came the dawn.

Dawn came fairly late, for this was January, but after breakfast on Sunday it was decided that we should all repair to the nearest beach for a little surfing and sea canoeing, because, as our SBS sergeant said generously, 'You blokes' – he meant Lou and me – 'have not yet had any fun.'

We loaded the canoes into a truck, drove to a steep shingle beach just east of Brighton, and met a problem. There was a hell of a sea running and great waves were dumping themselves on the beach and obscuring the horizon. There was also a keen wind blowing; the day was grey; and it all looked, well, uninviting.

However, the Royal Marines Commandos are not easily discouraged, and we decided to give it a go. For the next hour we attempted to get the canoes launched through the surf, only to find ourselves hurled back on to the beach, time and time again, by the waves. This was pretty tiring and it did not do the canoes much good, but it was quite funny. I still retain a vivid memory of Terry Brown, spouting sea water from every orifice, rising cursing from the foam just as a canoe, complete with paddlers and set in the midst of a wave like a fly in amber, came surging in behind and smashed him down on to the shingle. Laugh? Hilarious!

I might add that it was bloody cold, and our canoeing rig was tennis shoes, denim trousers, shirts and life jackets, none of which did much to keep the wind out, especially when we were soaking wet.

Eventually, I came up with the notion that the only way we were going to get off this damned beach was if we swam a canoe through the surf and got into it further out, where the sea was less violent. Since this was my idea I was the one who had to try it, so Lou and I duly leapt into the waves, each with the canoe in one hand and a double paddle in the other. Well, it worked ... after a few minutes of turmoil we found ourselves beyond the surf and swimming out to sea, clutching the canoe, the paddles, and spouting sea water. Once well away from the beach, we bailed out the water and climbed into the canoe, Lou first, into the rear cockpit, and myself into the bow. All this took some time, but eventually we were both on board and grasping the paddles; all we had to do now was turn the canoe and ride the waves back to the beach ... super! Next stop Hawaii.

We couldn't do it. Every time we attempted to turn across the waves the canoe turned over. We tried several times, turning over and repeating the bailing-out-the-water-and-getting-back-in process each time. The trouble was that the canoe would not steer. Eventually, I swam round to the stern of the canoe and discovered that the rudder was jammed fully across and, try as I would, I could not move it. It is not easy to exert leverage while swimming in freezing seas and it seemed that the only thing to do was to remove the rudder from its mounting and steer with the paddles. Then we found that we could not remove the rudder either; it must have been damaged one of those times when a wave flung it on to the beach and was now stuck. Bugger! I eventually managed to bend the blade straight, but we still turned over if we got across the waves.

Then Lou noticed another problem. We were now perhaps a quarter of a mile offshore and being carried steadily down the coast by the tide. Visibility is not good in a canoe and Lou could only see what was going on when we crested a wave, but he saw something up ahead he did not care for. When I hauled myself into the canoe again and took a look, I did not like the look of it either. About half a mile away, a solid concrete wall – part of what is now the Brighton Marina – lay across our path, with waves breaking over it and hurling themselves about in all directions, creating a positive maelstrom. If we went in there, and were battered against that concrete wall, life might get a little tricky, and yet that was the way we were heading – and fast.

We then debated the options. We could not turn and get round the obstacle by heading out to sea because whenever we attempted to turn we flipped over – and getting sorted out took time, the very thing that we were rapidly running out of. Moreover, we were getting pretty chilly and, if we abandoned the canoe and tried to swim ashore, we might not make it – or we might end up pinned against the sea wall along the shore, against which most of the waves which swept past were pounding. The choice was death or do something, so somehow or other we had to get ashore, somewhere. So I went back over the side and, taking the canoe by the bow, swam it round until the bow was pointing to the shore. Lou kept it that way with massive sweeps of the paddle while I got back in again.

Incidentally, it was much warmer in the sea than sitting up in the wind, so if anyone were to get hypothermia on this caper it was not going to be Sergeant Robbie.

Meanwhile, Terry and Co., on shore, had noticed our plight, and we could see them running along the sea wall. Then Terry stopped and semaphored the letter 'H' – 'Here' – to us. We were still going up and down on the waves and could only see the shore intermittently, but Terry was indicating a narrow gap in the sea wall, which offered us the fleeting chance of a safe landing.

I cannot say that Lou and I would definitely have died that morning, only that it was a strong possibility. Perhaps it would all have ended well anyway, but Lou and I have discussed it since and we do not think so. We had to do something or we were stuffed, and what we did, what we still believe kept us alive, owed everything to discipline and training – Royal Marines training – rather than skill and experience. Maybe a little nerve came in useful as well, at least in not losing it at the crucial moment. Our plan was to wait for a low wave, one that was not going to smash us into the sea wall, and then go for it, riding that wave on to the shingle. Then, with any luck, we could make a dash for the flight of steps where Terry and the others were standing by. A series of big waves swept under us and then Lou cried, 'This one,' and we went for it.

For a couple of total tyros, canoewise, I think we did pretty well. Somehow or other we stayed on top of that wave and rode it in to the beach, paddling hard and going like a train. About fifty yards out I saw a line of crooked, rusting angle irons sticking up out of the waves right ahead of us, but there was nothing to be done about it. In Marine parlance this was 'shit or bust'; anyway, the wave carried us over them and we ground to a halt on the shingle, at the very foot of the steps. Terry came leaping down, yelling 'bloody marvellous', and hauled us out of our cockpits and we were halfway up the steps when the next big wave swept in, picked up the canoe and took it back out to sea. By the time we were safely on the promenade the canoe was hooked on those reinforcing angle irons and being torn to pieces. This destruction was being watched by our SBS sergeant, who seemed to be taking a rather gloomy view of our survival.

'Cheer up,' I said, 'Lou and I are fine . . . no bones broken.'

'Glad to hear it, Robbie,' he replied sourly. 'I suppose you realise I signed for that canoe . . . and now I'll have to bloody well pay for it.'

1

WHAT IS THE SBS?

'Time spent on reconnaissance is never wasted'

Old military maxim

The short answer to the question at the start of this chapter is that the modern SBS – or Special Boat Service – is a unit of the Royal Marines, but to tell the full story of the SBS, what they do today and what they have done since SBS units were first created in the Second World War, is rather more complicated. The history of this unit spans many years, all continents and several wars and embraces the exploits of a great many other units, now sadly defunct.

John Lodwick, who served with one of these 'parent units', the Special Boat Squadron, in the Aegean during the Second World War wrote that, 'To write the story of the SBS in something approaching chronological order is like making one of those tiresome naval splices; you tuck one strand of rope away and another immediately wrestles free.' (*The Filibusters*, p. 49.)

This is very true, but one has to start somewhere, and the point of departure for this book is AD 1664, and the formation of the Corps of Royal Marines, all of which will be covered in a later chapter. The Royal Marines have always been, and still are, Britain's amphibious soldiers, soldiers trained for service at sea. The 3rd Commando Brigade, the sole survivor to the great commando brigades of the Second World War, is the cutting edge of the Corps and the modern SBS provides the Brigade with amphibious reconnaissance, plus a number of allied skills, as well as having its own role in ship attack, sabotage and, recently, counterterrorism.

For the sake of instant clarity, the SBS is best imagined as the maritime equivalent of the Special Air Service, but not all SBS men would agree with that. 'Good as the SAS are,' says one experienced SBS officer, 'I always felt that we [the SBS] had our feet more firmly on the ground, were more open-minded, modest in what we did, certainly more enthusiastic and keener, had a better sense of humour, had better officer–NCO relations (Hereford seems to be run too much by the NCOs) and we enjoyed the benefits of having a common Royal Marine and Commando basic training.'

To tell the story of the SBS in all its glory we must go back sixty years, move beyond the operational confines of the present SBS and recount the story of those small units and 'private armies' created in the Second World War that are, directly or indirectly, the parent units of the modern SBS. These units, and the men who served in them, took the risks and tested the equipment and tactics that the SBS deploy today, with sixty years of hard-won experience at their backs.

To describe the SBS as a form of maritime SAS is a loose definition and an inexact comparison, for although the two units employ the same selection procedures, often work together and share many of the same standards and some training, there are a large number of differences, not least that the SBS are closely integrated with the Commando forces of the Royal Marines and with the main body of the Corps. SBS officers, NCOs and other ranks are not an exclusive club within the Corps, but an integral part of the Royal Marines family. A man may well be SBS qualified and spend every other tour – or 'commission' – with an SBS section, but he will always be rotated back to the normal duties of his rank as part of his overall service career. With that much said, most

SBS-trained ranks remain close to the SBS units throughout their service and only SBS-qualified ranks are chosen to fill promotion vacancies within the ranks of the SBS.

Having said all *that*, everything may change. Newspaper reports of 28 December 1997 state that the SBS and the SAS are to merge in what the *Sunday Telegraph* describes as 'a far reaching change for Britain's Special Forces'. The report makes the point that, other than for a few weeks of basic training, the units have effectively been merged anyway, since after selection most of the SBS training is carried out at the SAS Hereford base and SBS personnel are then under the overall command of the director of Special Forces, a senior Army officer, for training and operations. The aim of the merger, it alleges, is to make the two units interchangeable for most tasks, though it concedes that the SBS retains a maritime specialisation and performs the most exacting waterborne tasks on its own.

The Army statement on which this report is based goes on to say that 'their [the SBS's] skills are too useful for us to be wasted on over-specialisation' – whatever that may mean. It is more than likely that the need for military effectiveness has yet again fallen before the Treasury's need to save money somewhere – especially on national defence.

The letters 'SBS' currently stand for Special Boat Service. In the past they have stood for Special Boat *Squadron* and Special Boat *Section*. The current SBS is a small unit, with no more than a hundred 'badged', or qualified, SBS men, that has synthesised many of the irregular, waterborne or underwater units that were created for reconnaissance or raiding purposes during the Second World War and taken on many of their tasks. The story of those units therefore forms part of the history of the modern SBS. The basic qualification for SBS work today is the rate of Swimmer Canoeist, or SC3, a grade (or 'rate' or badge) awarded after successful completion of the basic, three-phase, 33-week SBS selection course, which covers everything from survival to parachuting, scuba work, close-quarter battle skills, jungle and demolition training, escape and evasion, raiding skills and a great deal of swimming and canoeing.

It is these last two elements, swimming (especially swimming underwater using breathing apparatus) and canoeing (especially in the sea-going, submarine-transportable folboat, or collapsible canoe) that make up the basis of SBS work in the present day. The main SBS roles are beach reconnaissance, ship attack, small-scale raiding and counterterrorism, especially in the guarding of naval establishments and offshore oil platforms, and action against hijackings or hostage-taking at sea.

Counterterrorism has been adopted fairly recently, and does not override the main role of the SBS, which is to pave the way for commando operations and amphibious assaults. It is necessary to put these various functions in context as this will give a good idea of what SBS work is really like.

Of all military operations, the most hazardous is an amphibious assault. Any attack is risky, for success can never be guaranteed, but an amphibious assault has also to cater with the hazards of the sea, in shallow, dangerous, tidal coastal waters. Therefore, before a major attack is launched, it is as well to carry out a careful reconnaissance of the beach and assess both the natural difficulties and the man-made hazards and obstacles erected by the enemy on any likely landing beaches to thwart an invasion. A good, and amusing, example of what can happen without beach recce is provided by Lieutenant Milton of No. 7 Commando, in his account of the Commando raid on Bardia, North Africa, in April 1941.

We were accompanied on this raid by Admiral Sir Walter Cowan, a real fire-eater, though already in his seventies and about five feet three inches tall. In those days the first assault wave got into the LCA (Landing Craft Assault) while it was still in the davits. We did that but, as we were being lowered into the water, the ship swung about and we smashed into its side, damaging our port engine. Therefore, though supposedly the leading craft, we were well to the rear as we went ashore. I could see the beach and could work out where we were but about one hundred yards off the beach we grounded on a sandbar and Admiral Cowan, thirsting to be at 'em, ordered our cox'n to lower the door. He complied and Admiral Cowan and Lt Evelyn Waugh – the writer who had come out with 8 Commando – dashed down the ramp, and disappeared under the water. Relieved of their weight, we scraped over the bar, and I held my men back until we arrived at the real beach.

Funny perhaps, but heavily loaded men, disembarking into deep water, can easily drown. That apart, a landing that takes place on a 'false beach', some distance offshore, can at best become a shambles.

During the early days of the Second World War the need for beach recce soon became obvious. On numerous occasions – at Termoli in Italy for the British, at Dieppe for the Canadians, at Tarawa in the Pacific for the Americans – an invading force came in to land and struck a false beach or a reef some distance offshore, often with disastrous results. Here is Marine Ken Richardson of 40 Commando at Termoli:

> We got ashore all right, but hit a false beach and had to swim the last bit, drowning all our radios crossing the deep channel between the 'false' beach and the real one. The enemy came in real close, throwing stick grenades, and I got hit. My left arm was shattered and I lost a lot of blood, very quickly . . . my fighting days were over.

The British got ashore at Termoli with the loss of their armour and radios, which had been drowned in deep water. Thanks to that error they were forced to fight the Germans without tanks and were unable to contact the main forces pushing up the coast to join them – but they survived, just. At Dieppe, in August 1942, the Canadians were not so lucky. Their landing battalions ran into unsuspected beach obstacles, both man-made and natural, and took terrible losses, with entire battalions being machine-gunned on the beach. At Tarawa in 1943, the United States Marines were faced with a long wade across a lagoon, under intense Japanese fire, after their landing craft grounded on an unmarked reef some hundreds of yards offshore; hundreds of young US Marines were killed or wounded before they could even set foot on the beach. To prevent this sort of thing ever happening again the US Marines created an Army–Navy Special Force, the Scouts and Raiders, to carry out beach recce, while the British created COPP, the Combined Operations Pilotage Parties to meet the same need. The modern SBS and the US SEALS count these units among their parent bodies and we shall hear more of them later.

The Germans and the Japanese were not content with leaving their beach defences to purely natural hazards. They began to use mines and build various kinds of obstruction to impede the passage of landing craft to the beach, and they armed these obstacles with mines and booby traps as well as covering them with machine guns. To counter this threat the British eventually created LCOCU, the Landing Craft Obstruction Clearing Units, comprising swimmers trained in demolition work, who would use the information supplied by COPP to prepare charges. They would then swim in, attach these to the obstacles and detonate them just before the landing craft ran in for the assault. In the US amphibious forces this role was filled by the men of the UDT, the Underwater Demolition Teams. During the Second World War many of these men used primitive aqualung equipment and swimming fins and therefore became known to the general public as 'frogmen'. Today we would call them scuba divers but, like most of the essential underwater apparatus needed to carry out these tasks safely, scuba equipment had not been invented when the Second World War broke out in

1939. The story of the SBS, therefore, is not just one of battling against the enemy. It also concerns their war against that most hostile of environments, the sea, and the difficulties of developing and testing the necessary equipment. In both of these tasks, men died.

Beach recce and the removal of underwater obstacles are still prime SBS tasks, part of their role in assisting the Commandos get ashore. So too is small-scale raiding, especially attacks on shipping. During the Second World War the Allied blockade was broken by commerce raiders or blockade runners operating out of French ports. To bomb these port areas, which were often in the heart of major cities, would cause severe loss of life among the French civilian population, so one way of solving the problem was to send in a small raiding party by canoe, as in the 'Cockleshell Hero' Operation *Frankton* of 1942, a classic raid conducted by the Royal Marines Boom Patrol Detachment (RMBPD), a unit that is still regarded as the direct ancestor of the SBS. The RMBPD was created by Major 'Blondie' Hasler specifically for canoe raiding. There was also the Small Scale Raiding Force, or SSRF, which swooped on the German-held coast of France from fast MTBs (Motor Torpedo Boats) and eventually sent many men, including the famous Danish soldier Anders Lassen, on to serve with the SBS.

Raiding by canoe was also employed when the British lacked air superiority, as in the Mediterranean in 1943–44 when a folboat section of the RMBPD attacked two German destroyers in the Aegean Islands. Similar tactics were also seen in Italy and Sicily in 1941–43 when the first SBS units created by Major Roger Courtney went ashore by canoe and attacked bridges, viaducts and railway trains, an activity pioneered by the indomitable Royal Artillery officer, Lieutenant Tug Wilson and his oppo, Marine Hughes. This sort of activity, recce and raiding, was facilitated by combining the canoe with the submarine, as Jim Booth of COPP explains, in an account which also indicates the kind of men this sort of work attracted and what the job involved:

13

I joined the Royal Navy in 1939 and served in convoy escorts in the North Atlantic for a while. Then I thought I would like to try something different so I volunteered for Chariots – human torpedoes – but I didn't get in, so I volunteered for COPP and got accepted.

COPP, the Combined Operations Pilotage Parties, was created after the Dieppe Raid fiasco in August 1942, partly because the tanks could not get off the shingle and some of the Canadian troops were off-loaded in deep water; no beach recce, you see. Anyway, our job was pre-invasion recce and we did a lot of it, in Sicily and Italy. We went in big submarines which surfaced offshore at night and then we went into the beach in canoes. There were always two men, a naval surveyor who did his stuff below the tidemark and a Royal Engineers officer who did the beach above the low-water mark.

We would put a peg in on the water line and swim about, taking offshore depths and gradients with a plumb line at 25-yard intervals and I suppose the army chap was doing the same on the beach itself. Then we would paddle back and rendezvous with the submarine and plot it all on a chart. I enjoyed it – jolly good fun.

Jim Booth went on to serve in X-craft, or midget submarines, and we shall meet him again. His account also mentions another method of underwater warfare that was pioneered in the Second World War and eventually became an SBS speciality – the Charioteers or human torpedoes. This method of attacking enemy shipping was actually pioneered by the Italians, who carried out a number of underwater attacks against the Royal Navy and British merchant shipping in Gibraltar, Malta and, most effectively, Alexandria in Egypt, where a team of Italian human torpedoes attacked and sank the British battleships HMS *Valiant* and HMS *Queen Elizabeth* in a well-defended anchorage.

The British created underwater frogmen units to

counter these attacks and, after Italy surrendered and joined in the war against Germany in 1943, these Italian frogmen joined the British units and carried out a number of attacks against German shipping, especially in the Adriatic. The Americans were also active in raiding and beach recce, as Matthew Kaye of the US Navy Scouts and Raiders recounts:

I started my war as a landing craft cox'n; it was boring, the circling was endless, our days on exercise were always the same. Then one day a small notice caught our eyes: WANTED, VOLUNTEERS FOR EXTRA HAZARDOUS DUTY. Not just hazardous, but *extra* hazardous. Anyway, four of us put our names down, and next day we were introduced to the Scouts and Raiders. Our job was beach recon and our training was very intensive and included the use of short-wave radios, hand-to-hand combat, body building, all sorts of weaponry, night-time silhouette studies, scouting, demolition, swimming, map reading, handling small rubber boats, raiding and so on. Slowly our edges got honed, and paddling a rubber boat all night through the Florida swamps, avoiding alligators, or crawling on our stomachs in the mud and mosquitoes began to harden and educate us. We had our share of casualties. Sergeant Zimmerman of the US Army – I was a sailor – lost his arm and a Scout and Raider died in an 'unloaded weapon' accident. Finally we boarded the USS *Tarazet*, a troop transport, and sailed into the North Atlantic, destination Arzew, Algeria, for Operation *Torch*.

The US Scouts and Raiders were not alone on *Torch*, the codename for the Allied invasion of North Africa in November 1942. British troops went ashore as well, including men from No. 6 Commando and paratrooper units, and the US Rangers were guided to the beaches by the canoeists of 101 Troop, No. 6 Commando, in which Stan Weatherall was serving:

On Wednesday 4 November we reached the bay of Arzew, near Oran, in the submarine HMS/M *Ursula* and began a periscope recce of the beach, finally surfacing six miles offshore, to off-load the canoes, on Saturday 7 November. The sea was very choppy and we shipped a lot of water as we launched the canoe over the buoyancy tanks. I bailed it out with my green beret. The dolphins were a nuisance, churning up a lot of phosphorescence but we made good time to the beach and dropped our kedge anchor about 200 yards off Z beach at around midnight. At 0115 hours we began flashing Z seaward in Morse, using an infra-red lamps and the US Rangers landing craft came sweeping past our starboard side about fifteen minutes later. All was very quiet for about an hour and then the first shots were fired . . . but as it got light we had done our bit for the moment and paddled back to sea to join the SS *Reina del Pacifico*.

At 2300 hours on Friday November 13 1942, the ship was attacked by a U-boat and a near miss was recorded as a torpedo passed twelve feet in front of the bow. A petty officer kept referring to some 'pongos' they had on board, and these turned out to be some members of our SBS who had been operating in Oran harbour, who had lost all their kit and were now in civilian clothes. We ended up in Gibraltar and I reported to the first lieutenant on HMS *Maidstone*, the submarine depot ship, who told me that another operation was in the offing. The rest of the SBS sailed for home on the SS *Etric*, but they did not get very far as the *Etric* was torpedoed and sunk 160 miles west of Gib. Fortunately they were picked up by a destroyer and brought back safely.

These men, and the units in which they served, were the forebears of the modern SBS. Many of the skills and techniques that the SBS employ today were developed by the men who rode the Chariots, paddled the early folboats, dived using the Davis Submarine Escape

Apparatus (DSEA), marked beaches using hand lines and destroyed beach obstacles with satchel explosives while under enemy-sniper and machine-gun fire.

They were brave men and great characters, and this book will feature some of them: Blondie Hasler of the Bordeaux Canoe raid, who later invented a self-steering gear for yachts and pioneered the Single-Handed Transatlantic Yacht Race; Lord Jellicoe of the Special Boat Squadron in the Aegean, who sent his men in by *caique* – Levantine schooners – to make life intolerable for the German garrisons on Simi and Samos and many other places that are popular holiday islands today. Here too are tales of canoe raiders, frogmen, the Charioteers and the men who took X-craft into guarded harbours to sink German battleships and Italian or Japanese cruisers. These men include people like Eric Newby MC, the travel writer; Anders Lassen VC, the fighting Dane, who died attacking a machine-gun nest at Lake Commachio; John Lodwick, the ex-Foreign Legionnaire and novelist; the tough and gallant Courtney brothers, who served in the Far East and the Mediterranean as well as Europe, and the Australian canoe raiders of the *Jaywick* and *Rimau* operations against the Japanese in Singapore. There were many more, but the common link in this book, and with the modern SBS, is that they went to war in canoes or submarines or as frogmen and have thus become part of SBS history. These men saw hard times and did great deeds; their stories ought to be remembered.

As the introductory account indicated, SBS training is always hard and often risky. So too are SBS operations and since SBS personnel were often regarded as spies or saboteurs their fate on capture was likely to be execution. Most of the Royal Marines who took part in Operation *Frankton* were brutally interrogated and then shot by the Gestapo under the terms of Hitler's infamous Commando Order. The British and Australian canoeists captured after the Rimau raid in 1945 were all beheaded by their Japanese captors, just a few weeks before the war ended.

In 1945, most of the Special Service units that had been created during the war were either disbanded or much reduced in size. The SAS was disbanded as were most of the other 'private armies' – the Long Range Desert Group, the Chindits, Popski's Private Army and the rest soon disappeared. Their task was done and their time was over.

Britain's two parachute divisions shrank swiftly to one Parachute Brigade, and the four Commando Brigades, which had served in every theatre of war from Europe to the Far East, were swiftly reduced to just one, the 3rd Commando Brigade. This brigade, which comprised two Army and two Royal Marine Commando units, had fought in Burma and was in Hong Kong, on the brink of disbandment, when it was taken up by Lord Louis Mountbatten, wartime Chief of Combined Operations. Mountbatten urged that the Royal Marines, Britain's sea soldiers, should take on the Commando role, which had proved so vital in the recent conflict, and retain it as one of their prime tasks. The 3rd Commando Brigade, Royal Marines, was duly formed at the end of 1945, taking on as its core units Nos 40, 42 and 45 Commando (Royal Marines) plus a sixty-strong collection of odds and sods from various maritime raiding units in what was then called the Special Operations Group (SOG). Some years later, this unit gave way to the SBS.

That the SBS came to take over the functions of its parent units – COPP, LCOCU, the Charioteers, the Small Scale Raiding Force and the X-craft – is hardly surprising. Many of the tasks that these units had been created to perform, beach recce and obstacle clearance to name but two, still needed to be done in peacetime, in order to get the Commando Brigade ashore safely on exercises. Landing heavily laden men on unknown beaches is a risky business at any time – if they fall into unexpected holes they can drown. So too can valuable equipment, but this can be more easily recovered if there are men around who can use diving equipment and know how to work in dangerous waters.

18

Moreover, new inventions, notably scuba equipment (*S*elf *C*ontained *U*nderwater *B*reathing *A*pparatus, invented and tested in the River Marne in occupied France in 1943 by the French Naval Lieutenant Jacques Cousteau) and the wet suit, meant that men could operate in safety at considerable depth and in chilly waters. These hard-earned skills had to be maintained, and kept up to date, and this role fell to the SBS and their US cousins in the UDT, which later became the US Navy SEALS. The bedrock remains the work done and the experience gained between 1939 and 1945, where this story really begins.

2

THE FOLBOAT SECTION
1941–42

'Are you tough? Then push off. I want buggers with intelligence.'

Notice on the door of Captain Roger Courtney,
Folboat Section, Army Commandos

One of the more curious facts about an invention or an innovation is that an idea is rarely confined to one man. Usually several people are thinking along the same lines and it is therefore hard to decide exactly where a story begins or, as in this case, exactly who should be credited with the introduction of canoe warfare at the start of the Second World War, one of the most technological wars in history. The prime candidates are Major H G 'Blondie' Hasler of the Royal Marines, Captain Roger Courtney of the British Army and Captain Montanero of 101 Troop, No. 6 Commando.

All three men had done a certain amount of canoeing before the war began, and all were quick to see the advantages of this sturdy craft in the raiding role. Any of these would serve as a true pioneer but, and as a Royal Marine myself (*et toujours la politesse*), one must give way to the Army here, and so this story can begin with the exploits of Captain Roger Courtney. Courtney, as the founder of the first unit, deserves the premièr place.

Lieutenant Colonel Godfrey Courtney, Roger Courtney's brother and another SBS officer, remembers the early days of the wartime Special Boat Section:

> Tug Wilson was our star turn. He was a mild and unassuming little man with an unequalled operational record, who was finally captured when testing an unpractical gadget. Another good man was Major Livingstone, a classics scholar, who used to read from the original Greek, which certainly impressed the submariners. He had an absolute passion for blowing things up. I never met Anders Lassen, who seems to have been a killer but admirable. Relations between the SBS and Royal Marines Boom Patrol Detachment were coolly official, owing to the contrasting characters of their commanding officers. Roger Courtney was a passionate, operational type while Blondie Hasler was more the professional technician and jealous of the reputation of the Royal Marines. Our relations with COPP were always very friendly.

Roger Courtney was an adventurer. Before the war he had worked in East Africa as a big-game hunter and gold prospector and had made a solo canoe trip down the Nile carrying all his worldly possessions, a spear and a bag of potatoes. He even spent his honeymoon in a canoe, on a trip down the Danube, and when the war broke out in 1939 he was anxious to develop his notion that the canoe, in skilled hands, could be a formidable weapon of war. He was then a sergeant in the Palestine Police, but he made his way back to England, joined the Army, volunteered for the Commandos and issued a challenge to Admiral Sir Roger Keyes, the then Chief of Combined Operations, that a canoe raider could infiltrate a harbour and sink a ship. He demonstrated this by boarding the Commando landing ship, HMS *Glengyle*, and carrying off two breech-block covers from one of the guns. This was impressive, but when he tried it a second time he was quickly grabbed by a pair of alert Royal Marine sentries.

Even so, this success at infiltration was enough to convince the admiral that there was some merit in this idea and Courtney was permitted to form a Folboat Section, of twelve men, to carry out reconnaissance and small raids for the Commandos. This was in the summer of 1940 and the Folboat Section spent much of the autumn and winter of 1940/41 training on the Isle of Arran in Scotland, which was then the training area for Britain's newly formed Commando forces.

Courtney intended to use his section for raiding, not just for recce, and it was with that function in mind that the section sailed for the Middle East in February 1941 as part of a Commando brigade formed from Nos 7, 8 and 11 (Army) Commandos. This brigade was under the command of Brigadier Robert Laycock, and was therefore known as 'Layforce'. Courtney's second-in-command in the folboat troop was a Royal Artillery lieutenant, Tug Wilson, a man who was to become one of the great canoe raiders of the war. Among the other officers in Layforce was a Scots Guards lieutenant, David Stirling, and a massive Ulsterman, Blair 'Paddy' Mayne: the founders of the SAS.

Layforce did not have a good time in the Middle East. The units were too small for service in the line and there was no shipping to spare to take them raiding along the North African coast. They put in a small raid against the port of Bardia and took part in the landings along the Litani river in Syria, when the British decided to take over that territory to deny it to the Germans, who were then advancing through Greece. Before long, the reinforcement officers were casting lustful eyes at Laycock's small brigade of superb infantry and, with no operations in the offing, the men themselves were getting fed up and anxious either to get into action or go back to their parent units. Stirling departed to form the SAS and Mayne, along with many other good men, soon followed him. By the end of 1941 Layforce had disintegrated. By that time, though, Roger Courtney had found another field for the folboat troop.

On arriving in Egypt, Courtney had managed to exercise the prerogative of all private armies and taken his force off to Alexandria, where he attached himself and his men to the 1st Submarine Flotilla, a small group of submarines based in the depot ship HMS *Medway* and operating against enemy shipping in the Mediterranean and the Aegean. Some time was spent training on the Great Bitter Lake near Kabrit, the first SAS base, and while they were there the Folboat Section became No. 1 Special Boat Section. Submarines are boats, not ships, and canoes were logically 'special' boats.

At this time Courtney also met Lieutenant Commander Nigel Clogstoun-Willmott of the Royal Navy, a man who was later to found COPP. Clogstoun-Willmott had taken part in the shambles of the Narvik operation in Norway in 1940, where a quantity of shipping had been lost on unmarked reefs, and he was determined to develop a force skilled in beach recce and obstacle clearance, for commando operations. The need to develop such a force had become urgent because, lacking any other employment, Layforce was about to be deployed for a landing on the Greek island of Rhodes.

No accurate charts or maps of the landing area were available and Clogstoun-Willmott suggested to the planners at GHQ that, in lieu of such aids, it might be an idea if he and Courtney went ashore on Rhodes before the invasion, to have a look round and examine the beaches. GHQ approved. Courtney thought this was a great idea and in March 1941, after a few weeks spent training Clogstoun-Willmott in canoe handling, the two men embarked with their canoe on HMS/M *Triumph* and sailed for the beaches. This affair, Operation *Cordite*, marks the start of effective beach recce, a prime SBS task to the present day.

The operation was not a great success. The two men were treated royally on board the *Triumph* but found boarding the canoe at sea from the submarine's fore planes extremely difficult. However, persistence paid off and they finally set out on their beach reconnaissance, the first of four. They paddled in until they could hear the waves breaking on the beach and then Clogstoun-Willmott, who had elected to take on the role of swimmer, slipped over the side and started to swim ashore. This was the Aegean, but the month was March and the sea was freezing. However, Clougstoun-Willmott got the first bit of useful information before he even got ashore – he discovered that the supposed sandy, gently shelving beach the planners hoped to land tanks on was in fact a jagged spit of rock, washed by the waves and quite unsuitable.

He continued his recce by swimming along the beach, just outside the breaking waves, but going in to land every hundred yards or so, calculating depths and gradients and noting the information down on a slate. He also detected a false beach some yards from the shore behind which the water was quite deep enough to drown a tank. Finally, and very chilled indeed, he decided to go ashore and probe inland. He crossed the beach, avoiding some Italian sentries who were having a chat and a smoke, and reached a road in the rear of the dunes. He then returned to the beach to collect sand samples before rejoining Courtney out on the water. He had been ashore for three full hours.

Flashing his infra-red torch, he swam back out to sea and, a few hundred yards beyond the waves, Courtney came surging out of the darkness and laid his canoe alongside the swimmer, hauling Clogstoun-Willmott aboard and handing him a very welcome flask of hot coffee laced with Navy rum. An hour later they were back on board *Triumph* and heading out to sea.

The two men continued their recce for another two nights, examining other possible landing beaches without detection, though on the final night, when Roger Courtney had done the recce ashore and was about to swim back to the canoe, he was seized with cramp and only made it back with difficulty, being rescued from the water by Clogstoun-Willmott just as his strength gave out. This British invasion of Rhodes never took place, but in 1944 the Special Boat Squadron were to raid Rhodes and many other islands in the Dodecanese. Courtney and

Clogstoun-Willmott's first operation had proved that beach recce was useful and quite feasible by canoe teams, a fact which lead to the creation of other beach recce units, like COPP. There was also the matter of canoe raiding: the possibilities of that activity were being demonstrated by another canoe-warfare pioneer, Roger Courtney's second-in-command, Lieutenant Tug Wilson of the Royal Artillery.

Tug Wilson was one of the great characters of canoe warfare, a regular Army officer with a trim moustache, an imperturbable manner, and the spirit of a buccaneer. Tug Wilson had gone to France with the BEF in 1939 and after the Dunkirk evacuation in June 1940 he volunteered for the newly formed Commandos and was sent to the Isle of Arran for training. There he met Roger Courtney and the two men hit it off, especially after Wilson had survived Courtney's unique selection process, which consisted of taking a would-be recruit down to the local pub and filling him full of whisky. Wilson poured the bulk of his whisky into a flowerpot whenever Courtney was not looking and eventually had to carry his new CO back to camp.

The two men took the Folboat Section to the Middle East and in April 1941 Wilson and his oppo, Marine Hughes, took their first crack at enemy shipping, when they were sent from Alexandria in a submarine to attack Derna harbour on the North African coast, by canoe and using limpet mines. Gales prevented the canoe being launched and this attack was called off, but on the way back to base they stopped and sank an enemy schooner after Wilson had paddled across to examine her cargo, which largely consisted of macaroni for the Italian troops in North Africa.

Wilson was then sent with Hughes on attachment to the 10th Submarine Flotilla in Malta. The Navy had quickly realised that having a few canoe raiders on board could add another dimension to a submarine's offensive capacity – and a few daggers, symbolising their cloak-and-dagger operations, were soon being added to the skull and crossbones that British submarines flew on returning from patrol. The officers and men of the 10th Submarine Flotilla in Malta were a remarkably aggressive bunch of pirates, eager to take on the enemy wherever he could be found, and in Wilson and Hughes they found a couple of kindred spirits.

Tug Wilson enjoyed blowing things up. He was especially fond of blowing up trains, and with his canoeing oppo and the assistance of the 10th Submarine Flotilla he managed to put quite a dent in the Italian dictator Mussolini's much-vaunted ability to make the trains run on time.

In late June 1941, Wilson and Hughes paddled ashore in Sicily from the U-class submarine HMS/M *Urge*, hid their canoe among some rocks and, carrying a quantity of explosives, climbed up a steep hillside to reach the railway track carrying the coastal line to Palermo. They walked along it until they found an unguarded tunnel and, since derailments in a tunnel are much harder to unblock than derailments in the open, they laid their charges well inside, scooping out a large hole under the rails, putting in the charges and finishing the job by attaching pressure switches to the track. They were just tidying up when Hughes tapped Wilson on the shoulder and pointed down the track to where a signal light had suddenly turned green. A train was coming and it was time to go.

They walked away from the charge in the approved Royal Engineers manner, which dictates that you never run because you might trip and end up lying immobile by a smoking charge. Once they had got a few hundred yards away they ran back down the slope of the hill, found their canoe and paddled hurriedly out to sea. They were back in the submarine, enjoying a late supper, when a soft hail from the conning tower had them back on top in time to see a massive explosion shoot flame and debris from the mouth of the tunnel. As the sound of the explosion boomed across the water, the submarine dived. A few days later this submarine had another success when the *Urge* encountered two Italian cruisers and four destroyers in the Straits of Messina. She put in an attack and sank the eight-inch-gun cruiser *Gorizia*.

Three months later, Wilson and Hughes did it again. Their target this time was a railway line on the west coast of the Italian mainland and HMS/M *Utmost* took them to the dropping-off spot. The crew helped to load nearly half a ton of high explosives into the canoe, which was duly ferried ashore and humped up to the railway line. Once again their target was a tunnel, but this time they were unlucky; they ran into an Italian patrol while they were still moving the explosives up the hillside. Having discouraged the Italians with bursts from a Tommy gun, Wilson and Hughes had to abandon the attempt and paddle back out to sea.

Fortunately, *Utmost* had plenty more explosives, 'canoe raiders for the use of', and three nights later the two men went ashore again, aiming this time for a railway bridge. Alas, this also turned out to be heavily guarded and, having shot a sentry and been shot at by a machine gun, the two men again had to retreat out to sea. However, Wilson remained undaunted, as evidenced by his patrol report to Courtney: 'Though tunnels and bridges are now well guarded there is plenty of scope for attacks against long straight stretches of line.' Before long, Wilson and Hughes were back on the rampage, demonstrating this fact, and we shall hear from them again.

Roger Courtney was not too interested in administration, the boring side of being a unit commander, and, like his second-in-command and the rest of his men, he preferred to get out on operations and lead from the front. In June 1940 he embarked on HMS/M *Taku* for a raid on an Italian fort and signal station on the Gulf of Sirte on the North African coast, near the town of Mersa Brega. A periscope recce revealed a lot of transport on the coast road and a satisfying amount of smoke indicated that the RAF were scoring plenty of hits on Italian dumps and transport parks. This also indicated that there would be plenty of targets for the raiders once they went ashore.

On the night of 7 June Courtney and his No. 2, Sergeant Major Barnes, paddled ashore from *Taku*. It was full moonlight, and since concealment was impossible

Courtney decided to march straight up to the fort and play it by ear. This led to the first disappointment, for when they reached the fort, lugging pounds of explosives, they found that the RAF had got there first and reduced it to rubble. They therefore turned towards their second objective, the signal station, reboarding their canoe for a seaward approach.

This was a mistake. An Italian patrol, sitting down for a rest behind the beach, watched them come ashore and greeted them with some accurate rifle fire, which Courtney managed to quell by standing up and bellowing, '*Basta!*' (Enough!) Thinking they were firing on some of their own side, the Italians stopped firing and, while they were discussing who should take the blame, Courtney and Barnes flung themselves back into their canoe and made a hasty retreat back to the submarine – urged on by more bullets from the infuriated Italians. Undaunted, such canoe raids continued, and every submarine sailing from Malta or Alexandria soon came to include one or two canoe teams.

Apart from raiding along the North African shore, Courtney and his chums soon added a new role to their expanding list of tasks by putting agents ashore on the enemy coast of Europe, especially in Albania and Crete. Tug Wilson had not yet exhausted the list of railway targets and, in October 1941, he and Hughes embarked on HMS/M *Truant* and set out for the Adriatic coast of Italy, aiming for the Milan to Brindisi railway line. They got ashore without difficulty after a long paddle and found the line unguarded and well supplied with trains, so many in fact that they had to abandon laying the charges twice to let trains pass by. Fortunately, by the time the third train came along the charges were laid and the detonators primed. The two men were back on the submarine when the explosion came and did not see or hear the blast, but next day a periscope reconnaissance revealed a satisfying amount of damage to the track . . . and a fourteen-coach train lying on its side at the foot of the embankment.

Meanwhile, even if Courtney and Wilson were having a

good time and making themselves useful, matters were not going well with Layforce. Men had left to return to their parent units and by the autumn of 1941 Layforce had, in effect, disbanded. Then, the remnants of the 11th (Scottish) Commando, under Lieutenant Colonel Geoffrey Keyes, was tasked to make a raid on the enemy-held coast, find the headquarters of General Rommel, commander of the redoubtable German Afrika Corps . . . and kill him.

The Folboat Section's share in the Rommel raid was quite small. Their task was to go ashore from one of the two submarines carrying the raiding party – HMS/Ms *Torbay* and *Talisman* – in two canoes, recce the beach and return with information for the lieutenant colonel. Keyes was the officer commanding the raiding party, though Brigadier Laycock was also going along. Four days after the raid the Folboat Section would also be responsible for checking the rendezvous beach, from where the raiders would be picked up.

The Rommel raid was a disaster. Rommel was in Rome, not in the headquarters attacked by Keyes's force, and it subsequently turned out that he had never been there anyway. Keyes was shot and killed inside the German HQ; another officer was shot accidentally by one of this own men; and most of the rest were killed or captured within a few days. Brigadier Laycock and Sergeant Terry took command of the remnants of the party and led them back to the beach, but the surf was too high to get the boats ashore and the rescue was delayed. Then the Germans turned up. Sergeant Terry and the brigadier got away again and made it to the alternative rendezvous, but the Germans were everywhere and, in the end, they decided to walk back to the British lines. It took them over a month, living on berries, and sometimes a goat, and using rusty water drained from the radiators of wrecked trucks abandoned after the desert battles. Lieutenant Colonel Keyes was awarded a posthumous VC, but the Rommel raid spelt the end of Layforce and, for a while anyway, the end of Commando operations in the Middle East.

Roger Courtney was not in good health and, in December 1941, he was sent back to the UK. In the absence of the Folboat Section, a canoe unit, 101 Troop, had been raised in the UK by Captain Montanaro, and that unit was employed in cross-Channel raids. Courtney's canoeing expertise proved useful at Combined Operations HQ, and he lost no time in forming another SBS unit – No. 2 SBS – also for operations against the Germans along the Channel coast. His place as commander of No. 1 SBS in Egypt was taken by Captain Mike Kealy, while Tug Wilson and Marine Hughes continued their merry way against a new enemy, German shipping.

In December 1941, Wilson and Hughes paddled their canoe into the harbour of Navarino in Greece and found it crammed with Axis shipping. They were paddling about, wondering which of these juicy targets they should attack first, when they were spotted, picked up by a searchlight and machine-gunned – though without great effect – from the shore. They escaped unscathed, but it appeared that German harbours were well guarded and, if the shipping was to be attacked, a new method had to be found. Wilson and Hughes mulled the problem over and came up with the answer – swimming in to the attack. An apron, capable of holding a couple of limpet mines, was run up and thus equipped. Just before Christmas 1941, HMS/M *Torbay* took them back to Navarino.

Periscope recce revealed a German destroyer tied up to one of the outer piers. The canoe was launched and, having paddled carefully to within 200 yards of the target, Wilson slipped into the water and swam back towards the submarine. The water was freezing. The only sound was the chattering of teeth, which led Marine Hughes to his numbed officer whom he found it necessary to retrieve from the harbour before he froze to death. Winter raids in freezing water would have to await the development of a suitable protective suit. Wilson continued raiding and, for a while, his luck held, not only in operations against the enemy. In April 1942, after being ordered home to

Britain, he was transferred from the submarine *Upholder* to her sister ship the HMS/M *Unbeaten*, which was in passage back to the UK: some days later, *Upholder* was sunk with all hands in an Italian depth-charge attack.

Wilson stayed in the UK until August 1942, testing some new raiding devices including a miniature torpedo, and then returned to the Mediterranean theatre to give the miniature torpedo some operational trials. In early September 1942, he sailed from Malta in HMS/M *Unbroken* to make an attack against shipping in the harbour of Crotone, Italy, accompanied by a new partner, Bombardier Brittlebank of the Royal Artillery. They got into the harbour without difficulty and launched the torpedoes against the assembled shipping, but no hits were recorded. They were then spotted and challenged, but got away to sea. However, they could not make contact with *Unbroken* and were eventually captured by the Italians when attempting to paddle the 250 miles back to Malta. After the Italian surrender in 1943, Wilson was taken prisoner by the Germans and spent the rest of the war trying to escape from a succession of prison camps. For his work in attacking enemy railways and shipping, Tug Wilson was rewarded with no less than two DSOs.

The story has now reached the autumn of 1942. The SBS had lost some good men but it had also 'chummied-up' with Stirling's new but rapidly expanding SAS. It had also taken on another role while in submarine transit – aiding the crew in boarding operations against enemy craft. When HMS/M *Torbay* surfaced to attack a merchant ship, SBS Corporal Booth gave covering fire with a Bren gun from the conning tower, shooting down the crew of the enemy's forward gun, then cutting down a party attempting to clear the ship's after gun and finally putting a full magazine of .303 into the bridge. At this point, the enemy captain decided to haul down his colours. For this useful bit of work, and some very accurate shooting, Booth was awarded the DCM.

The SBS also established a new escape-and-evasion record when two men, Captain Ken Allott of the

Middlesex Regiment and Naval Lieutenant Duncan Ritchie, having been sent in to recce the beaches east of Tobruk, were unable to rejoin their submarine. Undaunted, the two men set out to paddle back to base. They made their way by night along the enemy-held coastline, coming ashore to lie up each day. They finally reached the British lines after paddling more than 150 miles.

After Courtney's departure to the UK at the end of 1941, the new CO, Captain Mike Kealy, strived to keep the SBS free from the expanding clutches of David Stirling's SAS, but the two units became ever more closely involved. The SAS had started as a desert raiding force, while during 1942 the role of the SBS gradually changed from that of a long-range reconnaissance unit, with a canoe-raiding sideline, to that of the canoe-raiding wing of the SAS. The SBS, post-Courtney, was also very small, amounting to just fifteen officers and less than fifty other ranks – the disproportionate number of officers being accounted for by the fact that SBS operations, if small in scale, were often complicated and usually needed an officer in command. Two SBS corporals were lost with HMS/M *Triumph*, which failed to return from patrol in January 1942, being sunk with all hands in the Aegean. Other losses in action reduced the SBS strength still further.

In June 1942, the original SBS, though still commanded by Mike Kealy, was tasked by Stirling to attack German airfields in Crete, attacks timed to coincide with SAS attacks on German airfields on the North African coast. Stirling's SAS now had its own, fast-developing seaborne arm under Captain Earl Jellicoe and, on reflection, Stirling decided that the SBS should attack three airfields and the SAS contingent under Jellicoe should tackle the fourth.

The SBS share in this 'show' went very well. Though Kealy's attack on Maleme airfield was thwarted by the strongly manned defences and he was forced to withdraw, George Duncan carried out a successful attack on Kastelli, destroying eight aircraft and a large quantity of stores. A large number of the enemy were killed when the bomb dump exploded, and on the following day – *pour encourager les autres* – all the surviving German sentries were shot for carelessness. The SBS attack on Timbaki was abandoned because the airfield was found deserted, but all the SBS withdrew from the island without loss. Jellicoe's raid on Heraklion, the major German airfield on Crete, also went well with sixteen aircraft and a large quantity of stores being destroyed before the raiders withdrew. Then matters deteriorated and some French soldiers of the party were captured by the Germans. Jellicoe and his Greek companion, Lieutenant Costi, reached the south coast after a march of 120 miles over the mountains and were taken off by a Royal Navy *caique*.

The good luck of the SBS on Crete was not to last. In August 1942, a seven-man SBS party from M Detachment, led by George Duncan and including Eric Newby and other stalwarts, was sent from Malta to attack airfields in Sicily. This strategy was part of a general attempt to reduce the number of Italian bombers available to attack the vital Pedestal convoy to Malta, which was even then forging east from Gibraltar. Duncan's detachment was tasked to attack an airfield at Catania, which was believed to contain a quantity of JU88 bombers, and they were transported to the drop-off point in HMS/M *Una*, part of the 10th Submarine Flotilla from Malta. One of the canoes was damaged as it was being brought up on to the casing, but the raiders got ashore and were soon on the way to their target, which lay just behind the beach.

The enemy were now fully alert to the possibility of such raids but, still undetected, the raiding party got on to the airfield with ease, after avoiding some obvious minefields and walking down a track until they found themselves among some well-lit hangers – the way that raiders were able to penetrate enemy airfields is one of the minor mysteries of the war. Then, just as the raiders were about to go out on to the airfield and plant their bombs on the aircraft, they ran straight into a large party of Italian soldiers.

Greetings were exchanged, but the Italians were unconvinced by George Duncan's German and promptly raised the alarm. Some bombs were hastily laid among engine spares and the party was just splitting up to seek out the bombers when they were fired upon. The airfield lights then came on, tracer began to bounce about, and the game was clearly up. After one man concluded Captain Duncan's thoughtful 'I think what we ought to do now is . . .' with the words 'Fuck off, that's what we ought to do', the party dispersed. One man was captured ashore; another canoe was damaged and Duncan, Eric Newby and the rest were picked up the following day, floating about some distance offshore in two overloaded and sinking canoes. By the time they were rescued by an Italian fishing boat, several men were suffering from exposure and in a very bad way. Unusually for an SBS operation, their submarine had failed to find them, probably because a nasty sea was running and in the darkness and rain the submarine could not see their signals; and so seven good and useful men went 'into the bag' for the rest of the war. Then Tug Wilson was captured, a real blow to the SBS, which was losing good men faster than they could be replaced.

These losses were to continue. In early September 1942, Lieutenant Tommy Langton and the rest of the SBS took part in a raid on Tobruk, tasked in their role of beach recce. This raid – Operation *Agreement* – was the brainchild of a Lieutenant Colonel Hasleden, who had been involved in the Rommel raid. Like that operation, the Tobruk raid was no small-scale affair. It involved a full battalion of Royal Marines, a squadron of the SAS, a patrol of the Long Range Desert Group, a group of German Jews serving in a secret unit, a cruiser, HMS *Coventry* and two destroyers, HMS *Sikh* and HMS *Zulu*, plus landing craft and MTBs. The plan was for the main force to drive into Tobruk, disguised as prisoners, and destroy the port installations before being evacuated by sea. It was an audacious plan and it went wrong from the start.

The Tobruk raid was, in fact, a total disaster. The Germans had probably been tipped off but were anyway fully alert by the time the main raiding party arrived. Their trucks were surrounded and fired upon – the raiders were cut to pieces. HMS *Coventry* and HMS *Zulu* were sunk by enemy aircraft and a great many men were killed, including Lieutenant Colonel Hasleden. Most of the rest were taken prisoner, but those German Jews who had played the part of guards were shot out of hand. Tommy Langton and his men tried to leave from the beach but found their MTBs under fire. Langton eventually led 25 men out through the Tobruk wire into the desert and set out to rejoin the Eighth Army across hundreds of miles of enemy-infested desert.

Only three men, Tommy Langton and two private soldiers, Hillman and Watler, evaded capture and made it to the British lines, which they reached in the middle of November, more than two months after they had set out to escape from Tobruk. It took them weeks of slow painful progress, moving mostly at night through country thick with enemy soldiers. After their boots wore out they marched on in bare feet, but they kept going and, for his leadership in the attack and during the subsequent escape, Langton was awarded a well-earned MC.

The Tobruk raid was one of a number of offensives mounted at this time and, at the end of August 1942, the SBS mounted their own major operation against the Italian airfields on Rhodes, which became one of the classic SBS raids of the war.

A major operation in SBS terms meant that just ten men, British and Greek, were sent into Rhodes, led by two captains, Ken Allott and David Sutherland, a young officer of the Black Watch. The raiders were taken to the island in a Greek submarine, HHMS/M *Papanikolis*, and tasked to attack the airfields at Marizza and Calato. The Calato attack went in on the night of 12 September, after the raiding parties had split into two groups. While the A group under Sutherland destroyed several aircraft and a quantity of stores, the B group did even better – until they

35

were spotted and surrounded by the garrison. They elected to fight it out and were never heard of again, all of them being either killed or captured.

A similar fate befell Ken Allott's party at Marizza. They got on to the airfield without difficulty but were soon surrounded and captured by a thoroughly aroused Italian garrison, which then went swarming across the country-side, determined to capture the rest of these impertinent and destructive raiders. The Italians had a pretty good idea where the raiders would head for.

Only three men were still on the loose, David Sutherland, Marine Duggan and a Greek, Captain Tsoucas. They made their way by night, back to the pick-up beach, but Captain Tsoucas was captured on the way. Any movement was difficult because the country was literally swarming with patrols. It took five days, moving only at night, entirely without food, for the remaining two men to reach the rendezvous. They had no canoe or Carley floats to take them out to sea, for the Germans had learned a lot about SBS tactics in recent months and, after the Calato attack, they had headed directly for the beaches and searched them thoroughly, finding all the raiding craft.

Sutherland and Duggan were determined to avoid capture, so they did the only thing they could do: on the night of September 17/18, after five days on the run and weak from lack of food, they swam straight out to sea in the hope that the submarine, HMS/M *Traveller*, would still be looking out for them. They swam out for nearly two miles, flashing a torch from time to time, until *Traveller* came looming out of the dark, picked them up and took them back to base – the only two survivors of a large party. Patrol reports of SBS operations never fail to record their thanks to the gallant and intrepid submarine crews that stayed on station, often under the noses of enemy patrol boats, in order to reach the pick-up point and bring their SBS passengers back to safety.

Kealy and his much depleted unit continued to raid airfields into the early months of 1943, still operating as a separate unit but drifting under the overall direction of the SAS. However, these heavy losses, sustained in just a few months, at Tobruk and in Sicily and Rhodes, effectively destroyed No. 1 SBS as a fighting force. To function at all, more men were needed – but it was difficult to recruit and train more men for SBS work while Stirling's SAS were also on the lookout for likely candidates. Since there was no real case for having two units carrying out the same basic task, the logical solution was that the SAS should fully absorb Kealy's detachment, and this duly took place in the autumn of 1942. Some men went willingly into the SAS and remained there but others, like Mike Kealy himself, preferred SBS work and eventually made their way back to England.

At this point, therefore, the story of the SBS in the Middle East and Mediterranean splits into two parts, the story of Z SBS and No. 2 SBS (Special Boat Section), which is related in Chapter 5, and that of Earl Jellicoe's SBS (Special Boat Squadron), which is related in Chapter 12. A beginning in canoe warfare had been made and the tactics tested and established. In another part of the Mediterranean, the second strand of modern SBS activity, underwater warfare by frogmen, was only just beginning.

It was now the end of 1942, and the much depleted SBS was now absorbed, for a while, into Stirling's SAS. The two units had both been based at Kabrit, where the water of the Great Bitter Lakes had provided some excellent training, and putting the two units together involved no more than shifting a few tents. The SBS element was now grouped into D Squadron of the SAS under George Jellicoe, which also absorbed the Greek Sacred Squadron, another maritime unit. When the Squadron was formed it went off to Syria and everyone in it went through the SAS training course, in order that all should share the basis of common training. To follow the actions of the original SBS – Courtney's force – we must go back to Britain and link up with Courtney and his new unit, No. 2 SBS.

Eventually, the SAS version was reformed into the Special Boat Squadron under Major Earl Jellicoe, and we shall pick up their adventures again in Chapter 12.

3

ENTER THE FROGMEN
1941–43

*'They worked alone, in the dark, in enemy waters. They
knew that the chances were they had taken a one-way
ticket, that there might be no return. But it was forgotten
knowledge, completely subjugated to thoughts of attack.'*

Tom Waldron and James Gleeson,
The Frogmen

While Roger Courtney and his men in the Folboat Section
of Layforce were pioneering canoe warfare in the eastern
Mediterranean and the Aegean, the second form of
modern SBS activity – underwater warfare by frogmen, or
what are now called swimmer canoeists – was developing
in the western Mediterranean, specifically in and around
the British naval base at Gibraltar. Here, the pace was
being set not by the British or the Germans, but from a
somewhat unexpected source, the Italian Navy, which had
experimented with underwater equipment and techniques
in the immediate pre-war period and were now about to
give the Royal Navy a number of very nasty surprises.

During the Second World War, Gibraltar was one of
the most important British bases. It provided a vital link
in the chain that supplied food, ammunition and fighting
men to the island fortress of Malta, and it supported the
escorts that guarded British convoys heading across the

Mediterranean and down the African shore towards the Cape. To maintain the war in Africa, Gibraltar was vital, but Gibraltar had a problem. Gibraltar is a small British enclave just off the Andalucian coast of Spain, a fortress acquired by Britain in the early eighteenth century and ceded to Britain in perpetuity by the 1713 Treaty of Utrecht. The problem was that the Spanish people and Franco's Government did not like having the British in Gibraltar. During the Second World War, Spain, though neutral, was broadly sympathetic to the German cause and willing to turn a blind eye to Axis agents and military personnel, who were either spying on the Gibraltar convoys or using secret bases in Spain to make attacks against British shipping in Gibraltar harbour.

This latter activity first became known on 19 September 1941, when underwater explosions rocked Gibraltar harbour and the outer roads, the blasts coming from limpet mines which sank the tankers *Denbydale* and *Fiona Shell* and badly damaged a supply ship, the SS *Durham*. Exactly what had caused these sinkings was not immediately apparent, but when submarine activity had been considered and excluded it became clear that the ships had fallen victim to either human torpedoes, whose existence had long been suspected, or some new form of underwater attack. Human torpedo activity had already been reported by intelligence sources in Italy, where underwater warfare had already reached an advanced state of development even before the war began, and where training for underwater attack was now taking place in the harbour at La Spezia.

The Italian Army and Air Force did not emerge from the Second World War with a high reputation. The Italian soldier was not warlike and the Italian Airforce was not one to be reckoned with when compared with the Luftwaffe or the RAF, but the men of the Italian Navy – professional, courageous and well led – were an entirely different matter. The Italian underwater flotillas, both frogmen and human torpedoes, were to cause the Royal Navy considerable problems in the next three years and

British attempts to counter their attacks and match their equipment took some time to develop ... but then the Italians did have a head start.

The Italian Navy had, been experimenting with underwater warfare since 1935, after two young Naval officers, Lieutenants Toschi and Tesei, had produced draft plans for a craft they called a 'human torpedo'. They had these plans professionally prepared and examined by marine engineers and then presented them to Admiral Cavagnari, the Chief of the Italian Navy, as the outline for a new form of attack craft. The thinking behind the idea was that, since torpedoes launched from ships or submarines were notoriously inaccurate, it might be better to have men actually 'ride' the torpedoes and guide them close to the side of the enemy craft. The 'torpedo' part of this scheme was not actually a normal torpedo, with men sitting on top and clinging on grimly, but a true, submersible craft, carrying an explosive charge. It would have a crew of two men who had the dangerous task of steering the torpedo to its objective and attaching the charge to the hull of the target ship, a task that would require skill, training, experience – and a considerable amount of raw courage. These were early days, and hardly any of the necessary equipment to do this job existed in a workable form. It was just an idea, but a brilliant one, and the Italians worked hard to turn it into a ship-killing weapon.

Admiral Cavagnari was certainly impressed with the idea. He ordered the construction of a prototype, which was tested in the harbour of the La Spezia naval base in December 1936. The entire project was fraught with risk, both navigational and technical, and a large number of snags had to be overcome, but the Italians persisted. By the time they entered the war against the Allies in June 1940, they had a number of trained and experienced human-torpedo teams at La Spezia, organised in a Special Force company called the H Group. Thanks to a great deal of hard, dangerous work, this group was equipped with efficient underwater breathing apparatus and adequate diving suits, equipment far in advance of that held, if at all, by other navies. In August 1940, human-torpedo teams from the La Spezia H Group were deployed against the British Mediterranean Fleet, when three teams were sent to attack the battleships and aircraft carriers of the Royal Navy, supposedly secure in the British Naval base at Alexandria in Egypt.

Compared with some later developments, these Italian human torpedoes were fairly primitive craft. A 1940 human torpedo is best imagined as a submersible canoe, 22 feet long, with a 500 pound detachable high-explosive warhead in the nose. The torpedo was driven by an electric motor powering twin propellers and had a top speed of about three knots – anything faster and the men riding the torpedo could be washed off. This weapon, with its pilot and co-pilot – normally an officer and a petty officer – would be launched from a large submarine some miles from its target. The men would approach the enemy vessel on the surface, the torpedo partially submerged, with just their heads above water. With care, and after dark, they were virtually invisible.

Their air supply was limited and they would not dive until they were only a few hundred yards away from the target. They would make their final underwater approach and attach the warhead of the torpedo under the target vessel by suspending it from a steel cable which they would hook on to the target vessel's bilge keels, the two shallow keels which project from the hull of most merchant vessels and warships. That done, and the limited air supply in their underwater breathing apparatus almost exhausted, the crew would withdraw, surface, and attempt to make their way back to their parent submarine. If all went well, and they escaped undetected, the explosive charge would go off some hours later, leaving wreckage and confusion behind.

The Italians' first attempt to attack the British Fleet in Alexandria failed because the parent submarine was spotted and sunk by British aircraft near Tobruk, with the loss of all crew and passengers. A month later, the Italians tried again, sending H Group teams to attack Gibraltar and Alexandria. When these harbours were found to be empty of worthwhile targets, the carrying submarines were ordered to withdraw. However, one of them, the *Gondar*, was spotted and depth charged to the surface by Royal Navy warships, and everyone on board was captured. This included Lieutenant Commander Eduardo Toschi, one of the naval officers who had pioneered the entire human-torpedo project in 1935. Toschi kept his mouth shut, and the two human-torpedo craft secured to the outer hull of the *Gondar* went down undetected with the parent submarine.

The British therefore remained in ignorance of the threat and two months later, in November 1940, the Italians tried again, sending the submarine *Scire* and three human torpedoes to attack Gibraltar. Here they found an ideal target, the British battleship HMS *Barham*, a mouth-watering sight to the Italian raiders viewing the anchorage through the *Scire*'s periscope.

Three human torpedoes were duly sent against HMS *Barham*, but two broke down inside the harbour and had to be scuttled and the pilot of the third craft, Lieutenant Brindelli, lost his no. 2 when his co-pilot's breathing apparatus went awry and the man became unconscious. Then the engine of the torpedo failed, but Lieutenant Brindelli, a very gallant and tenacious officer, continued swimming *and pulling* his submerged craft toward the *Barham*, on his own – until his breathing set also failed, and he was forced to abandon the attempt and swim to the quay. There, he was promptly captured, but he went into captivity without revealing what he had been doing, swimming around Gibraltar harbour in the middle of the night.

These attacks continued, without success, and for a while without detection, with another attempt on Gibraltar in May 1941, and an attack on the Grand Harbour of Malta in July 1941. This last attack was a disaster, for the defenders were on the alert, destroying one torpedo with its crew and capturing another of the inventors, Lieutenant Commander Tesei. By now the commander in chief of the Mediterranean-based British Naval Forces was fully aware of the threat of underwater attack and had ordered nightly patrols of all harbours, plus the formation of a diving group to examine the hulls of ships that may have been victims of clandestine attacks in neutral ports.

In Gibraltar this signal was marked for the attention of Lieutenant William Bailey, then RMSO (Render Mines Safe Officer) for the naval base. Lieutenant Bailey had previously been concerned with destroying mines floating in from offshore minefields or mines dropped by enemy aircraft, and he would later work with P Parties, clearing mines from harbours in France and Belgium after D-Day, but he now decided to form an underwater group of volunteers, made up of men qualified in shallow-water diving. Shallow-water diving was taught to selected volunteers in the Royal Navy, ratings who were then expected to go over the side of ships in harbour, either to free a cable caught around the screw, or pick up some valuable object or piece of equipment dropped overboard by some careless hand. A shallow-water diver would use an airline from the surface and anything more complicated – or deeper – required the attention of a properly trained helmet diver. Free diving, as it is now known, did not exist because the necessary free-diving equipment – the aqualung, demand valve and wet suit – had not yet been invented. Finding some way to swim and survive underwater during these hull inspections was one of Lieutenant Bailey's first tasks.

Volunteers came from the shore establishment in Gibraltar and included Lieutenant L K P 'Buster' Crabb, a man who would become one of the legends of underwater warfare, and who would come to an untimely end after the war. Buster Crabb had tried to enter the Royal Navy in 1939, on the outbreak of war, but he had been rejected on medical grounds. He therefore went off and joined the Merchant Navy and came back into the Royal Navy via the Reserve, any of his physical shortcomings being overlooked. Crabb was an experienced helmet diver who had worked as a clearance diver in Palestine before the war, and his experience and strong, cheery personality was to prove a real asset to Bailey's newly formed force.

Bailey's group, which was first known simply as the Underwater Working Party, was quite small to begin with, just two officers and three petty officers. Their designated tasks included 'countering Human Torpedoes and Limpeteers [swimmers attaching limpet mines to shipping], finding bilge bombs [explosive charges attached to the bilges of ships], the removal of depth charges from sunken ships and aircraft, and the recovery of dead bodies'.

This last role provided their first task, when they had to remove the bodies from the crashed aircraft carrying the Polish General Sikorsky to London after it fell into Gibraltar bay. This diving work was extremely hazardous, and was made much more so because the divers still had only the most primitive swimming and breathing equipment, adapted from that supplied for other purposes. For clothing they wore swimming trunks and tennis shoes. For arms they carried an assortment of knives. For underwater breathing they used the Davis Submarine Emergency Apparatus (DSEA), exactly the same as the kind supplied to the crews of submarines but with two air canisters instead of one. This gave them an underwater endurance of about twenty minutes – if they controlled their breathing carefully. They had goggles which helped them to see underwater, but no swim-fins or any form of protection from the hazards they might encounter underwater such as from barbed wire, depth charges or questing sharks. Even so, they were soon extremely busy, and out in the harbour by day and night.

The bulk of their work consisted of examining the hulls of newly arrived vessels for limpet mines that might have been placed on these ships during a stop in a neutral port in Spain or Portugal. All ships arriving in Gibraltar had to have an underwater search and before long this vigilance paid dividends, when a limpet mine was found on the iron-ore carrier SS *Imber*, newly arrived in Gibralter after a stop in the Spanish port of Seville. Limpet mines were found and removed from other ships, all of which had made previous landfalls in Spanish ports, and for a while it was thought that this was the only way the enemy were sinking ships in protected British ports.

Then came the disaster of 19 September, when, as described above, three British merchant ships were sunk within hours. Three months later, on the night of 18 December 1941, the Italians struck again and finally scored a major success against the British Fleet in Alexandria.

The targets at Alexandria were two British battleships, HMS *Valiant* and HMS *Queen Elizabeth*, both major units of the Mediterranean Fleet. Three human-torpedo teams were launched from the submarine *Scire* and made their way into the harbour, one for each of the battleships, and one for an oil tanker. Commandant Count Luigi de la Pene was tasked to attack HMS *Valiant* and though his no. 2, Petty Officer Bianchi, was swept from the craft and forced to the surface, de la Pene went on alone and managed to jettison his explosive charge under the bows of the British warship. He was then forced to abandon his craft and, along with Bianchi, was captured and taken on board *Valiant*, to be confronted by Captain Charles Morgan.

Morgan interrogated the two Italians, who refused to say what they had been doing. Morgan then ordered that the two men be taken down to the bilges, in the lowest part of the ship, and kept there until they agreed to talk. If they had indeed sabotaged the ship, they would suffer the full effect of the resulting explosion. The two Italians sat there for two hours, saying nothing, until Captain Morgan relented. He then had the two Italians brought to the wardroom, where they were all having much needed gin and tonics when the explosive charge went off beneath the hull.

A few minutes later, the charge laid under HMS *Queen*

Elizabeth also went off and, badly damaged, both vessels sank. Fortunately, since they were in shallow water, the ships only settled a few feet to the bed of the harbour, and there they sat. The tanker was also sunk, but all the Italian raiders had been captured and subsequent Italian air reconnaissance failed to notice that the British ships were resting on the bottom. The report that went back to La Spezia therefore stated that the human-torpedo attack had failed. It was in fact a major blow to the British Fleet and might have had even more serious consequences had the Italians found out how successful the raiders had actually been.

This attack on the two British battleships in Alexandria was a great feat of arms and the two battleships were out of the war for some time. These was also an interesting sequel when, in March 1945, the Italian Government awarded Commandant de la Pene the Medaglio d'Ora, Italy's highest decoration for gallantry, for sinking the British warships. Italy had capitulated in September 1943 and was now an ally of Great Britain, and Captain Charles Morgan, now Admiral Morgan, happened to be with Count de la Pene when the medal arrived. Claiming that no one knew better than he did what these gallant Italian seamen had achieved, Admiral Charles Morgan insisted on pinning the decoration on the chest of the man who had sunk his ship three years before. Commandant de la Pene remarked later that the British are a curious people.

Italy did not enter the war on the side of the Allies until 1943, and until that time their underwater attacks continued. The Italians made another attempt against HMS *Queen Elizabeth* when she was under repair in a floating dock, this time losing all of the three crews involved. They also tried a new tactic by sending twelve specially trained swimmers, equipped with limpet mines, against a British convoy in Gibraltar. Four ships were damaged and all the swimmers escaped to their secret base just across the bay from Gibraltar, at Algeciras.

This attack represents the next development in the underwater war. The Italians were now using frogmen, suited swimmers using underwater breathing apparatus. In the summer of 1942 Lieutenant Bailey encountered one of these frogmen in Gibraltar harbour and attacked him with a knife, ripping the Italian's rubber suit before he got away. This is the only definite account of hand-to-hand underwater combat, of the type so often depicted in James Bond movies. Shortly after this Lieutenant Bailey was injured and had to leave his Gibraltar command, which passed to Lieutenant Commander Buster Crabb. Bailey was awarded the George Medal for his underwater work in Gibraltar, and he was to receive another one – and the DSO – for mine clearing off the beaches of Normandy in 1944.

Finally, in December 1942, the British in Gibraltar discovered where all these Italian frogmen and human torpedoes were coming from. This lucky discovery came on 7 December when two Italian frogmen – out of air, chilled to the bone and exhausted – were discovered sitting on the mole in Gibraltar. This was soon after the Americans had landed in Algeria and Morocco on Operation *Torch*, the Allied invasion of North Africa, and the harbour contained several US troopships loaded with American reinforcements bound for the American First Army, as well as the British battleships HMS *Nelson* and HMS *Rodney* – all prime targets. Crabb and his men were immediately ordered into the water to search the bottom of every ship, while small craft surged about trying to track down any other intruders. Several swimmers were soon encountered and three human torpedoes were detected and destroyed by explosive charges or machine-gun fire. The men captured declared that they had been launched from a submarine, but it transpired that they had in fact come from a secret base in Spain, established by the Italians in the Spanish port of Algeciras a few weeks after the start of the war

When Italy entered the war in June 1940, the Italian tanker *Olterra* was in Algeciras where, fearing that she would be seized by the British as soon as she left Spanish waters, she was immediately scuttled by her crew. They did this by opening the sea-cocks and, largely undamaged, the *Olterra* settled on the bottom with most of her upperworks out of the water. There she stayed until September 1942, when an Italian salvage crew arrived and commenced work, telling the Spanish that they intended to refloat her. In fact, they were busy turning the *Olterra* into a half-submerged base for their human torpedoes and frogmen teams. Once a hole had been cut in her hull below the water line, a quantity of human torpedoes were moved on board, ready for despatch against any likely targets that appeared in the harbour at Gibraltar. It is unlikely that the Spanish authorities were unaware of all this but, since the British – being completely unaware – made no formal protest, the Spanish let the Italians carry on.

The frogmen captured in December 1942 had come from the *Olterra*, as did the three human torpedoes who attacked Gibraltar in May 1943, sinking two ships before returning safely to base. In August 1943, the Italians did it again, sinking three ships without loss – but that was the end of the Italian attacks against British and American shipping. In September 1943, Italy requested an armistice; the dictator Mussolini was deposed and Italy soon entered the war on the side of the Allies.

This event brought various advantages to the Allied underwater effort. Quite apart from gaining the support and experience of the courageous Italian frogmen and human-torpedo crews, who quickly turned their skills against the Germans, Crabb and his men were now able to enter the *Olterra*. This had to be done discreetly, for the Spanish were still hostile and would not have permitted British frogmen to operate as they had those from Italy. Among a quantity of useful loot, Crabb and his men were able to retrieve an intact human torpedo, which he and his men used for tests and trial runs in and around Gibraltar harbour.

This craft was soon lost, but Crabb was then told to round up any Italian frogman who was willing to carry on the fight against their former German allies and enlist them on to the Allied side. This did not prove difficult as most of the Italians were more than willing to fight the Germans, and their ranks included Commander Belloni, head of the Gamma (or frogman-swimmers) Group in the Italian Underwater Forces. It is therefore fair to say that this new form of warfare was introduced by the Italians, who took the lead in training, equipment and operational techniques, certainly for the first three years of the war. Crabb spent more than a year with the Italians and made good use of his time, examining their equipment and organisation, conducting experiments and suggesting or making improvements in both equipment and techniques.

All this was most useful and encouraging, but the British in the UK faced problems that the Italians had been able to ignore. A decent, reliable and undetectable breathing apparatus must be developed. Some way must be found of inserting human torpedoes or frogmen undetected, and quickly, and a lot of technical problems needed serious study. Not the least of these was for some form of suitable clothing. British underwater units needed a warm, waterproof suit for their swimmers, divers and human-torpedo crews operating in northern waters.

The Italians, operating in the relatively warm waters of the Mediterranean, could stay in the water for several hours without discomfort, at least in the summer months. However, there were other targets which rested in less hospitable climes, most notably the German battleship *Tirpitz*, which represented an ever-present threat to the North Atlantic and Russian convoys and therefore had to be destroyed. *Tirpitz* lay at anchor in the chilly waters of a Norwegian fjord and her destruction at the hands of British X-craft is recounted in Chapter 11.

It is surprising that neither the Germans nor the Japanese, both highly technical nations, took any real part in this underwater war. The Germans had a miniature submarine, the *Beiber*, and had several trained underwater frogman units, but they made no real effort to employ them. The Japanese had midget torpedoes but, again, rarely used them. The Germans also had Commando units, not least the one led by Otto Skorzeny, and an SAS-style unit, the Brandenberg Force, which gave the SBS a certain amount of trouble in the Aegean, but, other than the Italians, the Axis played no significant part in underwater warfare. Some men, drawn from SS punishment battalions and formed into the SS Underwater Swimming and Assault Group, were employed in human torpedoes, using equipment taken over from the Italians after 1943. Another force, the German Swimming Unit, attempted to float mines down the River Waal, to be used against the bridge at Nijmegen during the Arnhem operation of September 1944. However, these instances apart, this area of activity was left to the Italians and the Allies.

The pioneers – Lieutenants Toschi, Tesei and Brunetti, Commander Count de la Penne and Lieutenants Bailey and Crabb – were operating at the extreme edge of underwater technology, and doing so not in peace but in time of war, when there were enough risks around without courting more in the depths of the sea or from hastily developed equipment. They had to make do with what they had, and fight a war at the same time. Their work was not widely appreciated and the crews were usually regarded, secretly if not openly, as expendable. If their attacks succeeded, all well and good; if not, the loss was small. Both sides, the attacking Italians and the defending British, still had a great deal to learn.

Even so, in 1940/41, a start had been made. It was on a small scale but it was a beginning, arising from the beliefs and guts of a few individual canoeists and frogmen who took the risks in these early days and who can rightly claim to be the forerunners of the later and more modern underwater warriors of the SBS. A great deal of work still had to be done, for a story of this sort of warfare is a story of constant struggle, not only against the enemy but also against scientific obstacles, the shortcomings of the equipment and, not least, the sea. Against this, the early pioneers had only ingenuity, courage and tenacity, but in the end those qualities were enough to get the job done.

4

SBS EQUIPMENT, TECHNIQUES AND TRAINING

'Down at a depth of thirty feet,
Lives a guy by the name of Oxygen Pete.'

Warning verse for divers, Gosport, 1942

At the end of the twentieth century the oceans of the world, though still the last, great unexplored part of planet Earth, are increasingly open to investigation by scuba divers and a wide range of submersible craft. In all the oceans, and in many swimming pools, trained divers from PADI, the US Professional Association of Diving Instructors, and the BS-AC, the British Sub-Aqua Club, pass on underwater skills to enthusiasts and holiday makers, and an offshore dive is now a common experience.

It was not like that sixty years ago. In the early years of the Second World War the oceans were regarded as treacherous, dangerous places. Other than the submariners or helmet divers, no one ventured below the waves voluntarily and all the techniques which people enjoy today had to be learned the hard way, and from scratch. The men who took Chariots into action, or dived to search for limpet mines in Gibraltar, or took their X-craft midget submarines into well-defended harbours to sink

German battleships, were not only risking their lives against the enemy – they were pioneering an entirely new kind of warfare in an inherently dangerous and little-known element.

Because their task seems simpler – it was certainly less fraught with physical hazards – it would be as well to start with the canoe raiders. Although the modern SBS uses submarines, canoes and scuba equipment, the roles of submariner, canoeist and frogman were all separate tasks in the Second World War and it is sensible, as well as accurate, to treat them separately, at least to begin with.

The first problem for the canoe raider was to find a suitable craft. This problem had to be tackled from various angles, for a decision on a suitable craft was largely conditioned by the task the canoe raiders had to perform. It should be appreciated that this was not a simple 'one man, a rifle and a 24-hour ration pack' operation. Canoe raiding was complicated and, since the operation might last days rather than hours, the craft would have to carry a quantity of stores including limpet mines, anchors, weapons and ammunition, food, dry clothing, navigation equipment and signalling apparatus. A canoe had to be strong, but not too heavy, a good seaboat, but virtually invisible ... the combination of requirements was not an easy one to fill. A final requirement was that the canoe could be put through the hatches or conning tower of a submarine. This called for a collapsible craft – and so the complications multiplied.

The Cockle II, as used on the Bordeaux raid and widely in service with Special Forces until the 1960s, was a sturdy craft, sixteen feet long and just over two feet wide, with a one-foot draft and a collapsed depth of six inches. The sides were rubberised fabric and the stout plywood bottom had two runners, or bilge keels, running the length of the canoe, which acted both as keels, to prevent the craft rolling over, and as protection for the hull, in the event of the canoe running on to rock or shingle. Unloaded, the craft weighed about 90 pounds, but this increased rapidly when the crew loaded the craft with weapons and stores. The Operation *Frankton* canoes each carried around 300 pounds of equipment, plus the two crew members.

Unloaded, or when carrying one man, this canoe would float even when full of water, but when both men were on board, or the canoe was equipped for raiding, shipping a lot of water would cause it to submerge. Then the only solution would be for one man to get out and stay in the water while the one on board bailed. Once in the canoe, sitting on low seats just above the bottom boards, the two crew members attached an elasticised cover round the top of the canoe and fitted the elasticised bottom of their canoe jackets to the edges of their cockpits, aiming to create a waterproof seal.

These canoes were not very stable. They had to be kept bows-to-the-waves as they could easily turn over if they got across them, and it was virtually impossible to roll a loaded canoe upright again. The craft had a small rudder, but it was usually steered by the front man, or no. 1, the commander and navigator, who could turn the bow by making wider, or more, strokes with his double paddle. The no. 2, in the rear cockpit, kept time with the no. 1 and also kept an all-round lookout.

Paddling a canoe for any length of time was hard work and it took a lot of practise and long hours on the water to build up the necessary strength and stamina. The normal practice, at least among British SBS men, was to use double paddles, which were feathered to reduce wind resistance. These could be unjointed to produce single paddles, which were quieter and less obvious when close to the enemy. Spare paddles were also carried as part of the on-board stores. The men rested every hour, bringing their canoes together to 'raft up', rest, chat or have a snack, before moving on again. For the Bordeaux canoe raid – Operation *Frankton* – the stores per craft included eight limpet mines, grenades, ammunition, a Sten gun with silencer, a boat compass, bailers, two pairs of double paddles, first-aid equipment, food, maps of the Bordeaux area and escape equipment including a supply of French currency.

Work on canoe development had never stopped. Before the Second World War ended, canoes were being equipped with outriggers, outboard motors and even Vickers K machine guns, and post-war developments have been speeded up with the use of modern materials like fibreglass resin. There was even a submersible canoe – the so-called 'Sleeping Beauty' – that the Australian raiders used on Operation *Rimau* in 1945, but the basic Klepper-style folboat, though constantly improved, remains the most popular craft. Steps have also been taken to improve the efficiency of post-operation pick-up by canoes and fast raiding craft.

The *Frankton* raiders could not be picked up after their mission to Bordeaux, but in the Mediterranean most canoeists expected to be picked up by their parent submarine after the raid, though it was tacitly understood that the submarine and her crew were more valuable than two SBS men and a canoe. If matters went awry, the submarine would have no choice but to dive deep and sail away – but this rarely happened. The main problem for the canoeists was in finding the submarine again, in the dark and often turbulent sea. All manner of methods were tried, from heading out to sea on a compass bearing to using an infra-red lamp, or a carefully shaded torch.

Understandably, it was thought that the canoeists would have a better chance of seeing a large object like a submarine rather than the submariners hunting down a small canoe. However, it did not work out like that since visibility from a canoe is very restricted. Eventually, in early 1943, the answer was found in a simple homing device called the 'bongle', which was a metal rod attached to a hammer. The bongle was held over the side of the canoe and turned rapidly. The hammer hit the rod and a noise was transmitted underwater to the submarine's Asdic, which was now so sensitive that it could pick up a 'bongling' canoe at a seven-mile range. Simply by following the sounds, the submarine swiftly came down on her charges. It was simple and it worked, and it has remained in service, though submarine insertion and extraction of raiding or recce parties now usually employs 'locking-out' and 'locking-in' techniques.

This modern method of search and find involves a submarine fitted with a Wet and Dry compartment – a form of airlock. The submarine approaches an enemy coast at periscope depth and the swimmer canoeists – usually four – enter the locking chamber and, on a given order, flood it. When the compartment is flooded the exterior hatch is opened and the men emerge, rise to the surface, inflate their rubber dingy and proceed to their allotted task. On returning to the sea later, they pick up the submarine and are either towed out to sea behind the submarine's periscope until it is safe for the submarine to surface and take them on board, or else they dive down and re-enter via the Wet and Dry compartment.

Though submariners were devoted to picking up their SBS passengers, surfacing near a hostile coast was clearly something to avoid if possible and the above solution was found during the Second World War in the Wet and Dry compartments used by the divers in X-craft, the miniature submarines.

This was clearly not a task for someone prone to claustrophobia and it needed men trained in diving and not short of nerve, but for despatching SBS and SEAL frogmen from submerged submarines, either resting on the bottom in shallow water or actually on the move, locking-in and -out was, and is, a highly effective technique. A more recent development is the Swimmer Delivery Craft, a mini-submarine developed for Special Force work which can carry a full SBS or SEAL team close inshore and insert and extract them without coming to the surface.

Some early work on this problem was carried out in the late 1960s by an SBS team based in Singapore. Their number included Major Pat Troy and Lieutenant Paddy Ashdown RM, and trials were carried out with the assistance of the 7th Submarine Flotilla. By this time all British submarines were equipped with an improved emergency breathing system known as BiBS (Built-in

Breathing System) in which every man carried a mouthpiece that they could plug in to any one of scores of breathing points set about the boat. These airlines led to two escape towers, and these towers also offered a way by which SBS men could exit and regain entry to a submerged craft. Under the codename *Goldfish*, trials took place in Singapore harbour, and they proved to be highly successful.

Further experiments followed. To cut down on operational time and save the submarine from serious overcrowding, a technique of parachuting into the sea and then diving down to lock-in to the submarine near the target was developed. Work also proceeded in developing some form of underwater motorboat that could get the frogmen quietly but quickly to their targets and back again, since swimming in, even with fins, was very slow and extremely tiring. The course of these experiments was always the same: identify and analyse the problem, work out a solution and develop the equipment and techniques that would work. This technique usually succeeded, but the process was not without risk and finding the solutions required a great deal of hard work – and some steady nerves.

There was then the matter of clothing. When Major Courtney made the first canoe recce of Rhodes in 1941, the swimmers were protected by coating their clothes with heavy grease, which did not prove very effective in keeping out the chill of winter seas. The Bordeaux raiders wore camouflaged canoe suits, which did little to keep them either warm or dry, and they had to carry badges and other Combined Operations flashes that showed clearly that they were members of a military unit and not civilian spies. Black woollen caps replaced their Royal Marine berets and their footwear was service-issue gym shoes. Modern Swimmer Canoeists have first-rate equipment using the latest scuba gear and the finest wind- and waterproof clothing.

These early canoe raiders did not carry scuba gear. They attacked ships with limpet mines, lowering them on a pole and attaching them to hull plates below the target vessel's water line with magnets. This done, they detached the rod, removed the magnetic anchor that had held their canoe in place by the ship's side and moved on to the next vessel. The need for diving equipment arose when it was found that many enemy vessels were so encrusted with seaweed and had hulls so foul that the magnets could not grip on the hull plates until a patch had been scraped clear.

Scuba gear was not even in existence until 1943, and did not come into general use until after the war. Before the Second World War, the bulk of underwater work had been carried out by helmet divers, who worked in shallow waters and were supplied with air at a normal pressure, piped in from a boat on the surface. The frogmen of the Second World War used a modified version of the DSEA equipment.

The normal use of this apparatus should be described as it will help explain some of the problems and difficulties of underwater swimming. Should a submarine get into difficulties and sink, the crew put on their DSEA equipment – basically just a nose clip and a mouthpiece connected by a tube to a canister of oxygen – and assembled at the escape hatches and in the conning tower. As the sea gushed in, the air inside the submarine was compressed until it equalled the pressure of the sea outside. At this point the hatches could be opened. In came the sea and the submariners, avoiding panic and the 'jumping wires' stretched above the outer hull, rose to the surface.

The hazards of this operation scarcely need stressing. In most submarine sinkings the majority of the crew drowned at once, dying a terrible death as the hull flooded, or they would be crushed by the sea pressure collapsing the hull as the submarine sank. Whether an escape was possible depended on how deep the submarine was and how badly she was damaged. A depth charge in the water would pulp any man swimming around it, and those who escaped from any significant depth had to make sure they did not rise too quickly or they could get the bends as nitrogen crystallised in their joints. Nitrogen makes up about four-fifths of the atmosphere and unlike oxygen has no life-giving properties. It is inert until it is put under pressure and then released, when it acts rather like a bottle of tonic water and forms bubbles in the blood-stream which lodge in the joints and cause the victim to double up in agony – hence the bends. It was to avoid the bends that divers tried using pure oxygen, but that too had its problems.

One answer to the bends, or decompression sickness, is to put the victim in a compressed air tank and restore the pressure. The only alternative would be to send him back to the original depth and have him come up slowly to the surface and normal atmospheric pressure. Neither is practical in wartime, so a controlled ascent from moderate depth was the best that could be suggested. As an aid to a controlled ascent the submariners were advised to deploy the apron that was attached to the front of the DSEA, like an inverted form of parachute, which effectively slowed their ascent.

Those who survived a sinking could expect to endure a terrible experience, and many reached the surface suffering from burst lungs or other internal injuries caused by pressure. The DSEA was of limited use and could only be used at shallow depths, but it was all there was and many men owed their lives to it. Every man volunteering for the submarine service went through a DSEA course in submarine escape procedures in the deep tank at HMS *Dolphin*, the submarine school at Gosport, and no man left until he was fully conversant with its use. However, the routine learned with difficulty in the tank at HMS *Dolphin* was a much harder routine to apply in the crowded, rapidly flooding hull of a stricken submarine.

When the underwater warriors began their mine-clearing work in Gibraltar, they soon found the DSEA equipment to be inadequate, and it was even less adequate for use by frogmen attacking enemy shipping. The main snag with it was that the DSEA used oxygen. The use of oxygen did have one advantage in that it did not produce surface bubbles and therefore did not reveal the presence of a frogman to vigilant patrols on the surface. However, on the other hand, oxygen under pressure and below a certain depth introduced the diver to a new enemy, oxygen narcosis – Oxygen Pete.

Underwater, it is only safe to breathe pure oxygen down to about thirty feet. Below that depth oxygen narcosis will most probably occur, since the metabolism of the body is changed by the increasing pressure – reaching two atmospheres, or 30 lb psi. The effects of oxygen narcosis are frightening, dangerous and rapid. The diver will suddenly experience hallucinations and physical spasms to the lips and extremities, followed by blackout and – if not removed and taken to the surface promptly – even death. Oxygen Pete is a killer and it severely limited the use of oxygen for most free-diving operations. Even today, the best way to avoid a meeting with Oxygen Pete is to stay above thirty feet when breathing oxygen.

In 1941 the Siebe Gorman company invented a form of the DSEA – the Amphibian Mark I – which allowed a diver to work underwater for up to an hour, though only down to thirty feet. The secret was a device known as 'pendulum breathing', which allowed the diver's exhaled air, rich in carbon dioxide, to be fitted and recycled back to the oxygen tank. Pendulum breathing was highly successful and remained the basis of underwater breathing apparatus for many years. This device enabled a diver to stay underwater for a considerable time, free of an airline, but some method still had to be found to help him stay down and move about.

Most humans – well over ninety per cent – are naturally buoyant. Left to their own devices most people who keep calm and lie on their backs will float, especially in the more buoyant saltwater – most people drown because they panic. Divers, especially those carrying air tanks, are therefore bound to come to the surface, so they have to be kept down with weights. Adjusting the weights to the diver's natural buoyancy and air tanks is a necessary diving skill which takes some time to learn – it varies with the individual, the salinity of the water and the equipment carried. Once the diver has got the buoyancy right, and can stay below the surface, he still has to move.

Swimming underwater is difficult and tiring – water is dense and offers resistance. In the early days it was envisaged that the divers would get about by walking along the bottom, as helmet divers did, and then float up to plant a mine on the hull of the target vessel. Experiments showed that this was difficult if not impossible and, anyway, far too slow. The solution was found among holidaymakers on the beaches of California – swim-fins or flippers, not unlike those provided naturally to the frog, and hence the name 'frogman'.

The frogman could now move and stay underwater for some time, but there was another limiting factor – the chill of the water, especially in northern climes. Water leaches warmth from the body and after a certain amount of time the frogman will be unable to function as his senses are overcome by cold. Clearly, some form of insulated suit was needed. The first effective model used by frogmen and Charioteers was the Sladen suit, named after the submarine officer who invented it. Two forms of diving dress were eventually evolved – the dry suit, where the diver was insulated from the water and, in 1941, the free-flooding or the wet suit, where water was allowed into the suit to be warmed by the diver's body heat, thus acting as another, and most effective, form of insulation. It proved almost impossible to keep a dry suit dry, and if it got torn its effect was immediately lost, so the wet suit eventually became the most popular.

Experiments to find out just how effective these suits were involved volunteers sitting or swimming about, sometimes for hours, in tanks of water chilled by blocks of ice. It was found that men could get used to low water temperatures but that it was impossible to work, place mines or cut wire when wearing gloves. To find that out, volunteers sat for hours with their hands in bowls of icy water; when they could stand no more and took their hands out, they were swollen to the size of boxing gloves.

Finally, the diver had to be able to see. Seeing underwater with the naked eye is very difficult, but put a layer of glass and trapped air between the eyes and the water and normal visibility is restored. Again, to begin with, the goggles used with the DSEA were called into play, but these offered only limited visibility and it was soon discovered that a full face mask was far better. Other items were added from time to time including a protective kapok jacket, which proved very effective in reducing the otherwise fatal effects of depth charges or explosives thrown into the water by the enemy to deter diving activity or when frogmen were known to be about. All these items, some commonly used today, had to be invented or discovered by an often painful process of trial and error during the years of the Second World War.

This frogman equipment – suit, air set, swim-fins and face mask – eventually became the standard equipment for underwater work, with small adaptations for those using it in X-craft, COPP, LCOCU or Chariot work. Something very similar is in use today by SBS units all over the world.

The successful development of the basic frogman outfit enabled work on the human torpedo (the Chariot) to proceed at some speed. The British began their experiments in 1942, after the Italians had shown the way. The big snag that hampered the work was our old friend Oxygen Pete and a great many brave men risked their lives, damaged their health and experienced some terrible blackouts in experimental work in the deep diving tanks at Gosport and in open-water work at sea and in the Scottish lochs. Slowly it was discovered that oxygen was less lethal when mixed with other gases, like nitrogen and helium, and a mixture of gases enabled the diver to work at depths of up to sixty feet – but the problem always needed watching.

So too did the salinity of the water. In early experiments in Scottish lochs many Chariot divers were alarmed when, for no apparent reason, their craft, creeping along just under the surface, suddenly lost all buoyancy and plunged out of control for the bottom. When this took place at night and far from the shore it left them in a dangerous position, and they were also at risk from increased pressure if they stayed with the craft and tried to control it. Some lives were lost before the problem was eventually traced to the matter of 'trim'.

Like the buoyant human body, most submerged objects tend to rise to the surface. The main task of the first lieutenant in a submarine is to adjust the boat's trim, by adjusting the amount of water in the buoyancy tanks, so that the submarine stays at the desired depth under the control of the hydroplanes, and therefore neither rises to the surface nor plunges to the bottom. This is known in the submarine service as 'putting on the trim'. Maintaining a level trim is a constant task and, during a normal dive, making slight adjustments to the basic trim is the responsibility of the officer of the watch. Chariots also had to maintain a trim, and the normal method of putting on the trim for a Chariot, after release from the towing vessel, was to go to the bottom and adjust the buoyancy there until the craft lifted clear and level.

The sudden dives arose because freshwater is far less buoyant than saltwater. Scottish sea-lochs, though open to the Atlantic, are also fed by streams from the hills, and where these streams entered the lochs the buoyancy changed abruptly, hence those alarming descents. Freshwater patches or patches of low salinity are not uncommon in all saltwater, especially in the fjords of Norway, and a constant need to watch the trim and take rapid action in the event of striking low salinity had to be added to the Chariot diver's skills.

The most refined weapon supplied to the underwater raider in the Second World War was the X-craft or midget submarine. This was a proper submarine and will be described in detail later, but to use and fight with all these weapons the crews had to be trained – and that itself was a dangerous and generally uncomfortable process.

The first Charioteers started with dives in the fifteen-foot diving tank at HMS *Dolphin*, where they were taught the basic DSEA techniques. They were then sealed in the pressurised diving tank at Siebe Gorman's works and taken down, artificially, to fifty feet – and a meeting with Oxygen Pete. They then moved on to diving in sheltered water, then the open sea, first by day and then by night. They also began to work in pairs and two became the accepted number for an underwater team. The training continued with a course in shallow-water helmet diving in the Solent. Those who wished to continue were then allowed to volunteer for Chariots.

Much of this training took place in the Scottish lochs and had three basic purposes. Firstly, the crews had to learn how to control their craft and handle emergencies. The only way to do that and gain confidence in the craft was to spend days and nights on and under the water. They then had to learn the approach skills, navigation, net cutting and the negotiation of obstacles. Finally, they had to learn attack procedures and practise them constantly, day and night, until they were confident that they could find their way into an enemy harbour whatever the dangers or difficulties. It took training, lots and lots of training, including hundreds of practice attacks.

An account given by an Australian Commando, Robert Butt, who undertook an SC3 course with the Royal Marines at Poole in 1975, provides an interesting insight into post-war SBS training. The Australian Commando Companies, which are Territorial Reserve formations, and the Australian SAS Regiment, have always had close connections with the SBS and the Royal Marines Commandos. When the post-war Australian Commando Companies were formed in the 1950s, Royal Marines instructors, including Sergeant Len Holmes of the SBS, were sent out to get them started and there has been a constant to-ing and fro-ing of personnel between Britain and Australia ever since, one of them being Lieutenant Robert Butt:

I was living in Britain at the time and serving with the Royal Marines Reserve in Bermondsey when I was called before a panel for SC training. The course was to last fourteen weeks and I was called for the week before Christmas. There was a bit of a problem with the paperwork since I was from another country, a reserve officer not a regular, and so could not be fully 'seconded' as a regular soldier might be. I won't describe the procrastination and general unhelpfulness of the military personnel at Australia House but, anyway, the Brits soon sorted it out and on 2 January I arrived at Poole.

The first two or three days were great. Morning PT started at 0600 hours, which at that time of the year means in the dark. The officers' mess was about half a mile from the start of every course activity, so from the first PT to the end of the day I was constantly doing a mile run-around trip, back and forth to my quarters. The others on this course were all Marines, about 25 of them, volunteers from the Commando Units, the two exceptions being myself and another Australian soldier.

After the first week, getting kit, PT and lectures, we were introduced to a large inland pool of water, not very deep, covered with ice and, at that time of the year, bloody cold. We had to plunge into this pool, every morning, cleanskin to toughen you up, or so they said, and we did not need much encouragement to sprint back to barracks afterwards.

The course introduced the student to complete basic training in canoeing, small boat handling, diving (both on air and oxygen), ship searches (defensive), explosives, specialist weapons, ship attack (offensive), small-scale raids, signalling and many other skills. All these were related to small team operation, raiding and survival. It was very intensive and extremely strenuous, requiring not only physical stamina but mental alertness and toughness as well. Only seven of the twenty-plus who started completed the course.

Our training took us to various locations around the south coast of England, including the naval base at

Portsmouth, the Royal Marine barracks at Eastney, Falmouth, Chatham and the Isle of Wight, with the final raid exercise taking place in the Thames estuary.

At Portsmouth there is – or was – a disused torpedo-range tank, like a colossal swimming pool, 1,500 metres long, a hundred metres wide and about ten metres deep. A lot of our diving was practised there and it was ideal for oxygen training, for the student or the experienced diver could not go below one atmosphere (33 feet), which is the limit in oxygen diving. However, swimming along in a 1,500-metre tank is quite boring, and many days and nights were spent here drearily logging up airtime.

Most of this was done wearing dry suits, instead of wet suits, and that was a different matter. We wore whatever we liked underneath, tracksuit, jumper, socks, whatever, and the suit only had three apertures, at the neck and the two wrists. The neck was sealed with a brass loop or neckband and the suit was really quite difficult to get into. In fact it took two people, 'dressers', to get each other into it and, until we got the knack, it took ages. We also had to make sure that the neck and wrists were absolutely waterproof because once in the water even a few drops turned you into a wet, miserable, submersible blob. The test for RN ships' divers, who were usually Marines but sometimes Navy personnel, was to get fully dressed in one of these suits and over the side *in two minutes*, which was no mean feat, I assure you.

It was winter, so picture this. We are at the diving point and I am in a dry-suit. I lower my tanks over the edge and, instead of hearing a splash, I hear a clunk. The dam surface is frozen! That is when I knew for certain that I was not imagining the cold and started dreaming of warm Australian waters.

Pure-oxygen diving is something else again. A canister of pellets (pendulum breathing) is attached to the diver's vest and sealed by rubber rings and metal clasps. It is essential that no water gets in here otherwise, instead of turning your expelled carbon dioxide breath into oxygen, it poisons you. Each time a new canister is used it is sealed and tested to ensure there are no leaks. Various gas mixes are used today, twenty years later, so the problem is not as complicated as it used to be.

We also visited and used the Royal Navy submarine evacuation test tank at Gosport. At the time it was the only one in the world and even Royal Australian Navy submariners came over to use it. It is not a dive but an escape hatch, used to simulate escapes from depths of up to a hundred feet – say thirty metres. Most submariners only want to do it once. It is quite spooky and something you don't want to think about if your work takes you down in submarines.

There were a number of interesting challenges as well, when working with the Klepper canoes during the weeks we were waterborne. Some good times were spent paddling various inland waters including sliding over waterfalls, some of which were three meters high. I was surprised at the amount of punishment those canoes could take. On another occasion we tried to paddle from Portsmouth to the Isle of Wight, about ten miles, but we did not make it. The sea was very rough and after an hour or so of paddling we were still not more than a mile or so offshore. When we rafted up – brought the canoes together – for a rest, we lost ground very quickly, so it was better to keep going.

The waves were very treacherous but, although drenched, we wanted to see if we could make it. A search-and-rescue helicopter was despatched by some well-meaning shore station that thought we were in difficulty, which was not really the case, though we were cold, wet and exhausted. It was really just another day's canoeing, and later we did a lot of canoe work around the coast which made up for this 'failure'.

Our final exercise was an 'attack' on some oil refineries at the mouth of the Thames. Each day we had to bring the canoes ashore, find a hide and lie up.

However, the only place to lie up was on some small and smelly mud flats covered with short scrubby grass about a metre high. This meant we had to lie alongside our craft all day, unable to stand or cook, or brew up. We did this for several days, and were we glad to see the end of that exercise.

A final word about our brothers in arms, the Royal Marines Commandos and especially the Special Boat Service. They were proud and professional and prepared to tackle anything that seemed to be a challenge. I hope that can be said of us too. We should all know that the physical rigours and mental challenges of our training will always stand us in good stead.

Those who want to join the SBS today begin by joining the Royal Marines, or the Royal Marines Reserve, and completing basic training and the Commando course. Regular Marines will then have to serve a full two-and-a-half-year commission with a Commando Unit before being considered for SBS training, since the type of man required must be both a trained Commando and a mature man. The first step is to volunteer for SBS training, take a two-week aptitude test and successfully complete the Joint Special Forces Selection Course in the recon Beacons in South Wales. The aptitude test comes in two parts, boating and diving, each lasting a week.

The boating phase includes swimming tests, canoe trials and the combat fitness test. The diving phase, arranged for non-divers, requires the candidate to show some aptitude for diving, 'confidence in the water' and an ability to absorb diving instruction. A number of volunteers either drop out or are rejected at this stage. Those who pass go on to the JSF Selection Course, which lasts around four months and involves tough physical work such as marching in the Beacons and in the jungles of Borneo. This is the standard SAS course, the core of which is a great deal of cross-country map marching involving ever-longer hikes with ever-heavier packs. There is another swimming test and another combat fitness test. Those who pass go on to Continuation Training in specialist tasks such as demolition and close-quarter combat, and all have to complete the service parachute course. The total process, from volunteering to passing the preliminary courses, takes about a year.

The students then depart for their parent units, the SAS to the Regiment, the SBS back to the Corps to start their SBS training. This takes a further two to three months and involves diving, canoeing, working with submarines, navigation, ship attack, small-scale raids and signalling. Only when all this has been successfully completed does the volunteer, now a badged SC3 Marine, join his SBS unit but, in reality, as in all good units, the training never stops.

5

2 SBS AND 101 TROOP IN NORTH AFRICA 1942–43

'Creep in, set the traps, hang about, collect the spoils and get away without being caught. The golden rule was "Don't make any slip-ups and have your line of retreat well thought out beforehand."'

SBS tactics, 1943, *SBS in World War Two*
G B Courtney

By the time Roger Courtney returned to the UK and formed the second SBS unit, his ideas on the merits of canoes and beach recce had been accepted. There was now a Combined Operations Headquarters (COHQ) which had been formed in late 1941, first under Admiral Keyes and then under Vice-Admiral Lord Louis Mountbatten. Apart from raiding the enemy coast and generally making life difficult for the occupying Nazi powers, COHQ had the responsibility of developing and testing amphibious warfare techniques and equipment for the forthcoming invasion of Europe, an invasion that must come if the Germans were ever to be defeated. Getting ashore could never be easy, but by the summer of 1942 the benefits of beach recce were obvious to all and Roger Courtney was the man who knew most about it . . . hence the formation of 2 SBS.

The first major task of 2 SBS was to recce the beaches for Operation *Torch*, the landing of US and British troops in Morocco and Algeria to open a second front in North Africa. This landing took place in early November 1942, a few weeks after the British Eighth Army had inflicted a great defeat on the Afrika Korps at El Alamein. *Torch* itself was a delicate operation politically, for Morocco and Algeria were then in the hands of the Vichy French, troops of the Pétain regime that then ruled in France and co-operated closely with the Germans. Killing Frenchmen was not part of the Allied plan, but the British were hated by the Vichy French, for the Royal Navy had sunk the French Mediterranean Fleet at Mers el Kebir in 1940, to stop it falling into German hands, and this action, though necessary, had not been forgotten or forgiven by the French. For this reason, American troops and American generals were in charge of *Torch*.

The SBS took part in four distinct operations connected with *Torch*. With the embryo COPP team, under Lieutenant Commander Clogstoun-Willmott, they marked the beaches for the two landings, *Torch* itself, in Morocco and Algeria, and *Reservist*, the subsequent landing at Oran. Prior to that, in the hope that the French in North Africa would not resist the Allied invasion, an American general, Mark Clark, was carried ashore in Algeria by the SBS to talk a deal with the French commanders.

This last affair, Operation *Flagpole*, was commanded by Roger Courtney's brother, Captain G B Courtney. His task was to get General Clark, and a party of senior American officers, ashore in Algeria for a (very) secret meeting with General Mast, the man commanding the French forces around Algiers and Arzew – the nominated landing area for the US First Army. To achieve this, Courtney had two SBS officers embark on HMS/M *Seraph*, which was commanded by an officer well used to clandestine operations, Lieutenant N L A Jewell. On the evening of 20 October the US officers were given a brief lesson in how to board a folboat in the open sea and at

0400 hours that night, just before dawn, the *Seraph* surfaced off the Algerian coast and the party went ashore.

The Americans duly met General Mast, but negotiations did not go speedily and Clark decided they had to stay ashore and carry on the discussions until some agreement was reached. This was achieved later that day and at 2200 hours the party returned to the beach, pulled the canoes from hiding . . . and found great waves pounding on the beach. Getting through the surf was a very dicey business and there were several capsizes before the American officers were safely on their way. *Seraph* appeared as arranged and before long everyone was below decks and heading for Gibraltar. Round One to the SBS.

Their next task was to rescue General Henri Giraud from the South of France. Giraud was considered vital to the Allied cause in North Africa because he alone could persuade the French there to abandon their links with collaborationist Vichy and come over to the Free French of General de Gaulle. Giraud had been captured by the Germans in 1940 but had escaped from his prison camp and was now living in the Vichy-controlled South of France while the Germans urged the Vichy leaders, Pétain and Laval, to return him to captivity . . . or worse.

HMS/M *Seraph* was again tasked to take the SBS to rescue the general but, since Giraud shared the popular French antipathy for the British, it had to appear that the *Seraph* was an American submarine and an American officer, Captain Wright, joined *Seraph* for this role. Quite why the British had to put up with this sort of nonsense and why General Giraud was not confronted with a starker choice – a German concentration camp or the best interests of his country – is open to question. The plan was that the general would come out to meet the submarine in a French fishing boat but, if there was any difficulty, or he was under guard ashore, the SBS would go in and get him.

Operation *Kingpin* went like clockwork. *Seraph* surfaced off the coast of Provence on the night of 4 November and again on the night of 5 November. Giraud was brought off in a fishing boat and joined the *Seraph*, where he was greeted by Captain Wright using his broadest American accent. On the following day he was transferred by canoe to a Catalina flying boat and flown to Gibraltar. Part Two of the SBS role in *Torch* had also gone well.

Now came the actual landings, which were to involve the SBS, COPP and 101 Troop of 6 Commando. Stan Weatherall, a canoeist with 101 Troop, had an adventurous time in the Mediterranean and his story gives a good picture of SBS operations at this time:

Well, as I told you, *Torch* was not a problem for us, though our Sergeant Major J Embelin was killed by the French in Oran harbour by fire from two Vichy vessels as he was preparing explosives. We marked the beach at Arzew, going ashore from the submarine *Ursula*, and the US Rangers came in and landed without much bother. Some of them thought we were a human torpedo and did not believe we were simply there to mark the beach. I was back in Gib and about to hitch a lift for Blighty when Captain Courtney and Captain Livingstone sent for me and said that another operation was now on and, on 20 November, Captain Livingstone and I boarded the submarine *Ursula* and sailed east for the Gulf of Lions and the coast of Italy.

As soon as we were clear of Gib, the klaxons sounded for diving stations, and we submerged to periscope depth. The 21st to the 25th November were spent sailing up the coast of Spain into the Gulf of Lyons, where the sea became extremely rough. The sub rolled to 55 degrees on the night of the 26th, scooping up water with the conning tower, which went down the hatch and flooded the control room. One of the diesel engine's big-end bearings went, then the Asdic, Sperry and wireless transmitter gave up. The klaxons sounded and the sub went down to 125 feet; the waters were somewhat rough at this depth and the vessel rocked. The engine-room artificers got to work on the engine and, with continuous effort, made and fitted new bearings. Other things which had gone wrong were also put right.

On the night of the 27th, the sub surfaced the sea was not as rough as before but one or two members of the sub's crew were sick, so I volunteered to do lookout on the bridge, using night glasses for scanning the sea, focussed on infinity. While travelling on the surface the sub changed course every five minutes, by five or ten degrees to port and then starboard, but at the same time keeping on a straight course. We reached the edge of the Gulf of Genoa, north of the Ligurian Sea, and while submerged on the 28th we did periscope reconnaissance of the beach where we were to land. The sub surfaced on the night of the 29th, and with the aid of Asdic depth soundings the skipper took us into a small bay to within about 1,200 yards of the beach edge. We slipped the canoe at 1000 hours and paddled to the sea wall, right on to the V of a Y-shaped road junction. One road followed the coast; the other went through the village, which was not far from Ventimiglia. In the V stood a large house with lots of bushes and shrubbery in the garden. Two large iron gates to the house directly opposite us were fastened with wire. A courting couple came down the road, and we were held up for over half an hour because they stood necking at the iron gates.

After they left and were well up the road, Captain Livingstone nipped across, cut the wire and opened one of the gates. We carried the canoe across the road into the garden, where we hid it among the bushes. Then, leaving the garden, we crossed the other road into an orchard on a sloping hill. We then located the railway track on a twenty-foot embankment and walked along the bottom of this for some distance before we crawled up the embankment on to the track and proceeded towards the tunnel. We came to a building with a veranda and were in position on the veranda, listening to voices inside, when suddenly the door opened and a man came out. He was talking over his shoulder to his comrades as he made water, not knowing that two knives were at the ready no more than a yard away. However, we knew that, as he had only just come from a well-lit room, his eyes would not be adjusted to the darkness outside and therefore he would not detect us. This was a guardhouse for the soldiers guarding the mouth of the tunnel, for we discovered that one sentry was at the top and one on the side of the track, and they called to each other occasionally. We backed off the veranda to the bottom of the track and crawled along a hedgerow, through which we heard something moving about and thought we had been detected, so we lay low for some time, but what we heard must have been animals.

Skirting the edge of the track for quite some distance, we got up on to it just as a very long train of wagons rumbled by, going westwards. We then walked further down the track and found that it curved ideally. We placed charges on the rail, positioned to blow a six-foot gap. We also placed charges on two iron posts which carried cables supplying the villages with electricity and also carried the feed cables for the railway engines; all charges to go off simultaneously with a pressure switch under the rail. It was now past 2300 hours and we had no time to lose in making our way back to the sub by moonrise. If we didn't get back by then the sub would have to leave and come back for us the next night. We cut our way through some wire netting and got back on to the main village road, down which we moved at a brisk pace, passing several soldiers talking together in a group.

Captain Livingstone was whistling some tune from an Italian classic when, twenty yards further on, we passed another group of people talking under some trees on our right, then a long figure came towards us, a drunken soldier, who looked at us as we passed him. We retrieved our canoe and ran down the beach with it to the water's edge, launched it and paddled back to the sub with no time to spare. We hurriedly got the canoe aboard, and the sub left the bay, moving away from the area. At about midnight the lookouts on the bridge saw a brilliant flash and heard the explosion from the charge we had laid. It was published in the *Gibraltar Chronicle* that the Blue Express line was blocked for some days. It would have been blocked for very much longer if we could have derailed it in the tunnel, but our orders were 'to let the enemy know we had been, only after we had gone!'

The sub then began the return journey, keeping fairly close inshore. The next night the sub cruised on the surface and by day submerged, following the coastline, when the periscope was used a great deal. At 0145 hours on Monday 30 November, a vessel was sighted and the sub's gun crew went into action and fired a few shots across its bows. It stopped and turned out to be an Italian Asdic schooner, looking for enemy submarines. We sidled up to it and found no one aboard; the Italian crew must have beat a hasty withdrawal in their dinghy after the first shot was fired. Captain Livingstone and I boarded the vessel with some plastic HE, which we placed in depth charges on the stern, while members of the sub's crew took off two Breda guns, with ammunition, two machine guns and several .25 rifles; also, the latest sea charts – very valuable to the navy. We set the delays going and got back aboard the sub, which hung about for around an hour while we blew up the depth charge. It was an enormous explosion, causing a huge black column of smoke which rose about 300 feet into the air. A little further down the coast we were spotted by the enemy who fired Very lights, so the skipper ordered diving stations and we crept away submerged.

We were waiting for a train to come along the coast to gun it. On Tuesday 1 December at 2230 hours, a train was sighted. The gun crew went into action, first firing a star shell which lit up the area, then shells were fired which hit the train amidships. The rear half caught fire while the other half was hauled by the train's driver into a tunnel and stayed there, no doubt until he thought it safe to emerge.

In peacetime, Lieutenant Laken RN had been on holiday in this area and knew the whereabouts of an olive oil factory, and so at 0100 hours on 2 December the skipper brought the sub under the lee of a sea wall and trimmed the craft so that the sub's gun was pointing just over the top of it. The gun took to action stations, first firing a star shell. The following shells hit the olive oil tanks, which caught fire the factory chimney was hit and collapsed, and a pillbox was demolished. The sub was creeping away from the wall when the enemy opened fire on us. The nearest shell fell fifty yards away, so we crash-dived to safety. The next night at 1830 hours, soon after surfacing, a vessel was sighted heading east. The gun crew went into action. I was below in the control room, assisting in handing the shells up through the conning tower hatch to the gun crew. Several shots were fired; the vessel stopped and one Very light was fired from it, which was the only armament on board. A torpedo was released, which passed harmlessly under the ship as, having no cargo, it was too high out of the water. The ship, the *St Margueritte II*, was manned by 23 Germans, most of whom had either never been to sea in their lives before, or were merchant seamen. They launched two lifeboats, but one was smashed and so they all had to cram into one boat, which was hauled alongside the sub. The captain and chief engineer were taken aboard as prisoners, but the rest were given a direction and told to row away. One man in the lifeboat stood up and, in English, asked for food and water, but the skipper told him we were not in a position to provide any, and they were only eleven miles from land – so they rowed away.

A rope-cum-wooden-ladder was made fast to the ship and sub, and several of the sub's crew boarded her to take anything valuable to the Navy in the way of radio and charts. Captain Livingstone and I boarded the ship with a 25 pound charge, which we could not place until the crew had taken off anything of value and were ready to reboard the sub. While they were doing this, I went into one or two of the ship's cabins situated on deck and put my loot into a leather satchel – lipstick, face powder, perfume, cigarettes, German and French currency. The crew got aboard the sub and we laid the charge in the forward hold below the water line and set a ten-minute delay fuse, which gave us ample time to get back on the sub. The charge went off, creating a big hole in the vessel's plating. The ship, of some 5,000 tons, was built in Dublin and was being taken by the motley crew from Marseilles to Naples. My loot had been intended by the crew as presents to their wives when they got home and had been purchased in Marseilles. This incident took place off the Isles d'Hyeres where the vessel, as far as I know, still rests on the sea bed.

The captain of the vessel was an arrogant pro-Nazi, while the chief engineer was a dear old soul, whose job in peacetime was fishing on the Dogger Bank. He had been a prisoner of war in British hands during the First World War. He had a son who was a prisoner of war in Canada, and another son on the Russian front at Voronesh. At the end of the patrol he asked to stay on the sub as one of the crew, which he preferred to a POW camp. The leather satchel, he said, belonged to him, so I gave it back to him.

On 6 December we were off the coast of Spain when a vessel was sighted by periscope. The submarine surfaced and ordered the ship to stop. The skipper hoisted a Nazi flag and, as we drew near the vessel, the ship's crew gave us the Nazi salute, which we returned. They lowered a rowing boat and came alongside the sub, and the navigating officer and a CPO got into it and were taken aboard the ship, which they found was laden with salt. They presented us with two loaves of bread and a bottle of wine, again giving us the Nazi salute, which we returned as we drew away. They must have thought we were a German U-boat.

Up to then the sub was making her way back along the coast of Spain to Gibraltar, but a radio message was then received, telling the skipper to alter course for Algiers, and we arrived there some time during the morning of 9 December. I went ashore with two CPOs and we made our way into Algiers and proceeded up the hill into the Casbah, which, unknown to us, was out of bounds for all troops; we were escorted back to the safety of town by the redcaps. The following day, HMS *Maidstone* arrived, which I boarded and berthed in the PO's mess. During the patrol I had saved my issue of neat rum in a water bottle, which was now about full. I stayed aboard the *Maidstone* until 16 December, and one night I took out my water bottle of rum and made many friends by offering it round the mess; the POs couldn't understand why anyone should want to give away his rum – unheard of in the Navy.

On 16 December, Captain Livingstone and I left the *Maidstone* and went by truck to Maison Blanche Airport, where we boarded a USA Douglas transport plane named *Old Crow* and took off. It was a good name to give it, for its wing tips went up and down about three feet. We landed at Oran Airport, a veritable quagmire of red mud. At 1100 hours we picked up some more passengers, took off again and landed at Gibraltar at 1530 hours after a very bumpy flight. I stayed in the Almeda RAF camp until 22 December, when Captain Livingstone and I boarded the mine-laying cruiser HMS *Adventurer*. The vessel carried numerous people who had fled from the Germans, a good many coming over the Pyrenees, escorted by guides who charged them a vast amount of money. By devious routes and methods they had reached the sanctuary of the British in Gibraltar, and were now being taken to England.

HMS *Adventurer* was a very fast ship, capable of doing forty knots. Christmas Day was just the same as any other day, as the ship was not provisioned for Christmas fare. We arrived at Plymouth at 1600 hours on 26 December. I found the family with whom I had stayed in 1940 and they made me welcome. The Axis bombers had literally flattened the whole of the shopping centre and some distance around. On 28 December, Captain Livingstone and I left Plymouth for Fareham, and on 29 December I went to our HQ at Hillhead, obtained my furlough form and went on leave to see my wife and baby son, who had been born on 7 October.

The Allied landing at Oran – Operation *Reservist* – was not as easy as the landings at Arzew. Since the French Navy seemed likely to resist, it was decided that the harbour boom should be charged by two British ships, HMS *Hartland* and HMS *Waleny*, both loaded with American troops. If the impact failed to break the boom, three men of 2 SBS would go over the side in canoes and attack it with explosives or miniature torpedoes. The two ships did fail to break the boom. The French opened heavy fire which sank both of them and, as related by Stan Weatherall, one SBS man, Sergeant Major Embelin, was killed and the other two captured. The French then capitulated and the surviving SBS men made their way to Gibraltar and embarked for England on the SS *Ettrick*, which was torpedoed. The SBS men survived and were taken back to England in an American Liberator bomber.

No. 2 SBS spent the rest of the winter in the UK, training and recruiting, but in March 1943 a new unit was formed under Captain Courtney for operations with the 8th Submarine Flotilla in the Mediterranean. Known as the Z SBS, and based at Algiers, this sub-section consisted of five canoes and their crews, all officers or senior NCOs.

After a couple of weeks sorting out stores and working on their tans, an operation arrived. Captain Courtney and his second-in-command, Lieutenant 'Sally' Lunn – who, modern readers should know, was a man – were tasked to take a party of Resistance fighters to Corsica and bring out a Resistance leader, Commandant de Saule, who had been 'blown' to the Germans and was now on the run. It seems odd that the commander and second-in-command of Z SBS should go on the same operation, for if both had been lost the group would have been leaderless, at least for a while. However, Courtney wanted to go on this first op and since Sally Lunn spoke fluent French, which might come in useful, the two men duly embarked on HMS/M *Trident* for Corsica.

Captain Godfrey Courtney has left an entertaining account of this operation, which he described as 'comparatively simple'. *Trident* reached the coast of Corsica where a periscope recce revealed no obvious hazards, so that night the party paddled ashore, Courtney and Lunn, in a canoe, leading the party of Resistance workers, who were in a rubber dinghy. The idea was that, when this party had disembarked, Commandant de Saule would get in the dinghy and the two SBS men would tow him back to the submarine. However, when they finally got to the beach, matters went a little awry.

Security seemed a little loose, for they found the commandant and his party were deep in noisy conversation with the newly arrived group. The wine was flowing and hilarity seemed general, and the two SBS men were told that, if they would wait a bit, a beautiful Corsican girl was hanging about somewhere who was most anxious to give them both a kiss. This sounded tempting but, since all attempts to hush the Corsicans proved fruitless, the two men ushered the commandant into the dinghy and set off back to *Trident*, arriving there safely after about two hours away. All was not yet over.

On the morning after they left Corsica the officer on periscope watch saw an enemy merchantman and put in a torpedo attack. Two torpedoes were fired, but no hits were achieved and only one torpedo was tracked leaving the submarine. Fearing that this failed attack would attract enemy warships, *Trident* made haste to leave the area, and the submarine headed for the Ligurian Sea off Genoa, hoping for better luck. Eventually, a small coaster was spotted, which was too small to waste a torpedo on so the submarine surfaced for gun action. Unfortunately, this coaster was prepared to fight and turned rapidly to come sweeping down on *Trident*, ready to ram. The diving klaxon blared; the gun crew scrambled back into the conning tower and down the hatch and, just in time, *Trident* dived under the waves. This ship – though apparently a small tanker – was actually a decoy, equipped with depth charges, and she subjected *Trident* to a severe bombardment, dropping over sixty depth charges before the submarine was able to creep away. Like everyone else on board, Courtney and Lunn stayed out of the way. They hung on to something strong and tried not to think about the pressure hull caving in under this hammering.

All was still not over. The Italian Navy was on full alert and a number of coastal craft had now come out from Genoa to patrol the area where the British submarine had last been sighted. Moreover, *Trident* needed to charge her batteries and could not stay down much longer. Eventually, long after dark and after listening carefully for the sound of propellers on the hydrophones, *Trident* came to the surface. The hatch was opened and the captain went up to the conning tower. Seconds later he was back, yelling 'Dive!' and lunging for the klaxon as the roar of aircraft engines swept through the hatch. The hatch had opened easily enough, but it had been damaged in some way by the depth charges and would not close again. As the submarine dived, water surged into the boat and, faced with the choice of bombing or drowning, the captain gave the order to surface again – and calm returned. The bombers were British aircraft making for Genoa, and a bit of urgent work in the conning tower improved the fitting of the hatch. The submarine crept away on the surface, charging her batteries . . . and then an inspection of the hull revealed another problem.

This was clearly one of *those* cruises, with one damned thing after another, but the current problem was unusual. The missing torpedo, one of those fired at the cargo ship off Corsica two days previous, was still on board – just. In fact, it was protruding from the forward torpedo tube and heaven alone knew why the depth charging of the last few hours had not set it off. It would not budge and it was difficult to judge if it was now armed and ready to explode. The patrol could not continue and, to everyone's relief, the *Trident* returned gingerly to the depot ship, HMS *Maidstone*, in Algiers, where the torpedo was carefully removed.

Sally Lunn and another SBS party returned to Corsica twice in May, again in *Trident*, on missions to the French Resistance, to pick up partisans and land stores, weapons and ammunition. The first operation was aborted through bad weather and the second failed when no one appeared to meet them on the beach. Lunn left the others in hiding and went inland for a look round, but he could find no one and eventually they had to reload all the stores and paddle them back to the submarine. More Italian coastal recces followed and then, along with teams of COPP swimmers and canoeists, attentions turned to the coast of Sicily, where the next invasion was imminent, following the Allied victory in North Africa.

The Allied planners were very anxious to conceal the fact that Sicily was the next point of attack, but this was difficult as it did present itself as the obvious target. One of the deception plans was Operation *Mincemeat*, better known as 'The Man Who Never Was' operation, when the body of a man who had died of pneumonia in a London hospital was dressed as a Royal Marine major in Combined Ops and, equipped with 'secret' documents concerning allied intentions to attack in Greece, was floated ashore in Spain. The papers were soon seen by German intelligence agents and copies were then sent to Germany.

Another attempt to deceive the Germans – Operation *Marigold* – was mounted by the SBS in Sardinia. This operation was in two parts. The first called for a landing by Captain Courtney and Sergeant Thompson, who would go ashore in Sardinia from the submarine *Safari* and leave some evidence of having been there in the form of marked maps and a notebook full of chat about beach gradients and enemy defences. With any luck, this would make the enemy look to their local defences and shift troops to Sardinia that might otherwise be deployed in Sicily. This part of the operation went without any trouble. The evidence was duly planted and the two men returned to *Safari* for the next phase in which the SBS were to act as boat handlers for a raid by eight men from the 2 SAS Regiment who hoped to take a prisoner. This part of the action did not go well. The party were detected and fired upon and in their retreat out to sea one of the SBS, Sergeant Loasby, was taken prisoner.

Acting as boatmen for the SAS was not entirely to the SBS's liking, but orders are orders and several operations of this nature followed, including Operation *Swan* in July 1943, when Captain Courtney went with an SAS party to attack the enemy airfields in Sardinia. The leader of the SAS was the artist and writer John Verney. The raid was not successful for, although the airfields were attacked and some enemy aircraft destroyed, most of the SAS, including Verney, were captured. The next SAS/SBS raid, on the island of Lampedusa, was also a failure. The canoes were spotted and engaged by the enemy and two men in one canoe – one SBS, one SAS – were killed. In July of that year a party of SBS was sent to extricate an SAS unit from Sardinia. This was yet another failure as the SAS party had already been captured and the rendezvous was ambushed by German troops. Captain Godfrey Courtney states in *SBS in World War Two* that the SBS/SAS co-operation at this time was not a success, basically because the two units had different roles, different priorities, different training and different attitudes.

The SBS was primarily a reconnaissance and small-scale sabotage unit, which operated in very small numbers – usually two – and relied on stealth, not only to avoid detection and get away afterwards but also to avoid compromising their carrier – the far more valuable submarine and its crew. The SAS, on the other hand, were far more aggressive and went in with all guns blazing; if they got away afterwards, fine; if not, too bad. The difference between the two units is expressed in their mottoes: 'Who Dares, Wins' for the SAS and 'Not by Strength, by Guile' for the modern SBS. Members of both units will probably acknowledge the truth of Roger Courtney's chosen motto, '*Escreta Tauri Astutos Frustrantur*' or 'Bullshit Baffles Brains', but then any old soldier would say 'Amen' to that.

6

ENTER THE ROYAL MARINES 1942

'Soldier and Sailor too'

Rudyard Kipling

The Special Boat Service of the 1990s is an entirely Royal Marine unit, though men from many other units, the US Navy SEALS, the Australian Commandos and SAS and Britain's own SAS Regiment, to name but a few, have taken the SBS course and served with the SBS on attachment. The Royal Marines have been involved in canoe and underwater warfare for the last fifty years, but they had been an amphibious unit for several centuries before that. Since their formation as the Duke of York and Albany's Maritime Regiment of Foot in October 1664, the Corps of Royal Marines has always been Britain's prime source of amphibious soldiers.

The Royal Marines have served as detachments on HM ships, provided boarding and landing parties, handled the big guns on Nelson's 'wooden walls', and modern capital ships, and quite often formed part of large, land-based forces, serving on the Western Front in the Great War and in all the campaigns of the nineteenth century. It is fair to say that, in all Britain's wars since the end of the seventeenth century, 'The Marines were there'. But in the early years of the Second World War, the Royal Marines' amphibious role took some time to develop.

Since the outbreak of war, men of the Corps had taken part in actions at sea, manning gun turrets in capital ships at a score of engagements, including the Battle of the River Plate and the hunt for the *Bismark*, but the Royal Marine Division, which absorbed much of the Corps' manpower, had hardly been employed at all and was largely concerned with coastal defence. Meanwhile, the army had taken over the Corps' amphibious role and formed the first Commando units, some of which, like Layforce, had already spawned a canoe raiding unit. Courtney's embryo SBS had been part of No. 8 Commando and there was another canoe unit, 101 Troop, attached to No. 6 Commando, which formed after Courtney took the first SBS unit to the Middle East. There were Marines in these early forces – Tug Wilson's canoe raiding oppo was a Royal Marine.

In 1942, the Royal Marines finally raised a fully volunteer Commando unit that became the Royal Marine A Commando, and later No. 40 (Royal Marines) Commando, and took part in the Dieppe Raid of August 1942. The Royal Marines were eventually to raise nine Commando units for Special Service in the Second World War and man most of the small landing craft that took the assault troops ashore in half a dozen major invasions. They also produced a canoe raiding unit, a small force of no more than thirty officers and Marines, known for security reasons as the Royal Marines Boom Patrol Detachment or RMBPD. The founder and leader of the RMBPD, the forerunner of the modern SBS, was a regular Royal Marines officer, Major H G Hasler, a man known throughout the corps and in pre-war yachting circles as Blondie. He was a tough-looking man, with a mass of blond hair and a cheerful nature that barely concealed the spirit of a pirate.

Blondie Hasler was something of an adventurer. Such people often find a niche in the Royal Marines, a Corps that has a great tolerance for minor eccentrics provided the eccentric in question also knows how to soldier and remembers that he is first and foremost a Royal Marine. Hasler was born in 1914, the son of an officer in the Royal Army Medical Corps who was killed in 1917. The family had very little money but Hasler's mother managed to send both her sons to public schools, after which both were commissioned into the armed services, the elder going into the Royal Engineers and the younger – Blondie – into the Royal Marines.

Hasler had already started his nautical career long before he joined the Corps. At the age of twelve he acquired a share in a small canoe and paddled it about Langstone and Chichester harbours, east of Portsmouth, risking his neck but getting a good grasp of tides and inshore navigation in the process. Sailing then became his principal obsession – and remained one for the rest of his life. Aged fourteen and a schoolboy at Wellington, he built his first sailing dinghy. Since he financed the work out of his slender pocket money this was not an elaborate craft, but it sailed and stayed afloat and in it Hasler made some creditable voyages along the South Coast and across the Solent to the Isle of Wight, often disappearing from home for days on end, sleeping in a tent made from the sail and living on fish he had caught or shellfish knocked off rocks. His mother got used to these absences and when he disappeared again later, during the Second World War, she assured those who came to offer their condolences that he would certainly turn up, 'for he always does'.

Hasler entered the Corps in 1932, but his interest in sailing was not abated by his military duties. In 1936, posted from Portsmouth to Plymouth, he elected to make the journey by dinghy and, having purchased a twelve-foot-long craft, he made the 180-mile voyage between these two naval bases single-handed and in six days, sleeping each night on the beach. When posted back to Portsmouth, he returned the same way. This activity was noticed and noted. By 1942, Hasler was a major on the staff of the Combined Operations Development Centre(CODC) at Portsmouth, an establishment charged with finding and developing new ways of carrying the war to the enemy. This was a revived version of the pre-war Inter-Services Training and Development Centre, which had been closed at the start of the war but was now flourishing again under the new Chief of Combined Operations, Admiral Lord Louis Mountbatten.

Hasler met Mountbatten on the day he arrived at CODC. He was first charged by Mountbatten with developing a British version of an Italian submersible attack craft – known to the British as an 'explosive motorboat' – that the Italians had been using against Gibraltar and Alexandria. Hasler took this task on but, given his small-boat experience, his role was soon expanded 'to study, co-ordinate and develop all methods of stealthy seaborne attack by very small parties'.

However, at first, the explosive motorboat was his main priority. The work of development was taken on by Vospers Marine, who were ordered to design a fast, semi-submersible motorboat that could be taken into an enemy harbour and aimed at an enemy ship. The cox'n would stay with the craft until it was right on top of the target – then he would leap overboard and the 500 pounds of primed explosive in the bow would do its work. If the crew were picked up and imprisoned by the enemy then it would be considered a worthwhile expenditure of both men and effort – the result was, after all, the sinking of an enemy naval unit. The Vosper development craft was known as the BPB, the Boom Patrol Boat, and some prototypes, thus disguised, were soon whizzing about the Solent on trials.

There were several snags with this basic idea. First, Hasler and his team were most unhappy with the notion that the BPB crew would inevitably be captured. Not only was this a waste of trained men but it also seemed to offer no incentive to volunteers. Besides, with such a visible and obvious method of attack it could only be a matter of time before the enemy worked out countermeasures. Far better if the attack could be clandestine, the men escaping undetected to fight another day.

There was also the looming problem of the German Commando Order, which came into effect at the end of 1942. In October 1942, infuriated with the growing number of Commando raids on German coastal positions, the German Fuhrer, Adolf Hitler, issued a secret order for the elimination of these raiders, who were to be 'ruthlessly exterminated wherever German troops may find them'.

The Fuhrer's Order continues thus:

> From now on all enemy troops which are met by German troops while on so-called Commando raids, even if they are soldiers in uniform, are to be destroyed to the last man, whether in battle or fleeing. It does not matter if they are landed by ship, plane or parachute. Even if they want to surrender no quarter is to be given on principle. Should single members of such Commandos, either as agents or saboteurs, reach the Werhmacht through capture by the police of the occupied countries they are to be handed over to the SD without delay. They are not to be kept even temporarily in military custody or POW camps.
>
> I shall have all commanders who do not comply with this order court-martialled.

That order was signed by Adolf Hitler and promulgated to all his area commanders. It arrived in France in time to authorise the shooting of the Royal Marines who took part in Hasler's *Frankton* operation. The SD were, in effect, the Gestapo and their operatives would have no compunction about torturing and killing any Allied Commandos who fell into their clutches, even without the *carte blanche* provided by the Commando Order. The Order was used to execute – or, to put it plainly, murder – a considerable number of British Parachute, Commando and SAS soldiers during the war and was a clear violation of both the Geneva Convention and the Rules of War. It did nothing to stem the activities of the irregular soldiers, who even revelled in the extra element of danger, but it clearly posed a severe burden for anyone ordering men to take part in a raid where the method would *inevitably* result in their capture.

While this problem was being mulled over, Hasler was beavering away at the problems of the BPB and another invention, still in the design and testing stage, the Chariot, which was an advanced and improved version of the Italian human torpedo. The big problem was not the attack on enemy shipping itself, which, given surprise and skill, would probably come off, but finding some way of transporting fairly large craft like the BPB and the Chariot to within striking distance of their targets. One obvious way was by air, but the problems of launching the craft into the sea seemed insurmountable, and then there remained the problem of recovering the crews after the attack.

Meanwhile, Hasler had not forgotten his first love, the canoe. As he mulled it over in what little time was left from this other duties, the possibilities of the canoe as a weapon of war began to intrigue him. There is no evidence that when Haslar started out to explore the possibilities of canoe warfare he knew what Courtney and his men were up to or, if he did know, that their activities influenced him. Although Hasler's mind began working on a different tack, based on the problems of employing the BPBs, he reached the same conclusion as both Courtney and Captain Montanaro. Basically, the canoe offered better possibilities for small-scale raiding and ship attack than other, more complicated craft.

Canoes might be frail but they were light and transportable. They carried a crew of two and could cover considerable distances in skilled hands. Above all, they were silent and easy to conceal. If a party of raiders got into a naval base in canoes they might do a lot of damage before they got away again, undetected, to strike another day. Hasler began to investigate the current state of canoe warfare and examine different types of canoe. He contacted Courtney and Gerald Montanaro and compared notes about canoes. The basic type currently in use by 101 Troop was the folboat, a collapsible craft with a rubberised skin, which Hasler did not find at all suitable for the task he had in mind.

Hasler eventually decided that the type of craft he needed had more in common with the Klepper canoes used by most of the pre-war canoe clubs. These were light but sturdy craft, which were speedy through the water and could be collapsed. A couple were found for experiments, but there were still a few snags, not least that the civilian Klepper was too long to go down the torpedo hatch of a submarine. In early 1942, Captain Montanaro came to Portsmouth to discuss canoe design. A month later Hasler visited 101 Troop at their base in Dover, from where they were mounting raids against the French coast in their own folboats, the Cockle Mark I. This provided a lot of useful experience on canoe raiding, camouflage and German reactions and routines, but it did not solve the problem of finding the right canoe. Hasler then decided that the only answer was to design and build his own craft.

Hasler wanted a sturdy craft for long-range operations, one that could be hauled over rocks and shingle without ripping its skin and be hauled from the inside of a submarine without breaking its frame. It needed to be a good seaboat, capable of working in waves or heavy seas, and it must have a low profile as an aid to escaping detection in enemy harbours. Hasler took his outline sketches and his problem to Fred Goatley, the man who had designed the Goatley boat, which the infantry used in river crossings. The result of their collaboration was the craft used on Operation *Frankton*, the Cockle Mark II.

All this work on canoes was private enterprise. Officially, Hasler had enough to do working on the Chariots and the BPB, but when work on the Cockle Mark II was put in hand Hasler decided that the time had come to get some official sanction. He approached his commander and suggested, firstly, that the experimental stage with the BPB was nearing its end and an operational training unit should be formed and, secondly, that since the BPBs could not easily cross obstacles on the surface, like booms, canoes could be employed to go ahead of the

BPBs and clear a path for their deployment . . . and rescue the BPB crews after their weapons had been launched. This proposal seemed to solve two chronic problems, and Hasler was given permission to recruit and train men for what, on 6 July 1942, became the Royal Marines Boom Patrol Detachment. Five months later the Boom Patrol Detachment paddled sixty miles up the Gironde River to attack German shipping in Bordeaux harbour.

7

OPERATION *FRANKTON* THE COCKLESHELL HEROES DECEMBER 1942

'The most outstanding Commando operation of the war'

German official report

Operation *Frankton*, the Bordeaux canoe raid of 1942, is the definitive SBS operation, the one that everyone has heard about, partly because of the best-selling book by General Lucas-Phillips and the subsequent film, and largely because the phrase 'Cockleshell Heroes' has passed into common speech and is still used to describe any small-boat exploit. Yet the men who carried out the Bordeaux raid were not SBS but members of Hasler's Boom Patrol Detachment; frogman techniques were not employed and the craft they used were not cockleshells at all but folboats. None of these minor *caveats* really matter; the Bordeaux raid is part of SBS history and the *Frankton* memorial to those who did not return stands today outside the SBS base at Royal Marines, Poole, in Dorset.

Hasler had always intended to turn his experimental team into an operational force and by the summer of 1942 he considered that the men were ready for war. They had put in hundreds of hours of training, their equipment had been tested and modified until it seemed to be ideal for any canoe raiding task and the moment had come to put it all to some practical use. Training and exercises, while essential, are of limited practical value in war; the real lessons are learned when a unit, a tactic or an item of equipment is put to the stress of battle.

Therefore, in July 1942, Hasler wrote to Combined Operations Headquarters (COHQ) in Whitehall, reporting his unit ready for operational service and requesting authorisation to start planning a strike against the enemy before the winter. COHQ kept a constantly updated file of information on possible raiding targets, and on his next visit to headquarters Hasler went through the file and studied the outstanding projects. Nothing seemed suitable for a canoe raid and he returned to Eastney and told his men to carry on training, concentrating on night work and long paddles.

In fact, a possible target for the RMBPD had already emerged and was under consideration. The planners at the War Office had recently become concerned by the activities of German blockade runners, fast ships which were running the gauntlet of British submarines and supplying the German war effort with scarce and vital raw materials, like chrome, tin, tungsten and crude rubber from Malaya and Japan. On their return trips to the Far East, these vessels were supplying Japan with weapons and ammunition. Most of these ships were docking in French ports, especially Bordeaux, and the problem was how to get at them.

Bordeaux is a large city at the head of the Gironde estuary, a centre for the wine trade and a considerable port. Intelligence sources, largely in the French Resistance, estimated that at any one time there were up to ten blockade runners unloading valuable cargoes of strategic material at the Bordeaux docks, and this trade had to be stopped. Air strikes were one possibility but the ships were quite small and the loss of life among French civilians was likely to be considerable if Bordeaux was subjected to a night raid by RAF Bomber Command. A daylight raid was considered impossible as the bombers would be harassed all the way there and back by the locally based Luftwaffe, and Bordeaux was too far from the sea to permit a Commando operation like the St Nazaire raid.

Clearly, something more subtle was needed, a method more like a stiletto than a bludgeon, and eventually minds turned to Major Hasler and his canoe teams now training in Portsmouth. If Hasler and his men could get up the Gironde and into the Bordeaux docks, the German blockade runners would be at their mercy. Hasler was summoned back to COHQ and invited to study the problem. He took his time over it, borrowing charts to study the tides and the sandbanks of the river in some detail, before declaring that he thought a canoe attack was feasible.

Even if it could be done, it would clearly not be easy. Bordeaux is a major port but it lies a long way from the sea, sixty miles or more up the fast-flowing Gironde estuary. Paddling that distance would take at least three nights and, apart from the obvious risk of detection by the enemy, the river was dangerous. Where the outflowing river met the sea there were tidal races and turbulent water, and this operation could not be launched in the balmy days of the southern summer. The canoeists would need every hour of darkness they could get, and that meant a winter operation, mounted in the dark period – the two or three days each month either side of the new moon. The only snag with that requirement was that this period is close to the monthly spring tides, the highest and the strongest in the monthly tidal cycle. To get up river at all, the canoeists could only move with the flood tide or in the hour of slack water before the ebb. Time and tide would be against them, even without the enemy.

Then there was the problem of from where to launch the attacking force. They could be taken south to somewhere off the Gironde estuary – a distance of some 600 sea miles from the UK by submarine. However, to avoid detection by coastal radar, the launch would have to be some distance offshore so then the raiders would have to cope with heavy seas and tidal outfalls, adding even more hazards to the growing list of obstacles facing Hasler's men.

However, COHQ had already accepted the idea that the blockade runners should be attacked and that the RMBPD offered the best chance of a successful strike. The attack had now acquired a codename, Operation *Frankton*, and a fat file of information at COHQ. Finally, in October 1942, Vice-Admiral Lord Louis Mountbatten requested formal approval for the operation from the Chief of Staff and his letter gives a good outline of what COHQ had in mind.

Steps should be taken to attack Axis ships which are known to be running the blockade between France and the Far East. Both seaborne and airborne methods of attacking these ships have been carefully examined and the plan now proposed is the only one which offers a good chance of success.

Between six and ten blockade runners are usually to be found alongside the quays in Bordeaux in addition to other shipping. It is hoped to deal with at least six of these ships.

Briefly, the plan is for one officer and five other ranks of the Royal Marines Boom Patrol Detachment to paddle up the River Gironde in cockles, moving during the hours of darkness only, and place limpets on the water line of the ships they find in Bordeaux. The cockles will be carried to within nine miles of the mouth of the river by a submarine which will be on normal passage to patrol duty and will not need to be specially detailed.

This outline plan was duly approved and its development and eventual execution passed to Major Blondie Hasler RM.

The RMBPD had now reached a strength of 34 men, including four officers; Hasler, his second-in-command Captain Jock Stewart and Lieutenants John MacKinnon and W H Pritchard-Gordon, the latter commanding the two sections into which the force had been divided. The bulk of the NCOs were regulars but most of the Marines were HOs (Hostilities Only), conscripts, who had volunteered for special service and found themselves in the RMBPD. Hasler said later that they were not remarkable men, but a good cross-section of typical Royal Marines, cheery, well-disciplined and fit, but by no means supermen.

Hasler proposed making the attack with just three canoes, six men in all, and his outline plan supposed that these men could get up the river in four days, attack on the next night and get back down and out to sea again to rendezvous with the parent submarine eight days after leaving it. He added that if that were not possible then the raiders should sink their canoes and escape overland towards the Spanish frontier, which lies some 150 miles to the south of Bordeaux, on the crest of the Pyrenees. It is notable that the explosive motorboat, Hasler's main charge at Portsmouth, was not considered for this operation, and that the Chariots were put out of court by the fact that the distance from sea to target was well beyond their range. If this was to be done at all, it had to be done by canoe.

It was now the end of October, and there was still a lot to do. The November moon period was too soon so the operation was pencilled in for December, which still left only a few weeks to do all that needed to be done. The RMBPD had only been in existence since July, so a lot of training was necessary, but at least they now had a specific target and could work on that. Hasler first made contact with the commanding officer of the 3rd Submarine Flotilla, based in Scotland, from where the party would sail. There he discovered that it would be both very difficult and dangerous for a large submarine to return to French offshore waters and attempt a pick-up after the raid. When Hasler's men left the submarine to start their attack they would be on their own, and they must make their own way to safety – or surrender. Hasler therefore added escape and evasion to the training schedule and resolved to teach all his men at least a few words of French.

Then came another snag. Hasler had always assumed that, when his men were finally sent on an operation, he would lead them. He was so sure of this that he never bothered to clear it with COHQ, but when his superiors discovered his intention they consulted Mountbatten and he refused to let Hasler go, ordering Hasler to entrust the raid to one of his officers. Mountbatten was not being difficult; Hasler was COHQ's canoeing expert and he knew a great deal about COHQ activities. He was, in short, too valuable to lose.

Hasler rejected those arguments and sent a memorandum stressing that the outcome of *Frankton* would affect all future operations for good or ill, that he alone of the RMBPD had sufficient small-boat-navigation experience to get the party up river and, finally, if David Stirling of the SAS could go on operations in the Western Desert why could he not go raiding on the coast of France? On 29 October Mountbatten duly summoned Hasler to a meeting in order to thrash this point out and only capitulated when Hasler claimed that he could not successfully develop raiding equipment and techniques if he never went on raids himself . . . and if his men went on this operation without him and failed to come back, he did not know how he could look their surviving comrades – or himself – in the face.

This was an argument any officer could understand and permission for Hasler to lead the raid was reluctantly given. He went back in triumph to Portsmouth where No. 1 Section, the ones chosen for the raid (though still unaware of that fact), were ordered to pack their kit for a period of intensive training in Scotland. However, Mountbatten did insist on one change in the plan – increasing the number of canoes from three to six. A T-class submarine, HMS/M *Tuna*, was detailed for the task of transporting the *Frankton* party to the mouth of the Gironde estuary and the sailing date was set for 30 November.

No. 1 Section, RMBPD, arrived in Scotland during the first week in November and joined HMS/M *Tuna* for what still seemed to be exercises. Hasler's particular concern was to get fully loaded canoes over the side of a submarine at night without loosing either men or equipment, or damaging the canoes. This is a delicate task even in a sheltered Scottish loch, but it would clearly be a good deal more difficult in the open, wave-tossed sea. The method used in the Mediterranean, where the crews climbed into the canoes from the forward hydroplanes, was not considered viable for heavily loaded canoes in the open Atlantic. On other, later operations, the problem was solved by setting up the canoes on the casing of the pressure hull and, after the crews had climbed in, the submarine would go slow ahead, blow her ballast tanks and submerge, leaving the canoes on the surface. This method is simple, but again not without risk. Hasler's men were finally put over the side of the submarine using a small, temporary beam attached to the submarine's gun barrel, from which the canoes and the already on-board crew were suspended in wire loops. The gun was traversed to lift the canoes over the side and they were then lowered into the water. It was still a tricky business but it seemed to work.

The men also spent a lot of time paddling about the loch at night, making practice attacks on the shipping. The method employed was simple and effective and involved a careful, silent approach using single paddles. Paddling and drifting, the raiders slowly closed with the target vessel and took shelter under the curve of the bow or stern. They then felt their way down the side of the craft until they were level with the engine room and, having attached their magnetic anchor to hold themselves in place, the no. 1 would place the first magnetic limpet against the ship's hull. Since ships have several watertight compartments several limpets had to be laid on each ship before the raiders paddled gently away to another target. Each canoe carried eight limpets and it was estimated that at least six ships could be sunk if these were carefully placed.

Practice continued, by day and night, in the confines of the loch and on the open sea. Long, exhausting canoe paddles against the wind and tide were included as part of the training and then, as a finale to all this, Hasler decided on a full rehearsal – Exercise *Blanket* – using the Thames and the Pool of London as substitutes for the Gironde and Bordeaux docks. The rehearsal was launched from Margate and was a total fiasco.

The standard of navigation was poor and a number of the canoes got lost – one was turned back when heading gamely out to sea, a full 180 degrees off course. After five nights, the crews – hungry, exhausted and having been spotted by the alert defenders – came ashore near the Blackwall Tunnel, thoroughly dejected. However, when Hasler told Mountbatten that the exercise had been 'a complete failure', Mountbatten was – or appeared to be – quite delighted on the grounds that since the raiders had made so many mistakes on the exercise they would easily avoid making them on the actual operation. This is a valid viewpoint: the exercise before the Commando attack on St Nazaire was also a disaster . . . but the raid itself was a great success.

Among the RMBPD personnel, though some might have suspected what was coming, no one but Hasler knew anything about the impending raid, even when they returned to Scotland on 19 November. The men had not yet been briefed and spent their last ten days ashore in endurance and navigation training, as well as exercising at sea with fully loaded canoes. Three days before they sailed, a messenger from London arrived with the latest information from Bordeaux including aerial photographs and updated charts of the estuary. Enough French money was supplied for every member of the party. The men were still told nothing, but they were advised to tell their families that they were 'going away for a while and might not be able to write'.

Tension was mounting and it is more than likely that, while none of the men knew exactly what was up, they all suspected that their current training was leading up to an actual operation. It has also been alleged that some of the men had a premonition of death, and said goodbye to their friends and families before leaving.

Finally, on the morning of 30 November, the crews were roused early to carry out one more check of their canoes and stores. That done, they went on to the upper deck of the depot ship, HMS *Forth*, and saw their canoes and equipment loaded carefully on to HMS/M *Tuna* which lay alongside. Then they went on board themselves and as *Tuna* slipped her lines and moved out to sea they fell in on their 'Stations for Leaving Harbour' posts on the outer casing. After that they went below, and Operation *Frankton* was fully underway.

The six canoes listed for the Bordeaux raid all had names and designated crews. Major Hasler and his no. 2, Marine Ned Sparks, crewed *Catfish*; Sergeant Wallace and Marine Ewart crewed *Coalfish*; Marine Ellery and Marine Fisher crewed *Cachalot*; Lieutenant MacKinnon and Marine Conway were in *Cuttlefish*; Corporal Sheard and Marine Moffat were in *Conger* and Corporal Laver and Marine Mills crewed *Crayfish*. These men had crewed up and been partners for some time, but in case anyone fell ill there was a spare man, Marine Colley, standing by to take over. The Marines were made very welcome in the cramped confines of the submarine, where thirteen extra men were quite a squeeze, and once the submarine had dived they were summoned to the forward torpedo space for a briefing.

Hasler began by telling them what they no doubt already suspected – that this was not another exercise but the real thing. He then told them the background to the operation and what they had to do, before drawing a map of the Gironde estuary on a blackboard and telling them in some detail how they were to do it. They would be dropped ten miles from the mouth of the estuary and paddle through the tidal races into the river, where they would turn south to start the sixty-mile paddle up to the city docks. He then handed out the charts and aerial photos and led a general discussion on likely lying-up spots during their approach to the target. The ebb tides would be so strong that they would only be able to get upstream on the flood . . . and then there was the enemy.

The Gironde was a German base and sheltered a number of German patrol craft, which worked the offshore waters or the actual estuary. These craft included armed trawlers, torpedo and motor gun boats (MGBs) and minesweepers, and there were observation posts, equipped with searchlights and shore patrols on both banks, which would be quick to spot any suspicious traffic. There were also a number of airfields around Bordeaux and along the Gironde, and the risk of being spotted by the aircraft crews when landing or taking off meant that their hiding places must be well concealed. It sounded daunting, but the Marines were not dismayed, one man describing it as 'Just like *Blanket* . . . tough but we can do it.'

The disasters on *Blanket* had not discouraged the men. As Mountbatten had predicted, they had learned from their mistakes and were very determined that they would not make the same ones again. Hasler had decided to make sure that all that could be done would be done to get his party to the target and so, with the *Blanket* experience behind them, the men listened carefully while he laid out the plans for their approach.

They would be launched as already practised, but in the open sea and in the dark. It would not be possible to use lights and the sea would probably be running and sweeping over the pressure hull of the submarine. If all went well, just before leaving the side of the submarine, the captain would give them a precise magnetic bearing to paddle on, which each crew was to set on its boat compass. Paddling on a compass bearing had been practised exhaustively in the last three weeks and the men had no worries about it. Besides, at this stage in the operation, Hasler would be in the lead in *Catfish*.

The canoes would head for the shore and then, within sight of the beach, turn north to follow the coast up to the mouth of the estuary. When that was in sight, then, depending on the time and the state of the tide, Hasler would decide where the party would lie up on their first day. When moving upriver the craft were to keep at least half a mile offshore, avoid the shipping channel and stay in arrowhead formation. Long before dawn they must be in a secure lying-up position and concealed from view. During the trip upriver, which Hasler estimated would take three nights, they were to concentrate on concealment. In their last lying-up position, close to the target area, they would arm the limpets, ditch any equipment they did not need for their escape, and go into the attack.

Hasler let them talk it over for a while and then returned to the briefing, filling in the gaps and stressing some of the most important points. The *Tuna* would arrive off the Pointe de Grave headland, close to the estuary, in five days' time, on the night of December 5/6. Should they be disturbed while the canoes were being offloaded the submarine would simply submerge, whether or not there were men on the casing, in which case those canoes already launched would proceed with the mission. The raiders would be mustered in two divisions of three canoes and proceed separately, to lower the risk of detection and double the chances of success. Hasler and Sparks in *Catfish* would lead *Crayfish* and *Conger* and Lieutenant MacKinnon in *Cuttlefish* would lead *Coalfish* and *Cachalot*. To redouble the chances of a successful attack, each division would direct one canoe to each of the three target areas. That way, even if one entire division was lost, at least one canoe would proceed with each phase of the attack. The aim was to sink eight to twelve ships, but they should avoid tankers, which were hard to sink since they had so many watertight compartments. They were to concentrate on the cargo ships.

This briefing went on for several hours and was to be repeated constantly in the days that followed, but when this first run-through of the plan had been completed Sergeant Wallace asked the one outstanding question: How did they get back?

Men who volunteer for Special Service know that their role will be risky. That much is obvious and nothing to complain about. The standard Special Service response to a difficult or dangerous situation is, 'If you can't take a joke, you shouldn't have joined.' There is, however, a certain difference between a dangerous mission and a hopeless one; Special Service soldiers are not fools and, while they will take any reasonable risk and quite a few unreasonable ones, they like to think that they have a chance to complete the mission, survive and get back to base.

When Hasler told them that the submarine could not return to pick them up and that after the operation had been completed they were on their own, some of the men were none too happy. Even without the Germans, France was an unknown country and the idea that they would have to make their way south and cross the Pyrenees was not one that immediately struck them as attractive or even feasible. Hasler then explained that each man would have a bag of escape equipment, including maps and money, and that they were to find and put their faith in the French Resistance, the Maquis, who would see them on their way to safety. Neither would they travel on their own: they had trained in pairs; they would raid in pairs; and they would escape in pairs.

Finally, he added, if anyone felt that this was a risk too far, then they were perfectly at liberty to withdraw from the entire operation. Naturally, no one did so. Once they got used to the idea, the thought of escaping across the Pyrenees was simply another adventure. If they were captured before the actual attack, Hasler stressed that they must keep quiet about the operation and the get-away plans, in order that those still at liberty had a better chance to attack the ships or make good their escape.

The first briefing gave the men a lot to think about and when it was over they were quiet for a while, thinking it over. Then the level of conversation rose; the charts and aerial photographs were consulted again and the men, fully committed to their task, began to work out how they would approach the job in front of them. Spirits were high and if anyone was scared – and most of them must have felt somewhat apprehensive – they did not show it. They had been well trained and they would give it a good shot.

As the submarine sailed south, much time was spent going over the plans, the charts and the aerial photographs of the docks, until the men had the entire area from the sea to Bordeaux imprinted on their minds. When the submarine rose at night to recharge her batteries, they practised setting up the canoes and swinging them over the side. This had been practised relentlessly in Scotland but now, out at sea in the pitch dark and with waves sweeping the casing, they could get their craft up and over the side in just thirty minutes. Finally, six days after setting out, the French coast appeared in the periscope and on the night of 5/6 December *Tuna* approached the launching spot – and met some problems.

First, the coastal waters were full of fishing vessels, some of them carrying German guards and observers. Second, the RAF bid to sink the blockade runners had comprised placing mines off the coast and, although the captain of the *Tuna*, Lieutenant Raikes, had a chart tracing of where these mines were, he did not trust it. He knew that the *Frankton* crews needed an accurate landfall if they were to have any chance of getting to the mouth of the Gironde. To give them one he had to get close inshore, running the risk of mines and detection by the fishing boats, and the large number of German aircraft that seemed to be constantly overhead. *Tuna* spent all day and most of the following night trying to get an accurate fix but Raikes finally had to tell Hasler that, as he was not sure of his position, the launch would have to be postponed until the following night.

It was not until the morning of 7 December that Lieutenant Raikes got an accurate fix and knew exactly where he was. That done, the launching spot could also be fixed and three hours after dusk that day, at 1930 hours, the submarine surfaced and the Royal Marines were told to prepare their canoes for launching. The canoes were rapidly assembled in the forward torpedo room and, lights having been doused, were passed through the hatch on to the casing . . . and then came the first setback. As Ellery and Fisher passed *Cachalot* through the hatch, a projection caught on the canoe's hull fabric and ripped it open. It could not be repaired and *Cachelot*'s crew were out of the raid. Marine Fisher was so overcome with disappointment he burst into tears.

Meanwhile, the other canoes were being passed up on to the casing, put into the slings and lowered over the side. In twenty minutes, as the submarine rolled gently in the swell, four canoes were rafted up alongside and it was time for Hasler and his no. 2, Marine Ned Sparks, to go. Raikes was worried that the submarine had already been spotted by German radar and hurried Hasler into his canoe. The *Frankton* raiders dipped their paddles and vanished into the night.

The last boat was waterborne at 2020 hours and at 2022 hours we said goodbye to a magnificent bunch of black-faced villains, with whom it had been a real pleasure to work, and withdrew to the south and west. (Patrol report, Lt R P Raikes, Commanding HM/S *Tuna*.)

8

THE FATE OF *FRANKTON*
1942–43

*'A fine operation, carried out by a particularly brave
party of men.'*

Lord Louis Mountbatten,
Chief of Combined Operations, 1942–3

The loss of one canoe before the raid was properly
launched was a severe blow to the raiders, and not least
to the crew of *Cachelot* who were left behind, bitterly
disappointed. It was fortunate that Mountbatten had
insisted Hasler double the size of his force to six or the
loss of this one craft could have made the raid unviable,
but there were still more than enough men left to do the
job, if the hazards presented by the sea, the river and the
enemy could only be surmounted.

On leaving *Tuna*, the five remaining canoes set out to
the east, heading for the coast, aiming to turn north some
way offshore and paddle to the mouth of the Gironde by
making their way between the Pointe de Grave and the
offshore island of Cordouan. The crews were relying on
Hasler to navigate this sector and he was alarmed to
discover that his compass had developed an error and was
at least twenty degrees out of true. Fortunately, it was a
clear night, if bitterly cold, and he was able to stay on the
right heading by using the North Star. He and Sparks also

discovered that their canoe was leaking slightly and Sparks had to bail it out and mop it out every half-hour. They still made reasonable progress and after three hours were over the Banc des Olives, an offshore sandbank, and picking up the flood tide. They were now getting into shallower water and the swell was now turning into big rollers. They turned north, keeping about two miles off the dim line of the coast.

The sound of surf took some time to identify. They were moving faster now and were swept along on the flood tide between Cordouan and the Pointe de Grave. As the booming of surf grew louder and white tops appeared ahead, it was clear that they were running into a rip tide, or tide race, where the sea swept through a narrow space or over shallow ground. They had met such places before while training in the UK, but never at night, or with such rough water. This obstacle was not shown on any chart and was therefore completely unexpected. Hasler had the canoes raft up and reminded the men that they had done all this before, and that the routine was to fit their cockpit covers snugly, paddle hard into the rollers and, above all, keep the canoes straight until they were in smooth water once again. The men did as they were told and, when they were ready, paddled hard into the surf.

It was alarming, exciting and even a touch exhilarating, fighting wild water on a dark night, but eventually the canoes burst free into smoother water and rafted up again . . . or four of them did. *Coalfish*, with Sergeant Wallace and Marine Ewart, failed to reappear. Hasler ordered the others to search about, but they were still being carried north by the tide and after half an hour there was still no sign of Wallace or Ewart. Eventually, deeply depressed, Hasler abandoned the search and ordered his men to get back on course towards the mouth of the Gironde. A quarter of his strength had already gone and the *Frankton* raiders were not yet even in the Gironde estuary.

They could now see the light marking the Pointe de Grave and the bulk of the Isle de Cordouan but, as they aimed for the darkness in the middle, they heard yet again the booming of the surf. This was yet another unexpected tide race, caused by the incoming tide meeting the outfall of the Gironde and the waves here were even shorter and steeper than the ones that had eliminated Wallace and Ewart. Another period of turmoil in boiling seas and this time they saw and heard *Conger* capsize, throwing Sheard and Moffat into the sea. Somehow the others came through intact and when the sea was calmer they found that Corporal Sheard and Marine Moffat were alongside, clinging to their upturned canoe, gasping with cold in the freezing water.

All efforts to right *Conger* failed. Heavily laden with 300 pounds of lashed-down stores she would not come over and eventually she had to be scuttled. Her hull was ripped open and she was left to sink, while Hasler and MacKinnon prepared to tow Moffat and Sheard ashore. It would hardly be surprising if Hasler was beginning to wonder if anything would ever go right on this operation – but if he had such thoughts he kept them to himself. He had now lost three canoes and if he did not get Sheard and Moffat ashore soon they would die of exposure. Seawater was freezing on the canoe decks and the water temperature was at best only a degree or two above zero; the men must go ashore but, if they were caught by the Germans and forced to reveal their mission, what chance did the rest of them stand?

While that problem was churning through Hasler's mind yet another tide race appeared ahead, the white caps of the waves clearly visible in the revolving beams from the lighthouse on the Pointe de Grave. This one was less violent than the rest and the men were now more used to dealing with such conditions so, even with Sheard and Moffat clinging to the backs of two canoes, all three came through without undue difficulty, and turned at last into the calmer waters of the Gironde estuary. Hasler had decided to hide up for the day on the north-east bank of the estuary, but then came another hazard – the pier of Le Verdon, which lay across their path and could hardly be avoided with two men hanging on to their canoes.

Hasler had intended to tow the men to the beach, but now he saw that there was no time for that. The men had life jackets and could swim and the beach was perhaps a quarter of a mile away – they must take their chance. He ordered the canoes to raft up and told Sheard and Moffat that they must strike out for the shore on their own. They knew the problem and they knew the risk. They shook hands swiftly with the men in the canoes and swam off into the darkness.

What Hasler had not seen, and what only came in view as the pier grew closer, was the three small German warships which were tied up to it. The raiders could not turn away or head out into the dark; they had to go under the pier and hope that no patrolling sentry or anchor watch saw them slip by. One by one, with Hasler and Sparks leading, the canoes slipped past the destroyers and into the darkness beyond ... or two of them did. *Cuttlefish*, with Lieutenant MacKinnon and Marine Conway, failed to appear on the far side. The others waited, keeping both canoes together in the darkness, straining their eyes and ears back towards the pier, but saw nothing. They heard, or thought they heard, a shout, but that was all. MacKinnon and Conway had followed the other lost members of the party into the dark.

By any standards, *Frankton* was now a disaster. The raiders were down from twelve to four; two men had never left the submarine and six more had been lost in the last four hours – and their target, the shipping in Bordeaux docks, still lay sixty miles away. Moreover, none of the losses so far had been due to the Germans; accidents, on the submarine or at sea, had reduced Hasler's force to just four men, but some interference from the Germans was almost inevitable sooner or later, and more natural hazards still lay between them and their target. In fact, though they did not know it, *Cuttlefish* had not been detected or overwhelmed by the sea. MacKinnon and Conway had lost direction and were even now out on the river, plugging towards Bordeaux, determined to make their attack.

Hasler had intended to cross the river, but now he decided to press on upstream, using every hour of darkness to gain distance. It was not until seven in the morning, when it was nearly dawn, that they found a suitable hide on shore in the reeds and marshes of the Pointe des Oiseaux. They had been paddling hard, fighting the sea and the cold for more than eleven hours, without food or drink, and they were now very tired. They camouflaged the canoes and were hoping for a few hours undisturbed rest when a new hazard arose.

Fishing boats were coming upriver and preparing to anchor just offshore and women from the village of St Vivien de Medoc, mothers and wives of the fishermen, were now coming down to the beach to meet them. Within a few minutes the raiders had been spotted and little groups of villagers were soon standing about, staring into their hiding place, clearly wondering what they were up to. Eventually, Hasler decided to go and tell them that they were British soldiers and ask them to remain silent, or, better still, go away. The women were not fully convinced, suspecting that Hasler and his men were Germans, but eventually they drifted away and, since no Germans appeared later, they must have kept their mouths shut.

The existence of the raiders was, however, already known to the Germans. German coastal radar had picked up the silhouette of *Tuna* and Wallace and Ewart had been captured by some German soldiers from a coastal battery. The soldiers treated them well, but they were clearly Commandos and the local area commander, a German naval officer, Admiral Bachman, ordered, in accordance with the Commando Order, that they should be handed over to the SD, the German security police, and shot. Before that, they should be interrogated – 'with no methods barred, including the subterfuge of sparing their lives' – to find out what they had been doing, if there were others in the party and where they had been heading. Under severe Gestapo interrogation, Wallace and Ewart said nothing. Two days later, they were taken by night to the woods near Bordeaux and executed by firing squad.

It was later revealed that while under interrogation Wallace had managed to convince the Germans that he and Ewart were alone, that only two canoes were involved, his and one which had been damaged on leaving the submarine and left behind. On 8 December, the Germans therefore issued a communique stating that 'A small British sabotage party was engaged at the mouth of the Gironde and finished off in combat', a statement that deeply depressed the people waiting for news at COHQ in London.

Hasler and the remaining raiders spent the day in sodden clothing, sheltering in the reed beds behind the beach at St Vivien. They got little sleep and had only cold food to eat. By the time dusk fell they were stiff and frozen, and more than willing to haul the canoes down to the water and warm up with a few hours of hard paddling. Sparks found and repaired the leak that had been a nuisance the night before and when the tide turned after dark they set out upriver, aiming to make at least 25 miles before the ebb tide brought them to a halt.

Twenty-five miles in six hours is not a great distance, but the men were heading upriver and each canoe carried 300 pounds of kit, quite apart from the crew members. That is a heavy weight to push along, hour after hour by arm muscles alone, and in addition the men had to keep a constant lookout, avoid any vessels on the river and plot a course that kept them clear of obstacles. It all took time and long before the ebb tide turned they had to find a hide to lie up in during the following day.

The night was very cold. Water froze again on the decks and ran down the paddle shafts to soak the men's hands, which were soon freezing. They plugged on, stopping every hour for a few minutes' rest, and the only hazard encountered was a small convoy of German ships that came up from behind and nearly ran them down. It took a lot of hard paddling to get out of the way but they were not seen and started upriver again, coming ashore on the east bank of the estuary near the tiny Portes de Calonges. They had made the desired distance in the time available and were now back on schedule, but they were very tired and in need of a good rest and a hot meal. Their hide, in a dry ditch, gave everyone a few hours' sleep, and they could brew a hot drink, but that was all the rest and comfort they could find before evening came and they had to push on again.

Hasler decided on an early start, for tidal flow changed daily and darkness now offered only three hours of flood tide to take them upriver, so the sun had not yet gone down when they carried their canoes down to the water and set off again. Within a few miles they were running among islands off the wine town of Paulliac, but it was now deep darkness and they were not seen. Neither were Lieutenant MacKinnon and Marine Conway, who were still plugging upriver, lying up each day and following their orders.

It was now their third night on the river, the 9/10 December, and the warmth and comradeship of HMS/M *Tuna*, let alone life in Britain, already seemed like another world. There was only the river, the drip of water from the paddles, the chill wind in their faces or pushing at their backs and the need to keep moving, driving the canoes through the night. That night they saw a patrol craft, a small motorboat, but otherwise there was no sign of any German activity. That night was a short one, for the ebb tide came down on them strongly, backed by the growing force of the river, and before 2100 hours they were forced to lie up on a small island. They got some sleep here but were up again soon after midnight to catch the first hint of slack water and push on again to the southern end of the Isle de Cazeau, just where the river Dordogne flows into the Garonne to create the Gironde estuary. They paddled along quietly, for the river had narrowed and there were houses about, but in spite of careful searching they could not find a suitable hide. It was not until nearly 0800 hours when the sun was rising and traffic could be heard on the roads that they found a suitable spot on the southern tip of the island, just twelve miles from their target. They spent the day by their canoes and were on the river again by 1900 hours, intending to get up to the edges of the port, lie up again and attack on the following night of 11/12 December.

The final approach went well and the raiders were encouraged by the sight of two fine motor vessels tied up in the Bassen Sud, one of their target areas. These ships were lit up and being unloaded so the raiders crept past on the far bank. There they found a small stream running out through the reed beds and they followed it into the perfect hide. There they spent the rest of the night and the following day, with at least two target vessels in plain sight across the river.

They had made it. Not easily or without loss, but all the effort and the sacrifice of so many good men would be worth it if they could sink some ships. Hasler spent the day brooding over his maps and in the later afternoon issued his final orders for the attack. They would leave their hide at 2100 hours, to avoid moonrise and catch the last of the flood tide, which would carry them through the docks. Then the ebb tide would, with any luck, carry them back again. Hasler and Sparks, in *Catfish*, would work up the west bank of the Garonne and attack the shipping on that side, while Laver and Mills would search the east bank towards the centre of Bordeaux. If they found nothing suitable there, they were to come back and attack the two vessels in the Bassen Sud. They had sixteen mines and they intended to make every one count.

When all limpets had been fixed they were to head back downriver, hell for leather, making as much distance as possible away from Bordeaux before sinking their canoes, going ashore on the eastern bank and attempting to contact the Resistance. They ate the last of their food, arranged their escape packs and, at 2000 hours, fused the limpets, setting a nine-hour delay. However, as Hasler reminded them, in the current low temperatures, the heat-and cold-sensitive fuses would take a few hours longer than that before they set off the mines. It was a cold, clear night with good visibility when a little mist and rain would have been very welcome. At 2115 hours they pushed their canoes back through the reeds and shook hands before setting off into the Bordeaux docks.

It took Hasler and Sparks about an hour and a half to paddle up to the docks. There, tied up, some of them lit up, were seven ships, tankers and cargo vessels. The lights illuminated the water but threw plenty of deep shadows, so the raiders went over to single paddles and crept across the river, heading for the first ship. They kept close to the sides of the vessels, so that someone would have to lean right over the rail to see them. They ignored the first ship, a tanker. The next two were marked down for future attention if neccessary, but the fourth vessel was a fine cargo ship, an ideal target. Sparks clamped the magnetic anchor to the side of the vessel and Hasler attached a limpet to the ship's side. They edged forward to midships and the bow, placing two more mines before they paddled gently away. They then attacked two more vessels and had just put two limpets on a small German destroyer, a *sperrbrecher*, when they heard a sudden noise from the deck above and a light shone directly upon them.

It was the German anchor watch, a sentry who patrols a warship in harbour at night to see that all is well. Something had attracted his attention and now he was staring down at them from just fifteen feet above, trying to make out what that oblong, lumpy object was, bobbing about beside his ship. Hunched over, their faces pressed to the deck of the canoe, Hasler and Sparks froze, letting the gathering ebb tide float the canoe backwards down the side of the ship. They dared not look, but as they floated back they heard the sentry pacing down the metal deck above and the beam of his torch stayed on them. Finally, they drifted under the bows and out of his sight. Sparks halted the drift by attaching the magnetic anchor to the hull – and there they stayed, hidden by the overhang above the anchor cables, waiting. The sentry was still up there, for they could hear him shuffling about and they could see the beam of his torch playing on the waters just ahead. They waited. He waited. Time passed.

Finally, they could wait no longer. Hasler nudged

Sparks and jerked his head. The magnetic grip-fast was pulled free and, still crouching over, they let the canoe drift away and into the shadow of another vessel. Only then did they sit up and dare to breathe deeply.

Their next target, a cargo vessel moored between the shore and a tanker, was hard to get at. They finally paddled in between the bows of the two vessels and, with Sparks about to lower the placing rod over the side, they noticed that the two ships were swinging together, threatening to crush the canoe between the hulls. It took their united strength, and a lot of hasty paddling, to hold the vessels apart while they got free, after which they drifted down to the other ships and placed some limpets there.

That was it. Had they had more limpets they might have gone on doing this all night, or until the ebb was running fully, but they had used all eight limpets and attacked five ships. *Frankton* had succeeded, in spite of everything, and all they had to do now was get away. Free of mines, their craft was light and, buoyed up with their success, they paddled out into the middle of the river and went downstream under double paddles, taking full advantage of the ebb. Tiredness and doubts had gone. The two men were elated with their success and even more so when, stopping for a breather, they heard the sound of paddles from behind and Corporal Laver and Marine Mills came storming gleefully out of the night. They had searched the right bank and, finding no targets, had come back and successfully attacked the ships in the Bassen Sud. Seven ships now had mines ticking away against their hulls, a good blow delivered by four weary men.

The plan now called for the crews to separate, but they stayed together for the rest of the night, paddling fast downstream. By dawn they were well downriver, back in the Gironde and nearing the town of Blaye. Then they rafted up for one last time. They had been together in enemy territory for five nights and now they had to part and take their chances on escaping. Laver and Mills went ashore about a mile north of Blaye and Hasler and Sparks went on a little before heading into the bank.

They came ashore on a mud bank and, having carried the bags containing their escape kit to the bank, they slashed open the fabric of *Catfish* and pushed it out into the river, hoping that it would sink. They then stripped off their wet canoe suits, put on dry clothes and walking shoes, and set out inland, heading not south towards the Pyrenees but north, into the centre of France. Their best hope of escape now lay in finding the Resistance and enlisting their help.

What happened after that lies outside the scope of this story, but must still be briefly told. Major Hasler and Marine Ned Sparks managed to contact the Resistance and, after many adventures, eventually crossed into Spain. By April 1943, five months after the raid, they were back in the UK, where Hasler was awarded the DSO and Sparks the DSM.

Marines Fisher, Colley and Ellery went back to Portsmouth on HMS/M *Tuna* at the end of her patrol and returned to duty with the Boom Patrol. Although the other men of *Frankton* were 'posted missing, believed killed', and all the relatives so informed, it was not until the end of the war that their fate was finally known.

The body of Marine Moffat was washed ashore in France on 17 December 1942, and this fact was communicated to the British by the Germans. Corporal Sheard must also have drowned, but his body was never found. At the end of December the Swiss Red Cross reported that Marine James Conway and Lieutenant MacKinnon were prisoners, and the same fate befell Corporal Laver and Marine Mills, who made it to the shore, sank *Crayfish* and made their way inland. They had covered over twenty miles when they were picked up by the French police and – still in uniform, with Royal Marines and Combined Operations flashes sewn on them – handed over to the SD who took them to the central prison in Bordeaux, which was under Gestapo control.

Laver and Mills were still in prison, under brutal

interrogation by the SD, when Lieutenant MacKinnon and Marine Conway were brought in. After losing contact on the first night of the operation, this crew had continued upriver, still intent on attacking the ships, on their own if need be. They continued to paddle on for the next three nights and would undoubtely have added their weight to the attack but for striking a submerged log near the confluence of the Dordogne and Garonne. They were forced to swim back to the Isle de Cazeau where they stayed at liberty, helped by the local people, until the end of December when they were betrayed into the hands of the SD and taken to Bordeaux.

Sergeant Wallace and Marine Ewart, lost in the first tidal race, had not in fact been overwhelmed by the sea. Like MacKinnon and Conway, they had become separated from the rest but pressed on towards the Gironde only to be upset in the second tidal race when they were forced to swim ashore by the Pointe de Grave, where they were captured by members of a Luftwaffe anti-aircraft battery. Their canoe was found and, as they were Marines, they were handed over to the local naval authorities. Then, as already related, they were handed over to the SD, interrogated and shot.

So, by the end of December 1942, two members of *Frankton*, Corporal Sheard and Marine Moffat, had been drowned, two had already been murdered by the Gestapo, and two were on the run in France, attempting to escape across the Pyrenees. The rest, Lieutenant MacKinnon, Corporal Laver and Marines Mills and Conway were still in the hands of the SD. What happened to them can never be known in detail. Perhaps they were murdered soon after capture under the terms of the Commando Order, but a German order dated 12 January 1944, which gave details of what happened to British Commandos captured during raids, records that the men captured after the Bordeaux raid were 'shot in accordance with orders, in March, 1943'.

These men were murdered. They were part of a legitimate military unit operating in uniform, not spies, and entitled to the full protection of the Geneva Convention and the Rules of War. To torture and murder them – and Ewart and Wallace were certainly beaten and tortured soon after capture – is a crime, punishable by court martial and, in the event of conviction, a sentence of death. Yet no German was ever executed for the murder of the *Frankton* Marines. The order that they should be handed over to the SD for execution was given by Admiral Bachmann, but he could not be found after the war, and was reported dead. Another admiral, Wilhem Meisel, wanted the executions delayed but was told by a Colonel von Tippelskirch of Hitler's personal staff that 'these men must be shot at once.'

Von Tippelskirch was brought to trial in 1948 as an accessory to the murders but was eventually acquitted, since Bachmann and Meisel were not obliged to follow his instructions. All the accused hid behind the Commando Order and offered the same *befel ist befel* – orders are orders – excuse that was given by many German officers to avoid punishment for their crimes. The Commando Order, which was used to murder many Commando soldiers during the war, was an illegal order, and all the Germans knew that. It was issued with strict orders that it was not to fall into Allied hands – though it very quickly did – and, to cover up the consequences of implementing it, many local commanders declared that their prisoners had been 'shot while escaping' or, in the case of the *Frankton* Marines, 'found drowned in Bordeaux Harbour'. A lie, contradicted by the German report of January 1944.

Operation *Frankton* was a fine operation, but the cost was high. The RMBPD had lost half its strength, but it would re-form, recruit more men and go to war again.

Major Anders Lassen VC MC**

Left British submarine: *HMS/M Alliance*

Below X-24. Midget submarine or X-craft. This vessel sank the Barenfels and the floating dock in Bergen

Above Italian human torpedo or chariot craft

Right Chariot controls

Right Rigid raiding craft move in to pick up SBS parachuting into the sea

Below left A Royal Marine canoeist bringing his craft ashore during an exercise in Arctic Norway

Below right SBS canoeists

Left SBS parachuting into Norway

Right SBS frogmen training

Below left SBS ambush exercise

Below right Frogman and canoeist of the Special Boat Squadron, Poole 1955

An SBS Marine in combat equipment

9

SBS AND SSRF
WESTERN EUROPE
1942–43

'You can do it some of the time for quite a while,
but you can't do it all the time for very long'

On raiding, Major Anders Lassen VC MC★★

It is now necessary to go back a little and sail with Roger
Courtney to the UK, the embattled island he returned to
from the Middle East in December 1941. By then a lot
had changed in Combined Operations activities, mostly in
the formation and expansion of major assault and raiding
units. The Commando units and the parachute battalions
had already been formed, and would eventually rise to the
size of brigades and divisions. Some had seen action, but
that outburst of creative soldiering which had inspired
Stirling and Courtney in the Middle East had been
duplicated in the UK with the birth of a number of small
Special Force units.

Among these was 101 Troop of No. 6 Commando,
commanded by a sapper (Royal Engineers) officer,
Captain G C S Montanaro. Captain Montanaro was one
of the pioneers of canoe warfare – his men appear in many
Special Force histories – and his troop had taken up canoe
warfare on behalf of the Army Commandos after Roger
Courtney took the folboat troops off to the Middle East

with Layforce. By the end of 1941, this troop was engaged in canoe raiding across the Channel, disembarking off the French coast from submarines and fast motorboats. However, some 101 Troop men were soon absorbed into Courtney's new unit, No. 2 SBS, which he formed at Ardrossen, Scotland, in March 1942.

Another unit in which a number of SBS/SAS volunteers had served at some stage in their careers was No. 62 Commando, a unit also known as STS 62 or the Small Scale Raiding Force (SSRF), which was at first largely recruited from the ranks of No. 12 Commando. The SSRF, another parent unit of the modern SBS, was formed in February 1942 at the suggestion of Lord Louis Mountbatten. This unit was an extension of the idea developed by 101 Troop, but submarines and two-man canoes were exchanged for a small, fifty-man, raiding force, tasked to strike across the English Channel in fast motorboats. The commander of this doughty band was Captain March-Phillips and his officers included two great fighting men, Anders Lassen and Philip Pinckney, both of whom went on to serve with the SBS in the Aegean under Earl Jellicoe.

The job of the SSRF was to attack small targets or carry out special small-scale tasks, such as snatching prisoners for interrogation or bringing back enemy equipment for examination – preferably without the enemy noticing that it was missing. This the SSRF proceeded to do. Their favourite craft was the fast MTB 344, which had exceptionally powerful engines and was known affectionately to members of the SSRF as 'The Little Pisser'.

Corporal Percy Cotter of 12 Commando served with the SSRF and his account gives some idea of what the Small Scale Raiding Force got up to:

After forming up, 12 Commando spent some time in the Shetland Islands making small raids in motor torpedo boats (MTBs) handled by the Norwegian Navy. The main purpose of these raids appeared to be to land and observe movement of German coastal vessels and during our observation period ashore the MTBs would hunt out enemy shipping and lay mines. Many years later, in 1985, when visiting Amsterdam, I met some Norwegians and it turned out that one of the party had been a skipper on these same MTBs and remembered his trips with the Commandos.

I also had the good fortune to be with a small party from 12 Commando who were detached to STS 62 at Anderson Manor in Dorset. This was the Small Scale Raiding Force, and while with them I took part in a raid on the French-occupied territory, near Cherbourg. Our target was a radar station, and the object was to snatch some defending enemy troops, establish the quality of the men on coastal defence and also destroy the station. Captain Rooney was in charge, but we were also fortunate in having the assistance of the highly experienced Major Appleyard. The force moved to Churston Hall in South Devon and we sailed in a very small, fast MTB, No. 344, from Dartmouth. Nine of us, including Sammy Brodison, Ellis Howells (killed later in an operation in Italy), Sergeant Bruce Ogden Smith (an instructor at the STS, who later went into COPP), Lance Corporal Joe Barry and Jim Connor, were shoehorned, for want of a better description, into a small equipment store in the bow of the vessel, with Major Gus Appleyard and Captain Rooney sharing the comfort of the bridge with the skipper and others of the crew. There was no lighting in our accommodation, and we had one bucket to use in case of seasickness or as a toilet.

Around midnight the hatch entrance was partly opened and a shaft of torchlight lit the interior. From behind the glare Major Appleyard informed us of difficulty in locating the island of Alderney, a vital navigation checkpoint, without which we would be unable to make the correct landing for the target area. As always though, the navy rose to the occasion and about twenty minutes later we were called out on deck to lower a small dory for our final progress to the shore.

The view as we moved into our position on deck was really beautiful. We were in a wide bay with the shore some 400 yards on our beam, and we could then see the high ground rising some hundred feet from the shore to the target. In silence we climbed down into the dory. There was eight of us paddling, Captain Rooney navigating, and one man standing by to drop a kedge anchor when we were about a hundred yards from our point of landing. The purpose of the anchor was to give us the means, after disembarkation, to leave one man in the craft, who then pulled the craft some eighty to a hundred yards offshore and so avoided possible detection by a shore patrol. On this occasion, our boat guard was to spend a lonely four hours awaiting our return.

Once on the shore, we scrambled up the cliff as quietly as possible, although there were some grunts and curses. As I was carrying a Bren gun with a considerable number of loaded magazines, I was more than pleased to receive a few timely thumps around the rear from Ellis Howells to assist me in the climb. On the top of the cliff our first job, having orientated ourselves with the target, was for one person to shin up nearby telephone poles and cut the communication between the radar station and a nearby village. We had been informed by Intelligence that our target was undefended but patrolled regularly by troops stationed in the village. In addition to our normal arms, i.e. rifle and bayonet, we had fighting knives, also a Sten gun with an odd attachment which was supposed to act as a silencer; we had little faith in this weapon. Captain Rooney had armed himself with a bow and arrows in case our information on the target was not correct. The force, myself excepted, now made a cautious approach towards the target and I settled down to cover them in the event of a German patrol coming from the village.

After about half an hour I heard a slight noise from behind me and, as I whipped round, a hoarse whisper, which in the silence of the early morning sounded like a roar, said, 'Cotter, it's me. Don't shoot.' I recognised the voice of Captain Rooney. He explained that the target, far from being undefended, was surrounded by the usual German triple-wire fence, behind which two enemy guards kept a watch. One remained in a position opposite where our men lay under cover, while the other man made a patrol round the camp. An undetected entry was not on.

Having reminded me to keep a sharp lookout for any activity from the village, Captain Rooney then made his way back to the rest of the force. After some time, the silence was suddenly shattered by a tremendous explosion. We had noticed a German sign at the top of the cliff reading '*Achtung Minen*', and my first thought was that one of the boys had trodden on a mine. Almost immediately, however, I heard the sound of automatics firing and voices, in German, saying '*nicht schiessen*', followed by more firing. Apparently, on the return of Captain Rooney, our party first thought of trying to eliminate one sentry with either the silent Sten gun or an arrow while the second man was on his patrol round the station grounds. This was dismissed because of the difficulty in trying to line up the target in the dark.

However, Captain Rooney had taken along a two-pound plastic explosive grenade, which was activated like a Mills grenade by the removal of a cap. As the grenade was thrown a tape unwound and withdrew the safety pin, thereby allowing the grenade to explode on contact. Captain Rooney decided to use the grenade when the two sentries were together having their periodic discussion. The grenade was thrown over the defensive wire and fell between the sentries, who were blasted to bits before they realised what had happened.

At this point Ellis Howells threw himself over the wire to make a bridge for the rest of our force to enter the radar station. German soldiers then appeared from a guardhouse and were engaged by our force. After a short period it became obvious that the radar station had sufficient men to defeat our purpose and, with the prospect of reinforcements coming quickly from the village, it was decided to withdraw. A speedy descent was made to the shoreline, where we were more than pleased to find the dory ready and waiting. Firing was still coming from the direction of the radar station as we paddled towards the approaching MTB, heading for home and safety, but alas, empty-handed.

In June 1943, I was attached to another small-scale force, again under Captain Rooney of No. 4 Parachute Troop, who were made up of men from B Troop, No. 12 Commando. Shortly after I arrived they took part in a small operation, parachuting on to the cliff top near Abbeville. The only others I can recall by name who took part in this raid were Jim Connor and Private Sims. The purpose of the operation was again to take prisoners for the object of identifying the type of troops manning that section of the German defences, and the parachute force would consist of a ten-man 'stick'. Pre-planning envisaged the force splitting on arrival, with Captain Rooney and seven men looking for the prisoners, while Jim Connor and another man would look after the escape arrangements from the cliff to the shoreline, from where they would be taken out by a small boat and to an MTB for return to the UK. The idea was for Connor to lower the other man down the cliff, as it was the task of the latter to contact the MTB for this part of the operation. Simple in practice. In the event, the 'stick' landed safely and the split-up duly took place.

Connor's partner had agreed that when he reached the cliff bottom he would signal to Connor, who would then throw down the remainder of the rope for his partner to collect. The idea was to leave no trace of their visit behind and deny the enemy knowledge of how their men had been snatched. The same rule applied to the parachutes, which were to be dumped at sea, but because these were made of silk, and the men preferred their ladies in silk, they decided to bring back these valuable pieces of equipment themselves. Connor had a further task, to prepare a rope for use by the rest of the force in their escape to the cliff base. A system had been devised whereby the main rope and a thin secondary line could be attached to the piton in such a manner that the last man down could release both ropes from the piton, pull them down, and both could then be brought back, leaving nothing for the enemy to find.

Now back to the raid. Connor paid out the rope attached to the other man, who proceeded down the cliff. The arrangement was that two tugs on the rope would serve as a signal that he was safely on the ground and all went well for about two-thirds of the way, when the rope became entangled in some growth on the cliff face. The man on the rope gave a couple of tugs to free himself and Connor, thinking this was the signal that the man was on the ground, threw the rope down the cliff, thereby expediting the descent of his colleague with sufficient force to render him unconscious. At the appointed time the MTB arrived offshore, but received no acknowledgment of its signal. Fortunately, the vessel remained on watch and was still on station when the main force arrived back at the cliff top and commenced the abseil to the cliff base.

A search was made amid some apprehension concerning possible shore patrols, and one of the party stumbled over the figure of the man they were looking for. The MTB was successfully contacted and sent in a dory to uplift the force. Due to tidal conditions this s was driven well away from the men on shore, who had to trail along the sand for about a mile as dawn approached, only to find the dory upside down in the waves with a tired sailor trying to make it seaworthy. The ladies had to go without their silk as the men had to dump the chutes and bury them in the sand. All duly returned safely and the injured man recovered. When the Commando forces were organising for D-Day, No. 4 Parachute Troop was disbanded and we were posted to 6 Commando, which had recently returned from North Africa.

The SSRF had a short but active career and many members went on to serve in other Special Force units apart from the SBS – Sergeant Ogdon Smith, for example, joined COPP and was one of the swimmers who marked the D-Day beaches in 1944. A large number of the SSRF, including Captain Peter Pinckney, went on to serve with Jellicoe's SBS in the Aegean, but many of these original SSRF were eventually captured by the Germans and shot under the Commando Order. Few SSRF officers or NCOs survived the war.

One of Roger Courtney's first tasks in forming No. 2 SBS in March 1942 was to recruit some more officers, among them his younger brother, Godfrey Courtney, a regular officer in the Royal West Kents, who had just been sent home as unfit for infantry service with the Gold Coast Regiment, since he suffered from fallen arches. The younger Courtney felt that, if his feet were not up to the military life, sitting on his backside in a canoe might be a useful alternative – and so it proved. Godfrey Courtney was to emulate the exploits of his brother and command SBS units in the Middle East and Far East with considerable success.

The nucleus of this second SBS unit came from 101 Troop, which had been raiding across the Channel from Dover, but such a small force was becoming a little lonely in the rapidly expanding world of Combined Ops. Fifteen men of 101 Troop joined 2 SBS and Captain Montanaro became Roger Courtney's second-in-command. During his brief tenure in this role he took the new unit on their first raid, a swoop across the Channel to attack a German merchant ship in the harbour at Boulogne.

Two crews were tasked for this exploit, the second one containing Sergeant Stan Weatherall, who gave this account of the operation:

This was in April 1942. The navy in Dover had picked the target, two merchants ships in Boulogne, so we sent in two canoes on ML102, each carrying eight limpets and all the usual gear. We adjusted our compasses with

128

the RAF at Hawkinge – they were RAF compasses and could be affected by all the metal in the canoes, the limpet mines and so on; we tried to use brass which is not magnetic but could not always do so. We also wore RAF survival suits that could keep a pilot warm if he ditched in the Channel. Then Captain Montanaro came back and he had some bad news – the Admiralty had said that Boulogne was too small to let two canoes operate and that only one would go in, and Captain Montanaro said that he and Trooper Preece, his no. 2, would do the job. I was pretty fed up about that and said so at length, but although the Captain was very sorry, it was his decision and we only got to go over in the ML and help out.

It all went well; we launched the canoe about a mile or so outside the harbour entrance, in pitch dark, and they were in and out in a couple of hours while we hung about outside. Apparently the only snag was that the ships were pretty foul and they had to scrape off the seaweed before the magnets would stick to the hull, but that was not unknown. Anyway, they sank the ship; we all got back safely and Captain Montanaro got the DSO and Preece got the DCM. That was the last time I saw the captain as he went off on some secret work and ended up in the Royal Navy.

As already related, at the end of 1942 a number of 2 SBS personnel went off to the Mediterranean and took part in Operation *Torch* and some canoe raids along the Italian shore. Most of these men were back by the end of the year, when the unit moved to Hillhead, on the coast of the Solent in Hampshire. The troop recruited more men, most of them volunteers from the Commando units, and began some intensive training for operations in 1943. The unit reached a total of some sixty officers and men all fully trained, by the end of the winter, when the raiding season began.

The raids began in March 1943 with an abortive reconnaissance to the Channel Islands. Also in March, as previously related, a detachment of ten Z SBS men under Captain Godfrey Courtney was sent to the Mediterranean to work with the 8th Submarine Flotilla out of Algiers. Operations continued in the UK and, in July 1943, Stan Weatherall, now a sergeant major, was compensated for his disappointment of the previous year when he was sent with three other SBS men on a 'cosh job' to Dunkirk, tasked to capture a German soldier and bring him back to the UK. Stan remembers it well:

Since we had to bring off a prisoner we used a normal Cockle Mark I, and a three-man canoe to carry the German. We rehearsed the job in Dover, using the pier as the Dunkirk quay. We had a climber's ladder, steel cables and steps to get up on to it, and an American rifle with night sights. We loaded all our gear on to an MGB on the night of 2 August 1943 and set off across the Channel for Dunkirk, getting there just two hours later, at about 2345 hours, when we hove to about a mile off the pier and launched the canoes.

There was a small light on the end of the pier and Captain Dickie Livingstone paddled towards it. Then it turned on us and, although I don't think they actually saw us, something must have bothered them because the light followed us in until Dickie Livingstone decided that we were not going to make it, and ordered the withdrawal. We went out to sea on a reciprocal course – 180 degrees from the one we had gone in on – but we could not find the MGB. We heard later that it had got into a scrap with some E-boats and decided to go back to base.

We got rid of the searchlight, but that was the best we could do, and after a bit Dickie told us that we would steer north until daybreak, to get well up the Channel, and then head due west until we hit the east coast of England. He had become very sick so at about 0200 hours I took over the navigation and the paddling, and at daylight, about 0500, we started to head west, still in company.

It was a bit rough and we were shipping a bit of water, but nothing to worry about, and then, at about 0800, we saw a Spitfire, which did not see our smoke grenade. At 1130 hours we saw two more Spits and lit a flare and this time they did see us, and started to circle. Then four more Spitfires arrived, escorting an amphibian aircraft, a Walrus, which landed and started to taxi up as the Spitfires suddenly peeled off and started diving and strafing something a few miles off. This turned out to be the three E-boats, probably the ones that had seen our MGB and were now looking for us. Anyway, too late; we got in the Walrus, sank the two canoes, and were back in Hawkinge by the afternoon.

As the summer of 1943 drew on to autumn, and then winter, small parties of British Commandos, COPP and SBS, began to go across the Channel regularly, night after night, to survey the German defences and bring back samples of sand, mud, wire and mines. These reconnaissance operations were not only made in Normandy, the actual site of the D-Day landings, but all along the French coast, so that, if any news of this activity got out or any parties were detected, the Germans – though in little doubt by now that an invasion was coming – would still be unaware of exactly where the blow would fall. The SBS role in this activity was to conduct small raids called *Hardtack* Operations and in two of these, one against the Channel Islands and one against Gravelines, two SBS men, an officer and an NCO, were killed. All this activity in the Bay of the Seine was designed to conceal the vital COPP surveys of the actual invasion beaches. COPP was small, reaching its maximum establishment of around 180 men just before D-Day, and the SBS assistance was invaluable.

Training continued even as the operations took place, and those in training, new recruits or experienced raiders, met the men returning from these forays and picked up a constant stream of tips and useful advice. Most of the volunteers were already trained Commandos, used to night work, explosives, radio, signals and small-boat handling. To these some more specialised SBS skills – navigation, booby traps, escape and evasion and ship attack – needed to be added and the result, on completion, was a highly trained and individual fighting man.

Such a unit deserved and needed employment, but after D-Day the field for their skills and talents suddenly shrank, for the coastline of Europe was now in Allied hands and, even if the Germans were making a fight of it in the Aegean and the Adriatic, that theatre of operations was in the capable hands of the 'other' SBS – Major Earl Jellicoe's Special Boat Squadron. There was also a plot afoot either to transfer the Army SBS to Royal Marines control or to absorb it totally by transferring all SBS personnel into the ranks of the Royal Marines. This distinguished Corps had – and has – many admirers, but not every soldier wants to join it and the ranks of the SBS contained men from many famous regiments who wanted to continue wearing their own cap badge – thank you *very* much – and they said so to the Royal Marines in no uncertain terms.

This plan had been formulated by Admiral Lord Louis Mountbatten, a long-time supporter of the Royal Marines, who by the end of 1943 had left Combined Operations for a new and even more important role as commander in chief, South-East Asia. Mountbatten swiftly saw scope for small-scale raiding and in January 1944 Z SBS were transferred from the Mediterranean to Ceylon to work with Force 136, the Far East equivalent of SOE. Z SBS were at first attached to the 4th Submarine Flotilla in Trincomalee but were then sent to form part of a new, shore-based Special Operations Group – SOG – under Royal Marines control. Here, over the next few months, the rest of the original SBS, from the UK and the Middle East, gradually arrived to join them. We pick up their story again in Chapter 15.

10

CHARIOT OPERATIONS
1942–44

*'The work . . . demanded great courage, cool wits and
determination and physical endurance of a high
standard.'*

Admiral Sir George Creasy,
C-in-C, Home Fleet

The development of underwater warfare by frogmen,
Chariots and midget submarines (X-craft) was inhibited
from the start by a lack of suitable equipment and an array
of technical and scientific problems, all of which had to be
overcome before men could move and fight underwater at
all. At best, the underwater world is a hostile environ-
ment. Those men who opted to fight there frequently
found themselves at odds with the sea and the technology,
far more often than they were in combat with the enemy.
Gradually, however, the problems were solved and the
underwater warriors began to take a steady toll of enemy
shipping. However, among all the targets proposed for
undersea attack by Chariots and X-craft, none was
suggested so often as the German battleship *Tirpitz*.

Before the war began the German Navy had constructed a number of capital ships which were far in
advance of their kind – faster, better armed and armoured
than any comparable British warship and able to operate

at sea for long periods. These ships – the *Graf Spee*, *Bismarck*, *Scharnhorst*, *Guisenau* and, above all, the 40,000-ton battleship *Tirpitz*, were designed for commerce raiding, for powerful sweeps into the North Atlantic or much further afield, to attack British convoys. These German ships were powerful enough to sink any convoy escorts and fast enough to avoid any number of capital ships the British Admiralty sent in pursuit.

Gradually, however, over the first few years of the war, these ships, notably the *Graf Spee* and the *Bismarck*, were eliminated, but the *Tirpitz*, though confined to the safety of a Norwegian fjord, was still intact and, therefore, a potential threat. To guard against a foray by the *Tirpitz*, large units of the Home Fleet were obliged to stay at anchor in Scapa Flow, so that even when unemployed the *Tirpitz* succeeded in immobilising units of the Royal Navy that might have been usefully employed elsewhere.

The only answer was to sink the *Tirpitz*. Various options were considered, including air attack, but the ship was in a snug anchorage in the Asenfjord near Trondhjem, and well protected by anti-aircraft guns and fighter aircraft; an air strike against *Tirpitz* promised only further losses to the RAF, so the task seemed to require a more subtle approach. The job was eventually handed over to the Royal Navy's Chariot force and the Special Operations Executive (SOE), which was in regular contact with the Norwegian Resistance.

The idea was that the SOE and the Norwegians would supply intelligence on the position of the *Tirpitz* and her defences in and around the Trondhjemfjord, and supply the means by which the Chariots could get within striking distance of the German battleship. If they could do that, the Chariot raiders would attack and sink her.

This is an instance, neither the first nor the last, of the SBS operating with the intelligence community. The proposal was discussed by the Norwegian section of SOE and the Admiralty, and an outline plan was drawn up for the attack. This called for two Chariots, with their crews and assistants – a total of six British officers and ratings –

to be transported from the Shetland Islands to the Norwegian coast in a fishing vessel, the *Arthur*, carrying Norwegian colours and manned by a Norwegian crew under the command of Lieutenant Lief Larsen DSM. SOE was running a regular, clandestine trawler service into Norwegian waters from the Shetland Islands, so regular it was known as the 'Shetland Bus', which supplied the growing Norwegian Resistance with arms and instructors.

Most of this Bus service was in Norwegian trawlers and, although they were stopped and searched regularly by German fishery patrols, they actually *were* legitimate fishing craft for most of the time and their hidden cargoes of men and arms usually escaped detection. The Chariots were too big to be contained in a conventional submarine and towing them across behind the *Arthur* seemed the only feasible way of getting them to the target area, though it clearly increased the risk of loss if the towing cables parted. When the plan was further advanced the decision was made to carry the two Chariots lashed on deck for most of the crossing and only lower them over the side when close to the enemy-held coast.

The *Arthur* would then run the gauntlet of the German patrol craft, with the Chariots under tow behind, the towing cables ostensibly attached to fishing nets, and their crews concealed aboard. The *Arthur* could not bring the men back again, so after the attack they would go ashore, contact the Norwegian Resistance and be hustled across the frontier of neutral Sweden.

These plans matured slowly throughout the summer of 1942, but there was a snag – there was always a snag – and this was a big one: the attack had been set up for the harbour at Trondhjem, but the *Tirpitz* had moved. She had made a few short forays out to sea, probably to exercise her crew and fire her main armament, and then returned to the Bogenfjord, where she remained throughout the summer and into the autumn. The *Arthur*, her crew and the Charioteers could do nothing but wait while the Norwegian Resistance kept up a watch on the *Tirpitz* and hoped that their plan was not discovered.

Finally, at the end of October, after months of waiting, good news came from Bogenfjord. The *Tirpitz* had steam up and was clearly getting ready to sail. News then arrived that she was moving south ... possibly back to Trondhjem. SOE and the Charioteers decided to wait no longer and, in early November, *Arthur* sailed from Shetland, carrying four Charioteers: Lieutenant Brewster RNVR, two seamen, Brown and Evans and a soldier of the Royal Engineers, Sergeant Craig. This indicates the typical composition of an irregular, volunteer unit – a temporary officer, an army sergeant and two naval ratings. Since all these men must have been on someone's 'ration strength', how they got together on a Norwegian fishing boat bound for the destruction of a German battleship remains a mystery.

These two craft en route for Norway were the most up-to-date Chariots available. About the same length as a torpedo, around twenty feet, a Chariot carried two men in an open compartment plus a 600 pound explosive charge in a detachable warhead. She had a range of about eighteen miles and a speed of about three knots. The craft was battery propelled and steered by a combination of a rudder and hydroplanes aft. The crew wore the Sladden diving suit and were fed oxygen from tanks on their backs.

The *Arthur* ran into very heavy weather in the North Sea and could only make two or three knots on the first day. However, it is not far from Shetland to Norway and on the following morning it was decided to unship the Chariots and tow them behind, an operation that took some hours of hard work in constant fear of German reconnaissance aircraft appearing overhead. The fishing boat entered the Trondhjemfjord early on the following day and, having passed a German patrol boat, halted at the moored German inspection boat for clearance. This was a nightmare half-hour while the Germans examined their papers and searched the boat for, while the Charioteers were well concealed under the cargo of peat, the Chariots were only just under the surface behind the trawler and might easily have been seen.

136

However, that hazard was passed and the trawler sailed on up the fjord towards the *Tirpitz* anchorage . . . and then came disaster. A German craft came past at speed, throwing up a heavy wake, and the trawler pitched in the swell . . . and the tow ropes to the Chariots parted. The Chariots plunged to the bottom of the fjord and the operation was over.

Sick with disappointment, there was nothing for the crew to do but take the *Arthur* into a quiet cove and sink her before going ashore and making their way to the Swedish frontier. Not all of them made it. Evans, one of the seamen, ran into a German frontier patrol. He engaged them with his revolver but was wounded and captured. When the Germans discovered what he had been doing in Norway, they shot him. The Commando Order had claimed another victim, but the Charioteers, having had one crack at the *Tirpitz*, would be back.

This tale displays the fact that not all Special Force operations are inevitably crowned with success. To succeed at all a certain amount has to be left to chance and, inevitably, things go wrong. None of this was viewed as a reason to stop the attacks – on the contrary, it provided a constant spur to more training and the refining of techniques. Besides, if the first *Tirpitz* attack had been a failure, the Charioteers were having much better luck in the warmer waters of the Mediterranean in the early months of 1943.

By then, post-Alamein, the Eighth Army were storming west along the North African shore and the main factor inhibiting an even faster advance was logistics – a shortage of supplies. Every round of ammunition and gallon of petrol had to be brought from Egypt along the single desert road. What the Eighth Army needed was a working port and the port of Tripoli, in Libya, would have been ideal if the Germans could be prevented from blocking it before they pulled out. As a preventative step, two Chariots were sent into Tripoli in January 1943 to attack several blockships which the Germans were preparing to sink across the harbour entrance. These Chariots were

137

carried to the attack in special hangers on the deck of the submarine HMS/M *Thunderbolt* and the attack went in on the night of 18/19 January.

Thunderbolt was supposed to drop the Charioteers two miles from the harbour but, in spite of a prowling German E-boat, the captain decided to take them even further in, guided by flares which the RAF were dropping as markers over the town. It was also hoped that, when the ships blew up, the enemy would attribute this to bombing rather than sabotage and that this would give the Charioteers a better chance of escaping inland, for, yet again, there was no means of extracting them once they had done their job.

This attack went well. One crew, Lieutenant Stevens RNVR and CPO Buxton, attacked two ships with limpets before abandoning their craft and going ashore, where they were captured. The second crew, Lieutenant Larkin RNVR and PO Berey – who was a cook when not engaged in sinking enemy ships – had a less successful, but equally exciting, time. Soon after leaving *Thunderbolt* they discovered that their Chariot had been damaged so, as they were unable to carry on with the attack, they set explosive charges and sent the Chariot out to sea. They then went ashore and headed through the suburbs of Tripoli for the open desert.

Tripoli is a big city, and getting out of town took some time. They hoped to steal a car or a truck, but all the transport they came across was heavily guarded, though they did their bit for the war effort by cutting every cable and telephone line they came across. They continued this useful task next day as they headed east, but they were eventually captured by the Germans who kept them under guard during the day but took them out for a meal that night. The evening was crowned when Lieutenant Larkin entertained his hosts with a German song. This lulled the Germans into a false sense of security and, later that night, Larkin and Berey climbed out of the lorry they were sleeping in and made good their escape. After a few more days, and a few more adventures, they regained the British lines.

After the conclusion of the North African campaign in

1943, the next Allied task was the invasion of Italy. This began with the invasion of Sicily and here the Charioteers found a new role, replacing COPP in beach recce, for which the chariots were found to be ideal. The Chariots were carried close to the beach on the casing of large submarines and were then led closer to the beach by canoe teams. The canoeists waited offshore while the Chariots were driven ashore. The Charioteers beached their craft in about two fathoms of water and then went ashore to examine the beach obstacles. With their task completed, they returned to their craft, went back out to sea, surfaced and contacted the canoes, which in turn contacted the large submarine. This combination of craft was used on a highly successful and undetected series of beach reconnaissance operations.

This useful work was in addition to more shipping attacks, notably when Chariot teams sank an Italian cruiser and a merchant ship in Palermo harbour. This was the first time that the Italians realised the British had become major players in underwater warfare and, as the Italians had invented this activity, this information came as an unpleasant surprise. Enemy disquiet was compounded when the Charioteers made a successful attack on the major Italian naval base at La Spezia, where the Italians had first experimented with underwater craft.

By the time this attack went in, in June 1944, Italy was an ally, but the target for the Chariot attack was an eight-inch-gun Italian cruiser, the *Bolzano*, which the Germans had taken over. By February 1944, the British had established a secret Chariot base close to La Spezia and had contact with an Italian torpedo-boat officer who was familiar with the harbour and its defences. The plan they concocted called for the Italian MTB to take a Chariot to within two miles of the harbour entrance, which was protected by a boom and nets. After attacking the *Bolzano*, the Chariot crew, Lieutenant Causer and AB Harry Smith, were to go ashore and make their way up the coast to a point where the MTB would come in and pick them up.

The operation began in Naples in June 1944, where the Chariot was loaded on to the MTB. This craft duly took them towards La Spezia, but on the way the Italian captain decided he had done enough and declined to take the Charioteers to their agreed dropping-off point. He would go no closer than seven miles, and as a result the Charioteers had to travel on the surface for two hours to close the entrance before starting their attack. They then dived to twenty feet and, after half an hour of underwater running, surfaced to find themselves well inside the approaches and heading towards the boom. They dived at the first net and cut their way through it only to run at once into another one. There were several anti-submarine nets guarding the entrance to La Spezia, and it took a lot of time – and a lot of guts – before the Charioteers had hacked their way through these in the dark of the harbour bottom. They finally surfaced inside the naval base. All they had to do now was find and sink a cruiser.

Thanks to their early drop off, and the delays caused by the nets, it was almost daylight, but at least there was no difficulty in finding the *Bolzano*, which lay at anchor in the centre of the harbour. Dawn was already breaking and the harbour was coming to life as the Chariot dived and the two men began to make their final approach to the target. They dived to twenty feet and went on until they were under the ship's propellers, the hull clearly outlined against the lightening sky. They then rose under the hull and pulled the craft along until they were in the centre of the ship, under the engine room. Magnets were then placed on the hull and the warhead was attached to them and released from the Chariot. That done, the men dived to thirty feet and turned towards the shore.

At this point it would be a good idea to consider for a moment what these two young men had done. They had now been in the water for nearly eight hours, in well-defended enemy waters. They had been let down by their transport vessel and forced into a long, time-wasting approach to the enemy harbour. They had then found not one net but a series, yet, undaunted, they had cut their way through them, one after another, dragging their craft through after them. The sheer physical effort alone, deep under the surface, must have been exhausting. They had then carried out a copybook attack on a large enemy ship and were now on their own, with the virtual certainty of capture and knowing that there was a strong possibility that they would then be handed over to the Gestapo and shot. Courage and devotion to duty hardly seems an adequate description.

The plan had been to scuttle the Chariot in deep water and then go ashore, dump the diving gear and lie low for a while before making an escape to open country. Then they discovered that the Chariot batteries were too low – they would not be able to make it to shore below the surface. They therefore scuttled their craft in the middle of the harbour and swam to shelter in the lee of a breakwater in the middle of the harbour. They were still there at 0630 hours when a massive explosion shook the harbour and the *Bolzano* rolled over and sank.

This epic of underwater warfare continued. The two men stayed on the breakwater all day, somehow undetected, until an Italian fisherman appeared and agreed to take them down the coast. They then stole a rowing boat and set out to row the ninety miles to Corsica. After a night of hard pulling they came ashore, only to find themselves just twenty miles further down the Italian coast. They then joined a band of Italian Resistance fighters and fought with them for two months until the band was wiped out in an attack by the Germans. The Allied armies were now fighting their way up the Italian peninsula – Rome had fallen in early June – so they then attempted to make their way south to the British lines, only to be picked up by the Germans a few miles from safety. The risk then intensified, for the Germans were suspicious that these two sailors were the saboteurs who had sunk the *Bolzano* and not, as they claimed to be, survivors of a sunken submarine. Both men stuck to their story under interrogation and survived the war.

After the end of the Italian campaign it was decided that

the best field for Chariot operations was in the Far East, and by the end of 1943 most Chariot crews were on their way back in Britain, and awaiting redeployment. Chariot operations were eventually superseded by X-craft, which were found to be equally efficient at penetrating enemy harbours and far more comfortable for their crews – though comfort in this connection is a very relative matter. The X-craft were actually extremely uncomfortable, but they had a good range and were apt for the completion of the main outstanding task – the destruction of the battleship *Tirpitz*.

11

THE END OF THE *TIRPITZ* SEPTEMBER 1943

'A most daring and successful attack, after a passage of a thousand miles from base'

Citation for the award of the Victoria Cross
to Lieutenants Place and Cameron

By the beginning of 1943, the SBS in its various forms – canoeists, Charioteers, X-craft and seaborne raiders – had succeeded in one of the long-term aims of all Special Force warfare: they were forcing the enemy on to the defensive and obliging them to deploy large numbers of troops on guard duties. Whatever the particular objectives of any Special Force operation, and however much or little damage they caused, the actions of all these raiders forced the enemy to maintain large numbers of men on tasks that kept them out of front-line units. The enemy also had to devote a great deal of time and effort to the construction and defence of military and naval installations.

Airfields, ships, transport and artillery parks, fuel and ammunition dumps, bridges, dry docks, anything that could be of use to the enemy, and in striking distance of the shore or a submarine, was liable to attack and therefore had to be guarded. Just how many men were tied up in such mundane tasks is impossible to estimate, but it must have run into tens if not hundreds of thousands, for everything had to be guarded, even though only a few bases were attacked and only a few bridges were actually destroyed.

Then there was the cost of constructing defensive positions and equipping them with mines, barbed wire, machine guns, searchlights and telephone links. All this occupied a great deal of time and effort and was quite often to no purpose – either the position was not attacked at all or the defences, constructed with such care and effort, proved inadequate to keep the raiders out. A far better means of defence was to remove such installations beyond the reach of Special Force activity, but as equipment improved and their experience grew, Special Force teams, naval and military, began to range far behind the Axis lines and operate almost at will.

Even so, the steady improvement in the enemy defences did call for further developments in equipment and the redeployment of more vulnerable forms of attack to less well-prepared defences. The canoe raiders shifted to the Far East and the Greek Islands, where the defenders were less used to such activity and therefore less alert, while fresh methods were found for attacking targets on the well-defended Atlantic coast. After *Frankton* and the St Nazaire commando raid, the Germans improved their defences against surface attack and canoe raiding tended to die out, though canoe reconnaissance continued. Beach recce remained an important task and grew in importance as D-Day came nearer. This task was entrusted to the men of COPP, the Combined Operations Pilotage Parties, who sent teams ashore night after night throughout the winter and spring of 1943/44 to examine the Normandy beaches and inspect the ever growing number of obstacles the Germans were preparing to check the invasion they knew was coming.

Recce was well in hand, but the raiding element in underwater warfare needed a new craft, something with long range and a fully submersible capacity, to extend the activities of the frogmen and the Charioteers. Conventional submarines were at the other end of the operational spectrum, too big for inshore operations and, at the time, without the ability to release men underwater, men who could deal with defensive nets and then return and enter the submerged submarine. Something smaller and handier than a full-sized submarine was required, yet something with a longer range than the Chariot. The eventual solution was the midget submarine – the X-craft. Midget submarines are still part of the SBS story, for the US Navy SEALS still use them to carry teams ashore for raiding and beach recon, but the concept was pioneered and tested in the Second World War, specifically in operations against the *Tirpitz*.

The X-craft were first developed in 1943. The specification called for a four-man craft, not more that fifty feet in length, with a maximum diameter of five and a half feet except – as a small concession – under the periscopes, where a man of average height might dare to stand upright and stretch. Otherwise, the X-craft were very cramped and life on board was never less than extremely uncomfortable.

These X-craft weighed fifty tons and were divided into four watertight compartments. The forward compartment contained the batteries, which provided the power while submerged. The second compartment was the Wet and Dry, basically an escape compartment but one which was used by the diver to get in and out of the craft when required. This compartment was crucial to the successful operation of the craft. The X-craft did not carry torpedoes, but two large 500 pound charges, known as side cargoes, which were attached to the pressure hull. It was the job of the diver, exiting from the Wet and Dry, to position and release these side cargoes if necessary; his other tasks were net cutting and the placing of limpet mines on enemy vessels.

Then came the control compartment, with the periscope, chart tables, compasses and controls. The last compartment contained the gyro compass and the other controls. There were two bunks, shared off watch by the crew. The four-man team typically consisted of a captain, usually a lieutenant, who did the chart work and handled observation via the periscope; a first lieutenant, who handled the engine and hydroplanes through which the X-craft moved and dived; an engineer, always an ERA or Engine Room Artificer, who kept everything working; and, lastly, a diver.

The diver was actually a frogman or shallow-water diver and his task was arguably the most difficult and dangerous of all. The diver's job was to leave the submerged craft, as ordered by the captain, and carry out such tasks as were necessary. These included anything from cutting anti-submarine nets to releasing the vessel's two explosive charges. They also found themselves repairing damage and removing mines, but at best the task of the diver was a difficult one. On board he shared the watchkeeping with the rest of the crew, serving as the helmsman during his watch – four hours on and four hours off, day after day, night after night, often for weeks.

Hardly any of the underwater tasks could be described as easy or even pleasant, so it is a matter of wonder that any men could be found willing, if not actually eager, to take them on. The idea of diving in a conventional submarine fills most people with a touch of claustrophobia, if not the horrors, yet a conventional submarine is well lit, warm and roomy compared with these midget craft. If death comes, it comes quickly, and life on a submarine in wartime compared favourably with that in a tank or a heavy bomber.

A midget submarine had no advantages in the way of comfort. Insulation took up valuable space and could not be fitted, so the X-craft were damp and bitterly cold in Northern waters and hot and stuffy in the tropics. Sketchy meals had to be cooked when possible on a single electric ring and condensation dripped relentlessly on to the men and their equipment. In an X-craft you were never dry, and once the hatch had been closed it felt very like a coffin.

And yet, uncomfortable as it was, the X-craft was a

useful vessel and a superb seaboat. They could stay submerged for 36 hours – though the air would be almost unbreathable by that time – and dive to a depth of 200 feet. They also had a long range on their batteries and were hard to detect on Asdic or any other anti-submarine detection device. They were, in short, ideal for the task for which they had been designed – coastal and harbour raiding. When crewed by brave and resolute men, they were a formidable weapon of war.

The prime task of these craft was to make their way, fully submerged, into enemy harbours and attack shipping, either by releasing the heavy side cargoes underneath the enemy vessel or by letting the diver out to attach limpet mines to the enemy hull. To do this, the diver would enter the Wet and Dry compartment wearing diving dress and equipment and flood it by opening the outer sea cocks. When the inner and outer pressure had equalised, the outer hatch could be opened and the diver could exit the craft and go about his business. It has to be appreciated that this work took place at night, in pitch-dark freezing waters and often under the hull of an enemy warship. The thought is enough to make the blood run cold.

His task completed, the diver re-entered the X-craft, closed and secured the outer hatch and then blew out the seawater through the sea cocks using compressed air. The cocks were then closed and the hatch to the main compartment opened. His comrades would then greet him with a well-earned tot of rum. He could not relax though, for an hour later he might have to do it all again.

When – rather than if – the submarine ran into defensive netting, the diver was again deployed. He exited the submarine as before and examined the net. If it was rope or manila cable, it might be possible to hack a gap in it with his diver's knife, but by now the Germans were using steel or wire cables and these had to be cut using power tools deployed from the hull of the X-craft. This often meant clambering all over the net like a human fly, and all this had to be done carefully and with the minimum surface disturbance to avoid the possibility of a patrol craft appearing on the surface and dropping grenades or explosive charges. Once a gap had been cut in the net the X-craft could proceed slowly through. The diver remained outside to keep the net from jamming in the hydroplanes or catching on the propellers.

In 1943, the submarine flotillas in the UK, especially the 12th Submarine Flotilla, which had midget submarines, were still concerned with the German warships lurking in the Norwegian fjords, notably the 12,000-ton cruiser *Lutzow*, the 26,000-ton pocket battleship *Scharnhorst* and, largest of all, the 40,000-ton *Tirpitz*. If these three could be eliminated, many big-gun capital ships of the Royal Navy would be freed for more vigorous action against the enemy.

Therefore, on 12 September 1943, six craft from the 12th Submarine Flotilla made a major foray into Norwegian waters, sending the X8 to attack the *Lutzow*, the X9 and X10 to attack the *Scharnhorst* and three submarines, the X5, X6 and X7, against the battleship *Tirpitz*. All of these ships were anchored in or near the Altenfjord, behind a wide minefield and a long way from the open sea.

It took these tiny craft eight days to get to the casting-off area. To get there, they were towed across the North Sea by conventional submarines, and manned on the way by passage crews. The task of the passage crew was both hard and dangerous – without the possible compensation of glory. Passage crews had to keep the X-craft in fighting trim before handing back to the attack crew. This meant a constant monitoring of everything on board, plus any necessary adjustments and repairs. As for the risks, on the fourth night the cable between X8 and the submarine *Seanymph* parted. The weight of the long manila cable pulled the X8 into a steep nose dive, which was only corrected by blowing the main ballast tanks. The craft was finally located and taken in tow by the submarine *Stubborn*, which was already towing X7. Towing dangers were driven home when another towing submarine, HMS/M *Syrtis*, surfaced to find that the tow to her charge, X9, had parted. Although *Syrtis* went back and hunted diligently along her course, no trace of X9 was ever found. The conclusion was that the weight of the heavy tow rope had upset the X-craft's trim and pulled the smaller craft into an uncontrollable dive; before this could be corrected the pressure of the water had crushed her plates.

Problems continued. On 17 Sptember, X8 lost her trim and became very difficult to handle. The problem was eventually traced to the starboard charge, which was leaking and eventually had to be jettisoned. Then, the port charge started to give trouble. Losing this charge meant that X8 was out of the attack. The craft was scuttled after her crew had been taken off by *Seanymph*.

Losing X8 removed the *Lutzow* from the attack plan and reduced the number of available X-craft to just four. X7 (Lieutenant Place) was still on course for the *Tirpitz*, along with X5 (Lieutenant Henty-Creer) and X 6 (Lieutenant Cameron), but the only one left for the *Scharnhorst* was X10 (Lieutenant Hudspeth). The operation was still producing problems and on 19 September, X7 became entangled with a German mine. This was caught on her bow and had to be removed by the commander, Lieutenant B C G. Place, who went out on to the wave-swept casing and kicked the mine free. Finally though, on the evening of 20 September, all four X-craft slipped from their parent craft and began to edge gently into the Soroy Sound on the west coast of Norway. They still had a very long way to go to reach their targets.

In spite of all the problems met on passage, the crews of the four remaining X-craft were in very high spirits and their craft, thanks to the efforts of the passage crews, were in excellent condition. The main worry was maintaining the trim when encountering the Norwegian fjords' notorious patches of low salinity. However, there was nothing to be done about this, and the craft ploughed on in company, negotiating the offshore minefield without difficulty. Lieutenant Place, in X7, sighted the *Scharnhorst* near Arroy Island on the afternoon of 21 September but pressed on, since his target was the *Tirpitz*, which lay at the end of the Kaafjord.

Eventually X6 and X7 arrived at the Bratholm Islands, close to the Kaafjord, from where the attack began just after midnight on 21/22 September. It took three hours for Lieutenant Place to get X7 through the nets and into the Kaafjord and though Lieutenant Cameron, in X6, started an hour later he caught up by following a German steamer through the anti-submarine nets *in broad daylight*. Once through, Cameron dived to sixty feet and commenced his approach to the *Tirpitz*. By 0730 hours he had passed through more nets and was close to his target.

A mile away, Lieutenant Place was in serious trouble. He ran into another group of nets, became entangled and decided not to put the diver out to cut them free. Instead, he tried shaking the nets off by blowing the ballast tanks. This caused a certain amount of commotion on the surface of the fjord, but it got X7 free. However, it also sent her soaring to the surface. Fortunately, she was not spotted and, restoring the trim, Place took her back down to periscope depth.

Cameron's crew, in X6, then had some bad luck, running aground on a sandbank. Cameron got her free, but not before X6 came briefly to the surface where she was spotted by an observer on the *Tirpitz*. Fortunately, this observer decided that that the 'long black object' was probably a porpoise. Cameron was able to close the *Tirpitz*, but then hit a rock and had to surface again. Cameron took her down again, but this time the German observers had recognised her for what she was and gave the alarm. When X6 surfaced again, under the bows of *Tirpitz*, she was greeted with a hail of small-arms fire and a handful of grenades. Lieutenant Cameron therefore put the screws into reverse and, when X6 was under the *Tirpitz*, released the side cargoes, which settled on the bottom close to the enemy hull. He then scuttled the craft, after ordering the crew to bail out, and by 0730 hours they were all prisoners on the *Tirpitz*.

The Germans were now fully alert, trying to get steam up on the battleship and on the lookout for more midget submarines. By now X7 had closed on *Tirpitz* but had become entangled in a net close to the bows. Place surfaced, only to find that his target was now more than thirty yards away – but the X-craft was now free of the net. He too came under heavy fire, but he ordered full speed ahead, struck the *Tirpitz* under her B Turret and released the side charges under the keel. That done, Place attempted to get X7 out again, running partly submerged and partly on the surface, under attack from gunfire and depth charges all the while.

At 0812 hours, the first main charge under the *Tirpitz* went off, followed a few minutes later by another tremendous explosion as the three remaining charges went off together. This explosion not only damaged *Tirpitz* but also severely damaged X7, which was only a few hundred yards away. Place surveyed the damage and then decided to abandon ship, and since they were being depth charged he decided to bring the craft to the surface rather than use the DSEA equipment. Place and one of his crew were rescued, but two more were lost in the sunken submarine.

Place and his men were picked up and taken on board *Tirpitz*. At the same time, and only half a mile away, Lieutenant Henty-Creer's X5 was depth charged and sunk. In spite of the explosions, *Tirpitz* was still on the surface and the Germans were able to move her away from the sunken charges by hauling in on the anchor cables. However, she had been severely damaged. Plates were sprung, the ship took on a list, and all the electrics went out. All the engines were shifted from their bearings and all the electrical and wireless gear was out of action, as were two of the gun turrets. The port rudder was jammed and the ship was in no state to move, let alone go to sea. *Tirpitz* stayed under repair for another six months and was then sunk in a bombing raid by RAF Lancasters.

X10, the midget submarine tasked to sink the *Scharnhorst*, developed various mechanical problems, including a jammed periscope and a leaking side cargo, and eventually had to break off the attack and return to sea, where she met the waiting submarines and was taken in tow by HMS/M *Stubborn*. She was eventually scuttled off Shetland, so only one X-craft crew – and none of the midget submarines – returned to the UK. Awards for this successful if costly attack included VCs for Lieutenants Place and Cameron, a just reward for their most gallant and persistent attacks, and a clutch of well-earned medals for the other members of their crews. The X-craft had shown what they could do, and before long they were to go back to Norwegian waters and do it again.

12

THE SBS IN THE AEGEAN
1942–43

*'Then the SBS became respectable . . . it began to keep a
war diary'*

John Lodwick, *The Filibusters*

From the time of its formation in 1941, Special Force
operations in the Middle East were dominated by David
Stirling and his Special Air Service. The new Special Boat
Squadron under Major George Jellicoe was an offshoot of
Stirling's creation, and the men in it wore the SAS
sand-coloured beret and the SAS wings. This being so, a
brief resumé of SAS activities, prior to the creation of the
Special Boat Squadron in March 1943, will be useful.

David Stirling, an officer in the Scots Guards, went to
the Middle East with No. 8 Commando, as part of
Layforce, and when that unit disintegrated in 1942 he
found himself unemployed. Many of the officers and men
of Layforce gave up the struggle to remain Commando
soldiers and returned to their parent units, but Stirling
had seen the possibilities of Special Force warfare and
stayed on to develop a plan for small-scale raiding in the
Western Desert.

He also ended up in hospital. While there, with time on
his hands, he worked out the basic plan for what was to
become the SAS Regiment and on release he presented it

to Middle East HQ. Stirling was always lucky, and on this occasion the powers that be, which had failed to find a good use for Layforce, happened to be looking for some kind of unit which would lead the Germans, via their spies in Cairo, to believe that the British were planning a parachute landing somewhere in the Middle East. Stirling was therefore permitted, even encouraged, to raise a small force of men – L Detachment, Special Air Service – borrow some parachutes, set up a base at Kabrit in the Canal Zone, and make himself as conspicuous as possible.

Stirling had other ambitions, which went far beyond simple deception. As soon as his men were trained, he organised a parachute raid behind the lines of the Afrika Corps, intending to attack enemy airfields. The weather was foul, the men were not well enough trained, and Stirling's first operation was a disaster. However, Stirling was not easily discouraged. He soon joined forces with another irregular but well-established formation, the Long Range Desert Group (LRDG), a pioneer reconnaissance force commanded by such splendid officers as Colonel Prendergast, Jake Eason-Smith and David Lloyd-Owen, which operated in vehicles behind the enemy lines. Stirling proposed that the LRDG should take the SAS behind the German lines and – after they had committed a certain amount of mayhem – bring them back again. The LRDG agreed . . . and the rest is history. What is less well known is how the SAS expanded from that original parachute and jeep raiding concept into various forms of guerilla activity.

Stirling's original raiding concept was based on the fact that in the Western Desert the German forces – and indeed the British ones – had two open flanks, the Mediterranean Sea in the north and the desert in the south. His first intention was to attack via the desert flank, in jeeps, and in this he succeeded brilliantly until he was captured in January 1943. By that time the SAS had grown considerably and sprouted a number of ancillary units. Among these was the remnants of Courtney's No. 1 SBS.

The situation, therefore, is that at one time during 1941 there was, in the Middle East, the SAS under David Stirling and the SBS under Roger Courtney. After Courtney went back to the UK in December 1941, No. 1 SBS operated for a while under the command of Major M R B Kealey, but this unit eventually lost so many men on raids that it was too small to function separately and came under the command of Stirling's SAS. Stirling was then in the process of forming a 'Boat Squadron', which was regarded by Mike Kealey as a rival to the SBS. This SAS squadron is the parent of the Boat Troop of the modern SAS Regiment, while No. 1 SBS, though an army unit, is seen as one of the parent units of the modern Royal Marines SBS – though the direct line of descent there is via Hasler's Royal Marine Boom Patrol Detachment.

Stirling's capture threw the SAS into total confusion. Stirling was a raiding genius, but organisation was not his forte; when he went into captivity, chaos reigned, for only Stirling really knew what was going on. Patrols would return from operations and no one knew what they had been doing. Others radioed in for fresh orders but no one knew what their original orders had been. Stores turned up, like jeeps and field artillery – ordered by Lieutenant Colonel Stirling, who could get these precious jeeps when no other man could – but who were these jeeps for? After a few weeks, the powers that be sat down with a blank sheet of paper and tried to shape Stirling's leaderless empire into some kind of effective form. One of the decisions taken was to split the original SAS into two units, the Special Raiding Squadron under that redoubtable Ulsterman, Major Blair 'Paddy' Mayne, and the Special Boat Squadron under Major the Earl Jellicoe DSO, Stirling's second-in-command.

Like Stirling, Jellicoe had come to the Middle East with No. 8 Commando, as part of Layforce. When that unit had broken up he had returned to his own regiment, the Coldstream Guards, and served with the 3rd Battalion in the Western Desert, before running into David Stirling at

Shepheard's Hotel in Cairo while recuperating from a wound. Jellicoe and a section of guardsmen had been cut off by a rapid advance of the Afrika Korps and he only got back to his battalion after being wounded in the shoulder by walking seventy miles across the desert to the British lines. This experience made Jellicoe ideal for 'behind the lines' operations, and he was promptly recruited into the SAS as Stirling's second-in-command.

Among his other assets, Jellicoe spoke good French, and the SAS had just acquired a number of splendid French parachute troops under Commandant Bergé, a body recently arrived from Britain which soon became the French Troop of the SAS. Jellicoe was charged with Anglo-French liaison and, as already related, went with Commandant Bergé and the French to attack the German airfield at Heraklion in Crete. Six months later the SAS split in two, and Major Jellicoe took command of the Special Boat Squadron.

It is with this latter unit that this chapter is concerned. This unit took up raiding in the Aegean, at first from fast motor launches (MLs) and later from Greek *caiques* (schooners). Jellicoe gradually expanded their operations to the Greek mainland, Sardinia, the Adriatic, Yugoslavia and Italy. From April 1943 it came under the overall control of Raiding Forces, Middle East, and lost all direct connection with any of the SBS or Special Force units operating in the Far East or Western Europe.

Jellicoe's force soon began to expand. There were a large number of gallant but under-employed officers from various Allied nations swanning about the Middle East at this time, and some of them soon began to make their way into the ranks of the SBS. Others had to be directly recruited and Jellicoe's first task on taking over command of the Special Boat Squadron was to send a request to Robert Laycock, now Chief of Combined Operations in the UK, requesting the immediate transfer of two officers, Captain Philip Pinckney and a Dane, Anders Lassen – two men who had served with the Small Scale Raiding Force. Pinckney did not stay long with the SBS. Within a few months he was sent to the 2nd SAS Regiment and parachuted into Italy, where he blew up the tunnel carrying the railway through the Brenner Pass. He was then captured by the Germans and later executed under the Commando Order.

Anders Lassen survived until almost the end of the war, during which time he made an unforgettable impression on all who met him and established himself as one of the great Commando soldiers of the war. According to his commanding officer, Lord Jellicoe, Lassen was:

> Very likeable, great fun, on the ball. He also loved the ladies and had a quick temper. I was having a drink with him once and suddenly I found myself on the floor; I had said something Andy took exception to, and he just lashed out. He had amazing endurance and had an ingrained tactical sense. He could size up a tactical situation very quickly and, it goes without saying, had a lot of guts. The chaps he worked with would have done anything for him and had he lived I think he could well have done great things after the war. He was a remarkable man among a group of remarkable men, people like Pinckney, David Sutherland, John Verney, Jock Lapriak, Ian Patterson . . .

Lassen came from a distinguished Danish family. Before the war he had been an officer cadet in the Danish Merchant Marine and when Denmark was invaded he made his way to Britain, drifted into the British Army and got involved in the West African campaigns organised by Captain March-Phillips of 62 Commando. He did so well and took such a leading part, though only a private, that March-Phillips decided that Lassen should be commissioned on the spot and he took Lassen with him when he formed the Small Scale Raiding Force. Jellicoe had met Lassen on a shooting party at the home of the Stirling family in Scotland, and decided that such a man would be ideal for his new SBS command.

Lassen rarely used his rank and only wore the ribbons

of his Military Crosses to attract the attention of pretty ladies. Otherwise, he rarely deigned to wear a proper uniform at all. He was an entertaining character and a great soldier, quite untroubled by such military niceties as saluting or polished buttons. While in the SSRF he had taken part in various raids along the French coast but was lucky enough to miss the raid on Boulogne in early 1943 when March-Phillips and most of the other pioneers of the SSRF were captured or killed. (Those captured were later killed by the Germans while 'attempting to escape'. In other words, in cold blood.)

Men like Lassen were to make the reputation of the SBS, but Lassen was an exception – in every sense of the word. Danes were not common in the British Army. A very large number of the men in the SBS, and indeed in most Special Force units, were of Irish or Scots origin. David Stirling, Lord Lovat, Paddy Mayne, Jock Lapriak, Fitzroy Maclean and David Sutherland are a small but significant indication that a surprising number of men in Commando forces and other irregular units came from the Celtic and Gaelic fringe, though many famous names came from the English shires and cheery Cockney soldiers formed part of every unit.

In April 1943, when Jellicoe took command of the SBS at Athlit, a camp close to Haifa in what was then Palestine, his first task was to divide it into three squadrons – the cavalry influence hung heavily over all Special Force units at this time – L, M and S, initials taken from the names of the detachment commanders, Captains Langton, Maclean and Sutherland. Each detachment numbered about sixty men, approximately two platoons, divided into five patrols. Each of the patrols was commanded by an officer. The rest, drivers, signallers, cooks, armourers and clerks, all fighting men when so required, were in Unit Headquarters, directly under Lord Jellicoe, who retained a fighting patrol for his own use. The total strength of the Special Boat Squadron was around 250 men.

Fitzroy Maclean would soon go off and make a great

name for himself fighting with Tito's partisans in Yugoslavia, and his place as commander of M Squadron was taken by Captain J Neilson Lapriak MC. Since Tommy Langton was ill, his Squadron was taken over for a while by Lieutenant John Verney. The Verneys are an old county family with long-standing military connections, but John himself was an artist and writer – and a considerable soldier.

The new SBS were soon in action. Their operations began in June 1943 with the now annual SBS 'fixture', a raid on the airfields of Crete. This was made by David Sutherland's Squadron, divided into three patrols – Sutherland's, one under Lieutenant Lamonby and one under Anders Lassen. Lassen attacked Kasteli airfield on the night of 23 June. He bluffed his way past three sentries before detection, shot the fourth, blew up some aircraft, shot another sentry, destroyed a bulldozer and, pursued by a hail of fire, withdrew into the darkness. While all this was going on the rest of his patrol attacked more aircraft, put delayed-action bombs in a petrol dump and withdrew with Lassen to the base in the hills established by Sutherland.

There they were joined by Lamonby, who had found no aircraft but had blown up a petrol dump, and Lieutenant Rowe, who had found Timbaki airfield yet again empty. The enemy had not learned to guard their airfields properly, but they had a good idea how to catch British raiders. This time, instead of searching the hills, they sent strong patrols to guard every beach on the south coast that might be a pick-up for a raiding party. They swiftly made contact with the SBS and killed Lieutenant Lamonby. However, two of their number were captured and taken back to Cairo in the MTB by Lassen and Sutherland.

Driving into the city, Lassen decided that he needed an ice cream, so he and Sutherland stopped at Groppi's, a fashionable café. They took their two German prisoners in with them and bought them both an ice cream; apparently, none of the other customers, servicemen or civilians, noticed that they had been joined, albeit briefly, by the enemy. That night, the SBS men charged with guarding these Germans decided to take their prisoners out on the town, so the Germans had quite a good time before they were handed over to the prison cage.

In the following month, the SBS struck again, this time in Sardinia, when L Squadron, still commanded by John Verney, was sent in an attempt to convince the enemy that Sardinia, and not Sicily, was the next place to be invaded. The squadron was to be inserted by submarine but, while half the party got ashore, the part headed by John Verney, in another submarine, had to turn back and was inserted later by parachute.

As he knew about the proposed landings in Sicily, Jellicoe was not allowed to go on this raid, but he went on the submarine tasked to pick them up. Verney's parachute party was dropped into Sardinia on the night of 7 July. This Sardinia operation met various problems, not least that a large number of men in the main party developed malaria on the submarine. Their objectives were the Sardinian airfields and, having landed without incident, Verney and his party made a night-march to their first target, which they reached by dawn. That day was spent lying up and studying the defences – which seemed negligible – and that night the attack went in.

The initial moves were a great success. The Italians were rapidly losing interest in the war. Soldiering had never been an Italian preoccupation and Sardinia had been a backwater, so the raiders met no sentries and were able to lay bombs on a number of aircraft, storage parks and petrol dumps without difficulty. Only when these bombs started to go off did the defence become animated. Verney then took his men to a nearby village, where they enjoyed a well-earned meal in a café. When he was accosted by an Italian patrol outside the village, Verney told them that he was a German officer and marched off, leaving the Italians scratching their heads.

To spare his men's feet, he then had them climb on to a haywain which was plodding along behind an Italian convoy and, if anyone noticed that a half a dozen heavily armed British soldiers were hitching a lift, nothing was said or done about it. However, the German garrison were now getting involved and making a serious attempt to track the raiders down. It took the Germans eleven days to capture Verney and the story of his subsequent escape forms a major part of his excellent war memoir, *Going to the Wars*.

Most of Verney's party were rounded up, but some men continued to evade the enemy or escaped from captivity on to the Italian mainland. Among these was Sergeant Scott, who met up with a party from 2 SAS Regiment and joined them in harassing the enemy, shooting up convoys, raiding dumps and cutting telephone wires. With the collapse of Italian resistance in September 1943, there were hundreds of British prisoners roaming about Italy – including that SBS officer, Eric Newby – all trying to regain the Allied lines. Eventually, Sergeant Scott and many of Langton/Verney's squadron returned to safety and were sent back to Britain, following the rule that an escaped prisoner could not again serve in the theatre from which he made his escape.

Part of L Squadron went to Sicily, where one aircraft despatched its load of parachutists ten minutes before the drop zone, luckily not into the sea. The rest, mustered by Corporal 'Safari' Summers, an NCO noted for his marching ability, landed safely and, finding themselves with a large supply of explosives, took to the hills, from where they descended regularly over the next month, shooting up German convoys, cutting telephone wires, abducting sentries and blowing up anything they fancied. After the Allied landing – and only then because they had run out of explosives – they called off their private war and returned to the Allied lines. These operations in Sardinia and Sicily in July 1943, though highly enjoyable, almost wiped out L Squadron, which had to be reformed when its leader, Tommy Langton, returned from hospital. Such troops, skilled in guerilla warfare, were now to descend on the German garrisons of the Dodecanese.

The Dodecanese are the eastern islands of the Aegean, lying close to the Turkish coast. Most of the Dodecanese

Islands are small, but the group includes larger islands, like Rhodes, the main island of the group. Before the war, the islands belonged to Italy, although most of the inhabitants were Greek.

The Italian Army garrisoned the islands in large numbers, but they were supported by considerable contingents of German troops, and therein lay the problem; these German garrisons were determined to hold on to the islands after the Italians had surrendered to the Allies in September 1943.

The story of Major Jellicoe's SBS, at war with the Germans around the Dodecanese, is an almost piratical tale of sailing ships and gallant crews sallying out from their bases in sheltered coves – or more often the Turkish mainland – to sink ships, land raiding parties on these scattered and beautiful islands, and generally make the lives of the Axis occupiers a living hell.

Unlike the activities of the frogmen, Charioteers and the X-craft crews operating in muddy harbours or the freezing, mine-strewn waters of Norway, the life led by the SBS raiders in the Greek Islands actually sounds like fun, but it was no less dangerous. Lord Jellicoe is on record as admitting that, 'This sort of warfare was great fun, I admit it. It could be frightening from time to time, but it was always interesting, and of course you met and worked with such splendid people.'

Like David Stirling, George Jellicoe was a man with large ideas. He thought strategically and was not content to lead the happy and mildly productive life of the guerilla soldier, striking here and there at the enemy whenever the chance arose. Jellicoe did not merely wish to harass the enemy; he intended to drive them demented. His method would be an unceasing series of attacks, but before that started he had another duty to perform.

When the Italians capitulated in September 1943, Jellicoe was in Beirut. He was hastily summoned to GHQ in Cairo and there he received orders to take himself off to Rhodes and talk terms of surrender with the Italian gvernor. GHQ suggested that he should go by sea but

Jellicoe, knowing that speed was of the essence, suggested parachuting in, taking with him two volunteers, a Major 'Dolbey', who spoke fluent Italian and turned out to be Count Dobrski, a Polish aristocrat, and a British wireless operator, Sergeant Kesterton.

Jellicoe felt that if these islands were to be taken over by the Allies they would have to move quickly, before the Germans intervened and occupied the islands themselves. The Germans could be relied on not to waste time and they were ruthless with their former allies: those who capitulated were imprisoned; those who resisted or were in the way were simply massacred. The Dodecanese campaign therefore became a race between the SBS and the Germans, and it produced some of the most interesting Special Force actions of the Second World War.

GHQ's plan was that the Italians were to seize certain parts of the main island, Rhodes, and most especially the three airfields, after which the 8th Indian Division from Egypt would land and drive the Germans into the sea. Once the British held Rhodes, the other islands of the Dodecanese should fall without difficulty, for Rhodes had the airfields and in this campaign air superiority would be crucial. This operation had been prepared in the knowledge that Italy was about to surrender. It was hoped that the 30,000 Italians would obey the orders of their King, hold their positions and surrender to the British, which would then enable the British troops to concentrate on the 7–10,000 German troops – a light division – who, with some seventy tanks, were largely concentrated around Rhodes Town and the three airfields.

Jellicoe and his party were to parachute in on 8 September, but it was foggy and the pilot could not find the island. During the flight Count Dobrski admitted that he had never parachuted at all and asked Jellicoe to push him out of the door if he happened to hesitate at the last minute. The party finally parachuted into Rhodes on 9 September, when Jellicoe and Kesterton were fired on by the Italians and the count, landing on a road, sustained a compound fracture of his leg. Thinking they were about to be captured, Major Jellicoe ate his operational orders, but they eventually made contact with the governor, Admiral Campioni and received a guarded welcome.

Admiral Campioni did not conceal his dilemma, for he was in an impossible position. His men were scattered in small groups all over the island. They lacked transport and were not thirsting for battle, though some units were willing to engage the German enemy. On hearing of the Italian Armistice, Campioni had contacted his German former colleagues and suggested that, until the situation was clear, they should hold their positions and avoid fighting. The Germans agreed to this, but promptly sent out strong patrols from Rhodes Town and showed every sign of taking over the entire island and disarming the Italians. Therefore, Campioni told Jellicoe, if he was to order his men to resist, he must be guaranteed immediate support from the British. These negotiations between the parties went on for some hours and Jellicoe gradually became aware that Campioni, after talking to the British in one room of his palace, was talking with the Germans in another. The seriousness of Campioni's position is underlined by the fact that he was later arrested by the Germans, handed over to the Italian Fascists, and shot.

Jellicoe sent an urgent message to Cairo, requesting immediate reinforcements, but overnight the position deteriorated as the Germans, acting with their usual energy, proceeded to occupy the airfields and any likely landing beaches. The Germans were sweeping the Italian garrisons aside, and Campioni suggested that Jellicoe and his team should leave the island immediately. Since he could do no more for the moment, Jellicoe withdrew in an Italian MTB to the island of Castelrosso, seventy miles east of Rhodes, where he was met by David Sutherland and where, a day later, he heard that the Italians on Rhodes had capitulated. The main island had gone but, if he acted swiftly, Jellicoe calculated that the other islands in the group might still be taken over. Therefore, on 12 September, GHQ ordered S Squadron – all 55 of them – to occupy the Dodecanese.

13

THE SBS IN THE DODECANESE, GREECE AND ITALY 1943–45

'The war is ending but, when the last day comes, SBS must be in the field and not at base'

Major David Sutherland
OC, The Special Boat Squadron, 1945

Lord Jellicoe's Dodecanese operation began on 12 September 1943. It was a bold plan, but Jellicoe had one initial advantage, which he intended to exploit to the utmost. With the capitulation of their Italian allies, the Germans had a lot of islands to cover and insufficient troops for the job. The Germans had Rhodes, with its vital airfields, but Jellicoe intended to take over everywhere else and his first landfall was on the island of Kos, just off the Turkish coast, where he found the Italian commander quite biddable but somewhat apprehensive about the German reaction.

Jellicoe could not hope to hold Kos with just 55 men but, if he could encourage the Italians to resist any German thrust from Rhodes, much might be done later when more troops arrived. Leaving some men of Sutherland's squadron to stiffen the Italian commander's spine on Kos, Jellicoe and his little fleet moved on to Leros, where the Italian commander, Brigadier Mascherpa, greeted the son of a famous British admiral with open arms and a banquet. Jellicoe had more practical moves in mind and, having found a couple of spots suitable for the landing of parachutists and supplies, he sent an urgent cable to the Raiding Forces' Middle East commander, Colonel Turnbull, requesting immediate support. The request was granted and by 15 September a British infantry battalion had arrived to reinforce Kos, Leros and Samos, while a few more troops had landed on Kalimnos, south of Leros, on Castelrosso and on Simi.

Thanks to Jellicoe and the SBS, the British now had a foothold in the Dodecanese. The British intended to hold Kos and Leros in force and defy eviction, but the Germans, unfortunately, had other ideas. The Germans also possessed the advantage of the Rhodes airfields and air superiority, their airforce, including squadrons of dive-bombing Stukas, redeployed to the Aegean from the Russian front. The British did have support from a few US Lightning fighters, but when these were withdrawn German air power began to tell and the British were gradually bombed out of their Dodecanese strongholds.

Meanwhile, another SBS force, M Squadron under Major Jock Lapriak, had arrived off Simi on 17 September. Lapriak sent Anders Lassen ashore by canoe to scout around. The Italians on Simi were in a high state of nerves and greeted Lassen with machine-gun and shell fire, opposition which he quelled with a tirade of curses. The rest of Lapriak's force then came ashore and surveyed the defences. They discovered a few prepared positions and a group of some 150 Italian soldiers, troops torn between fear of the invading Germans and fear of the native Greeks. Lapriak put them to digging trenches and stringing barbed wire and sent another officer, New Zealander Lieutenant 'Stud' Stellin, to recce Rhodes and see what the Germans were up to.

Stellin returned after five days, to report that the

Germans seemed to have enough on their hands at the moment but needed to be watched. At the end of September Stellin went to Rhodes again for another fruitful recce, while Lassen was sent to Calchi, an island a few miles from Rhodes, and told to prepare it for attack. Lassen told the defenders of Calchi, twelve unwarlike Italians, that they could either fight the Germans or fight him, and delivered his message with such force that, when the Germans sent a landing party over from Rhodes a few days later, the Italians put up a stout fight.

By early October the situation in the Dodecanese was becoming clear. The Germans held the larger islands and had both superior airpower and superior numbers. The British and their Greek allies had some of the smaller islands and most of the *caiques*, but they were in urgent need of reinforcements, artillery and, above all, air cover. No one doubted that the Germans would attack the smaller islands and attempt to drive the British away as soon as they could round up sufficient *caiques* to carry a large enough force. The only force capable – or at least large enough – to make any kind of prolonged resistance to a German assault was the Italian garrisons – but would they fight? On 2 October, after several hours of Stuka dive-bombing, the Germans invaded Kos and the answer was made plain; some Italians would fight, but the majority would not.

As a result, Kos fell in just 48 hours. All resistance was over by 5 October, all the Italians and 900 British soldiers going into captivity. The Germans had complete air superiority and their fighters strafed anything that moved, while the Stukas bombed the defenders, pinning them down as the enemy came ashore. Lord Jellicoe and David Sutherland watched the fighting on Kos from the island of Kalimnos, a few miles away, and they decided to evacuate the SBS defenders before they were overrun. This was done, but the respite was only temporary. Two days after taking Kos the Germans proceeded to attack Simi.

Here they met stiffer resistance, for Jock Lapriak was

ready for them. The Germans arrived at dawn on 7 October, their advance party sailing into Simi harbour in a *caique*, which was immediately spotted and driven off with loss, its decks raked by Bren-gun fire. However, this frontal attack was a diversion. Within the hour, reports were reaching Lapriak's HQ that German troops were coming ashore in quantity on various beaches and pushing across the island. Italian resistance to these attacks was encouraged by Lassen, who stood behind the Italian gun crews with a pistol and threatened to shoot any man who ran away – and he meant it. Even so, the enemy pushed on across the island and by 0800 hours had taken up position on the outskirts of Simi Town. Lapriak then counterattacked and drove the enemy back. The upshot was that by the end of the afternoon the Germans were in full retreat and were later evacuated from the island, leaving over fifty dead or wounded men behind, for the loss of one SBS man killed and two wounded. Again, this respite did not last long. The Germans decided to soften up the garrison and three days later, after two days of Stuka dive-bombing, the Germans returned, overran the defences and the island was evacuated.

With the SBS driven from Kos and Simi, German attention now turned on Leros. This island was garrisoned by three battalions of British troops, a number of more or less well-organised Italian units, a large contingent of LRDG under Jock Eason-Smith and David Sutherland's squadron of the SBS. What was lacking was air support, for Leros had no airstrip for any defending fighters. Leros is small, just ten miles long by three wide, and the Germans blasted it from end to end with strafing fire and high explosive, keeping the bombardment up for days before they sent in their troops.

They started bombing the island on 1 November and invaded on 11 November, first from the sea at dawn, and at midday by dropping a parachute battalion. The SBS managed to keep the Germans occupied in their area, but more and more of the enemy came ashore. After three days of pounding from the air, and steady pressure on the ground, losses totalled 400 killed and over 1,000 wounded – the SBS share of this amounted to just seven – and the officer commanding the British and Italian forces on Leros decided to surrender.

Some 3,000 British troops and 5,000 Italians went into captivity, but not the SBS, who all escaped from the island at night by *caique* and withdrew to safe havens on the coast of Turkey. So this worthwhile attempt to take over the Dodecanese failed. The operation was probably doomed without the rapid capture of the Rhodes airfields and by the end of November the Germans had occupied all the islands of the Dodecanese with the exception of Castelrosso. That was not, however, the end of the matter. Under the direction of Colonel 'Bull' Turnbull, the officer commanding Raiding Forces, Middle East, Jellicoe and the SBS set out to make the German stay as difficult as possible.

Raids on the scattered German garrisons commenced at once, with an attack on Simi led by Lapriak and Lieutenant Bob Bury. Splitting their force in two, they blew up the governor's house, killed twenty Germans and injured many more, destroyed a power station and silenced some machine-gun posts; SBS life was back to normal and the other islands were soon feeling the effect of SBS activity. Lapriak landed on Piscopi and destroyed the telephone station and then took three patrols back to Simi where more mayhem was committed. Then the Germans on Leros got a pasting, followed by the garrison of Kos. These operations were not without loss, and it was necessary to fetch more men from the base at Athlit, where another outstanding SBS officer, Major Ian Patterson, formerly of the Parachute Regiment, was in charge of training and making things hum by sending unsuitable volunteers rapidly back to their regiments but getting any likely soldier rapidly ready for action.

Duly reinforced, the SBS swarmed about the islands, where the Germans had been making life miserable both for the Greek inhabitants and their former comrades in the Italian Army, who were faced with the choice of soldiering on under German command, being shot or sent to concentration camps. Nobody knows how many Greeks or Italians were murdered by the Germans at the end of 1943 but it must have been a very large number. The task of cowing the Italians completed – it proved impossible to cow the Greeks – the Germans proceeded to garrison the islands in some strength, sending 4,000 men to Leros, 2,000 men to Kos, and manning the other islands in proportion to size. A full division, with some tanks, was retained on Rhodes, but only 150 men defended little Simi.

With the exception of Rhodes, these garrisons had to be supplied by sea and this shipping provided perfect targets for British submarines and SBS raiders. The raiding forces were now comfortably – and illegally – installed in neutral Turkey, just south of Bodrum. The Turks knew that British soldiers were living on their coast but did not seem to mind too much. The SBS usually stayed on their *caiques*, but it was possible to go ashore and get supplies and take exercise. Now and then, when the German ambassador in Istanbul, Von Papen, got upset about this and complained to the Turkish Government, the local policeman would ask the SBS to go away for a few days, until the coast was clear.

It was from this base, in January 1944, that Lassen descended on Calchi, where he and his men were disappointed to discover only six Germans. They took them prisoner anyway and were in the process of blowing open the safe in the German pay office when they heard the sound of engines and saw a German supply *caique* entering the harbour. This was greeted with bursts of Bren-gun fire, which wounded two. After taking four prisoners, Lassen and his team took the *caique* back to Turkey with a useful amount of loot.

This activity continued. A few days later Captain Anderson, a South African SBS officer, took his patrol to Stampalia, where Corporal Asbery destroyed a German seaplane and sank two German *caiques*. Then David Clark went to Simi and wiped out a party of Germans. Bruce

Mitford went to Archi, a harbour on Patmos, and sank two German *caiques*, one by raking it along the water line with Bren-gun fire, the other with high explosives. They were celebrating this action in a dockside taverna when a third *caique*, under charter to the Germans, came in unawares and tied up at the quay outside. The crew were subdued and when the *caique* was boarded it was found to contain some delightful goodies including six cases of champagne, ten cases of beer, thirty kegs of wine and a large quantity of perfumed purple toilet paper. All this was sent back to the SBS base in Turkey, while Mitford continued to raid Patmos, shooting up the defenders and having a high old time.

Sergeant Summers was also busy, raiding Piscopi and staying ashore for some time to remove a quantity of stores from German dumps about the island. Major Patterson, bored with training men in Palestine, decided to go operational and led a seven-man patrol to Nisiros, where he arrived in time to stop the Germans removing the children from the local school and taking them away in a *caique*. The SBS occupied the school; the children were removed to a place of safety and an obliging Italian, dressed as a Greek priest, stood on the steps to welcome the Germans. Twelve Germans were killed, wounded or captured in the ensuing gunfight, after which Patterson took his men down to the harbour and shot up the *caique*. Seventeen prisoners and a large quantity of stores were sent to Turkey and a lot of food was distributed among the hungry Greek inhabitants. Patterson then took his squadron back to Athlit and David Sutherland took up the task of harassing the enemy.

John Lodwick, sometime Foreign Legionnaire and historian of the Special Boat Squadron, was also in action at this time, shooting up a German patrol in Stampalia. Lieutenant 'Nobby' Clarke captured ten Italian Fascists on Patmos and Lieutenant Balsillie and Marine Hughes – Tug Wilson's old oppo – attempted to kidnap a German officer on Piscopi. Unfortunately, the German appeared at their ambush site with three guards. When he refused to surrender, Marine Hughes emptied a full magazine of Bren – 28 rounds – into the group, killing all four.

And so it went on, night after night, week after week, month after month. If the Germans had hoped that taking over the Greek Islands would ensure a quiet time in occupation they were quite wrong. Nowhere was safe from SBS infiltration, and the German death toll mounted steadily. However, it was not all plain sailing and these raids were not without loss. Lieutenant Bill Blythe, with Sergeant Miller and Privates Evans, Jones and Rice were detected on a raid to Calchi and all five men were taken prisoner. Blythe was taken to Rhodes, interrogated and then sent to a prison camp in Germany, where he survived the war. The other four were taken to Salonica, where they were interrogated for a few days and then shot under the Commando Order. Nobody knows exactly what happened to them before they were executed, but Commandos caught on Simi were handed over to the SD and murdered and two LRDG signallers captured on Istria in 1945 were promptly shot by their captors.

Lassen had been accidentally shot and slightly wounded by one of his own men and the wound had kept him out of action for a couple of months. By April 1944, he was back and he went to attack Santorini, in the Cyclades, a new area for SBS attacks. The SBS attacked various places on Santorini, but Lassen reserved the Bank of Athens in Santorini Town for himself and his oppo, Sergeant Nicolson. The rooms above the bank were occupied by Germans, but they entered without difficulty and went from room to room, working their well-established routine. First, Nicolson would kick open a door. Then Lassen would throw in a grenade and close it again, while the two men flattened themselves against the walls outside. After the grenade exploded, Nicolson would enter the room and spray it with Bren-gun fire and Lassen would then finish off any aggressive survivors with his pistol. There were 68 German or Italian soldiers billeted in the bank on Santorini and only ten of them survived this encounter. Two of the raiders, Sergeant Kingston and a popular Greek officer, Lieutenant Stephen Casulli, were killed in the fighting and on the following day the Germans took and shot six of the Greek inhabitants as a reprisal for German losses.

While Lassen was getting his hand in again on Santorini, Lieutenant 'Nobby' Clarke landed on Ios, where he proceeded to stir things up, detonating a dump of shells, capturing a number of German officers and killing a few more, destroying the radio station and post office and sinking two *caiques*. He then went to the nearby island of Amorgos, where he killed eight Germans before making a quiet withdrawal to Turkey. In this one raid the SBS killed or wounded 68 Germans, took a score of prisoners, sunk ships, blew up dumps and communication centres and played havoc with the surprised garrisons – all for the loss of two men killed and three slightly wounded.

The Germans decided to reinforce their garrisons in the Cyclades, but before these could get established Lassen struck again at Paros, where the Germans were busily constructing an airstrip. Lassen took a full patrol of thirteen men to Paros and split them into two- or three-man groups, each with a separate target. It was not possible to destroy the airstrip but several Germans were killed and a quantity of stores and equipment destroyed before Lassen and his men drew off into the night. David Sutherland had meanwhile attacked Siphnos, sinking a *caique*. Then, with a good tally of stores destroyed and enemy killed, Sutherland and Lassen turned the Cyclades over to Jock Lapriak and his crew. With the SBS squadrons taking it in turns to raid, rest and plan fresh attacks, their war continued unabated.

The SBS had succeeded in making the Greek Islands a most uncomfortable billet for the enemy soldiers, many of whom had arrived in these beautiful islands determined to have a good time and very glad that they were somewhere warm and not soldiering on the Russian Front. Then the *verdammt* SBS arrived and spoiled it all. The Germans had no option but to look carefully at their defences and, by the time Jock Lapriak was turned loose, both the

Dodecanese and the Cyclades were well fortified and fully alert. He therefore decided to raid the Sporades, a dozen islands off the upper Peloponese which had been left alone so far and might therefore be more easily overcome. This campaign began in June 1944 when Captain Jimmy Lees attacked one of the smaller islands. Finding no Germans, Lees installed himself in an empty villa and had a good night's sleep. On the same night, Bob Bury was searching for Germans in Skopelos and Gioura, but, like Lees, could find no trace of the enemy. Bury then heard that there was a small German garrison on Skiathos, so he took his men there. This proved better, for the Germans were on the alert and proved quite aggressive – until they were killed.

Jimmy Lees had reported his failure to find the enemy and was sent to Calino; here he was assured of better luck since there was a sixty-strong force in residence. After Sergeant Horsfied had carried out the recce and met a certain amount of opposition, it was decided that a major assault might be needed, and the ten-man SBS patrol was reinforced by a group of twelve men from the Greek Sacred Squadron. This squadron could trace its origins back to remote antiquity but the 600 men in the Second World War regiment were long-time allies of the SBS, and their redoubtable leader, Colonel Tsigantes, was a great friend of Earl Jellicoe. The SBS soldiers were commanded by Sergeant Dryden and the overall commander was a Greek officer of the Sacred Squadron, Major Kasakopoulos, with Major Richard Lea going along as liaison officer.

The raid in the Sporades, on 1 July 1944, turned into an all-out battle. SBS and Greek patrols were moving about, firing into the German defences from all sides, killing the enemy but also taking casualties, including Sergeant Dryden and two other SBS men, wounded by mortar fire. German re-inforcements then came pouring into the area and the SBS and Greeks wisely withdrew, though Dryden and the two wounded had to be left behind. One died in captivity, but both Dryden and his oppo Private Doughty, a medical orderly, later escaped. Lapriak's squadron were not finding it all that easy in the Sporades so they decided that their next operation would be a major strike by the full squadron against Simi, back in the Dodecanese.

Quite apart from strong defences and alert garrisons, raiding in the Dodecanese had been inhibited by the fact that the Germans had moved four destroyers into the islands, well-armed ships, fast enough to run down the sailing *caiques* used by the SBS. This force had been gradually whittled down, one destroyer being sunk by a British submarine, another hit by a bomber from Cyprus. Then, in July 1944, a party of Royal Marine canoeists from the RMBPD arrived. They paddled at night into Portolago in Leros, and blew the two remaining German destroyers out of the water.

This section of the RMBPD was commanded by Lieutenant Pritchard-Gordon RM and was one of the units serving in Brigadier Turnbull's Raiding Forces, Middle East. Part of this force, six men with three canoes, under Lieutenant Richards, were installed on a *caique* anchored off the Turkish coast forty miles from Leros. Their Royal Marine 'spit and polish' and daily canoe and keep-fit exercises attracted a certain amount of derision from the SBS and SAS personnel, who rarely wore cap badges, let alone polished them. The Royal Marines needed an operation to show what they could do, and the German destroyers in Leros were the perfect opportunity.

Planning for the raid began on 16 July 1944 when aerial photographs of Leros revealed that the harbour of Portolago contained two destroyers and two supply ships. That night, Richards and his men embarked on a Fairmile Motor Launch, ML No. 306, and sped across the sea to Leros where the canoe crews – Lieutenant Richards and Marine Stevens in *Shark*, Sergeant King RM and Marine Ruff in *Salmon* and Corporal Horner and Marine Fisher in *Shrimp* – were launched for the attack. Each canoe carried eight limpet mines and the men carried a 24-hour ration pack, Sten guns, fighting knives and a camouflage net.

The canoes got into the harbour without difficulty, though it was a bright, starlit night, with Corporal Horner heading for one of the supply ships, the *Anita*, and the rest heading for the two destroyers. As Horner approached his target he was spotted and hailed by a group of men on board. He kept paddling, shouting back, 'Patrola,' which he hoped would sound sufficiently foreign to pass muster. It did. The men on board shone a torch on the canoe, but he was able to shelter under the bow overhang and after a while the men on board wandered off. However, rather than risk arousing further suspicion, or capture, which would ruin the entire operation, he decided to break off his attack, withdraw to a cave outside the harbour and lie up.

This was a sensible decision, for the other two canoes were inside the harbour and closing on the two German destroyers. Lieutenant Richards and Marine Stevens heard the shouts of the Germans hailing *Shrimp* but got alongside their target and placed seven limpets along the hull, enduring a nasty moment when a sentry appeared above them and peed over the side. They withdrew without detection. On the way out they met up with *Salmon* and learned that their attack on the other destroyer had been equally successful. These canoes and crews, all well camouflaged, lay up on a nearby island during the following day and heard their limpets detonate, followed by a considerable amount of confusion. The Leros canoe raid was the last the RMBPD carried out, but it was a considerable success, 'One of the rare occasions when six men went out to do a job and six men came back,' as Pritchard-Gordon said later. Canoe raids were not common in the Aegean and the Germans were not expecting one, but the skill and professionalism of the well-trained RMBPD played a big part in this successful operation. With the destroyer threat removed, SBS operations in the Dodecanese were once again on the cards, and the first target chosen was an old one, Simi.

Brigadier Turnbull took personal charge of the Simi raid. His was a large force, some 200 men from the SBS and the Sacred Squadron, divided into three parties, one under Captain Clynes, one under Captain Macbeth and the third under Turnbull himself, with Jock Lapriak as his second-in-command. This force went ashore, quite undetected, on 13 July and attacked Simi Castle at dawn with mortar and machine-gun fire. The island fell within the day, and the booty was considerable: nineteen German chartered *caiques* were sunk, various barges blown up, gun emplacements destroyed, fuel dumps and ammunition stores destroyed and the entire German garrison of 200 men either killed or captured. Greek and SBS losses totalled six men wounded. Flushed with this success and loaded with booty, Lapriak and his men went off to Beirut for a well-earned spot of leave. SBS involvement in the Aegean ended here, at least for a while. Their tasks were turned over to the capable hands of the Greek Sacred Squadron, while the SBS sailed off to find fresh fields of endeavour in the Adriatic, though Jock Lapriak stayed on as adviser to Colonel Turnbull.

There was, however, one final foray, the 'annual outing' to Crete, which began on 23 July 1944 and involved men of Ian Patterson's squadron. They landed after a recce by a small patrol consisting of Patterson, John Lodwick, Dick Harden, Marine Clark, and Sergeant Summers. The raiders dealt the Germans a solid blow: seven petrol dumps destroyed, 35 Germans killed or wounded, staff cars and trucks shot up and general confusion spread – all for the loss of two men, Private Nixon and Captain John Lodwick, both taken prisoner. The two men had a hard time on Crete, being threatened with execution, but were eventually sent to the mainland, and then to Yugoslavia, where they managed to escape. After helping the local partisans to destroy a train, both men made their way back to the SBS after an absence of four months.

Jellicoe's SBS arrived in Italy in August 1944, where they came under the command of Brigadier Davy, commander Raiding Forces, Adriatic. Their task here was to carry out raids in Italy and Yugoslavia, and this they began to do at once. Lassen's patrol was sent to blow up a bridge at Karasocici in Yugoslavia. Lassen's report on this operation was extremely brief. 'We landed, we reached the bridge and blew it up, and we came back, that is all.' Lord Jellicoe demanded a fuller account, and subsequent investigation revealed that this was by no means all. The landing party, all twelve of them, had been intercepted by around 400 German and *Ustachi* (Yugoslav Fascists) troops whom Lassen dispersed by charging them with a Bren gun and throwing grenades, killing several of the enemy before the SBS party got back to the beach and withdrew.

SBS parties under Stud Stellin and Nobby Clarke were infiltrated into Yugoslavia. Though they did good work and certainly earned their pay, they might have done much more but for the sullen opposition put up by their supposed allies, the Yugoslav partisans commanded by Marshal Tito, the post-war ruler of Yugoslavia. The partisans were Communists to a man, and with the Germans now clearly losing the war they felt that they no longer needed any help from the 'Imperialist Capitalists' of the West. They were only waiting for the arrival of the Red Army, when they would be able to drive the Germans out, extract a suitable revenge on the Chetniks of the rival right-wing resistance movement, and take over the country.

This enthusiasm for the Soviets took a knock when the Russians entered Belgrade and celebrated their arrival in Yugoslavia with a three-day orgy of rape and violence, but for the moment the Yugoslavs were devoted admirers of Marshal Stalin and Soviet Russia, and they regarded the SBS as unwelcome intruders. However, the SBS had their own orders and they got on with attacking the enemy, including the Ustachi, or the Chetniks. A leading light in this activity was Ambrose McGonigal, who went ashore in Yugoslavia at the end of August 1944 and stayed ashore for two months. During that time the SBS blew up a railway line and tunnel, derailed a train, killed large numbers of Germans and Chetniks, shot up convoys and laid ambushes, withdrawing to Italy with the loss of just one man.

This activity was in full swing when Jellicoe received orders to take a squadron of the SBS back to Greece. He was to take command of a joint force, rejoicing in the unlovely name of *Bucketforce*, consisting of the SBS, a troop of the LRDG, a squadron of the RAF Regiment (equipped with anti-aircraft guns and armoured cars) and a detachment of sappers. His task was to drive the Germans from the last of the Greek Islands and the Peleponnese. With the defection of Albania from the Nazi cause and the Yugoslav partisans cutting their escape route through the Balkans, the Germans in Greece were in an untenable position and had to withdraw. Jellicoe's task was to make that withdrawal as costly as possible.

This campaign began on 24 September 1944, when Major Patterson and his sixty-strong squadron parachuted in to seize the airfield at Araxos in the north of the Peloponnese. The Germans had already left, so this part of the operation went without difficulty. Jellicoe, now a lieutenant colonel of the SBS Regiment, arrived next day by air, and the seaborne contingent, largely composed of the RAF Regiment, landed that night at the port of Katakolon on the west coast of the Peloponnese.

When all were ashore, *Bucketforce* moved on the town of Patras, where the Germans and three 'Security Battalions' of Greeks – largely anti-Communist – were currently being contained, though not attacked, by Greek Communist partisans, or ELAS. Pattterson sent a messenger to the German commander, pointing out that since they could not escape they might as well surrender – he did not reveal he had exactly 62 men. When the German declined this offer, Patterson tried the commander of the 1,600-strong Security Battalions, who was willing to surrender but worried that his men, once disarmed, would fall into the hands of the ELAS partisans who would certainly shoot them out of hand. Jellicoe was also concerned that the partisans would exact reprisals on the inhabitants of Patras, many of whom were also known to be anti-Communist.

That night the Security Battalions surrendered and

were herded on to the elusive safety of a small peninsula behind Patras, while Patterson and his force, with a company of the RAF Regiment, entered the town of Patras, roaring up and down the streets in jeeps, SAS fashion, shooting up any Germans who showed themselves or showed fight. The Germans evacuated the town that night and withdrew in boats to the Greek mainland, while Patterson and Jellicoe went along the coast to Corinth, taking prisoners as they went, hoping to prevent the Germans blowing up the Corinth Canal. Jellicoe was also trying to prevent the ELAS partisans, who might have been usefully employed fighting the Germans, from murdering fellow Greeks in the Security Battalions or taking hostages from the population of Patras. ELAS were more interested in taking control of Greece before the legal government could re-establish control. The Greek Civil War of 1945–47, which was to claim hundreds of thousands of lives and cause untold suffering, was just beginning.

Having done all he could, Jellicoe joined up with the newly arrived 4th British Parachute Battalion, which had just dropped at Megara, and while this battalion pursued the Germans he embarked in a *caique* with Patterson and his squadron and sailed for Athens. The *caique* docked at Scaramanga, on the outskirts of the city, where the two officers mounted the only transport on hand – a pair of bicycles – and entered the city from the south as the Germans left from the north. Jellicoe installed his men in the Hotel Grande Bretagne and declared the day a holiday. The SBS had helped drive the Germans out of southern Greece and had a lot to celebrate.

Within a few days the SBS were back on the road north again, harrying the retreating Germans towards Yugoslavia, as part of a motley band called Pompforce. This consisted of the 4th Parachute Battalion under Lieutenant Colonel Coxon – so his part was called *Coxforce* – a group of SBS, the RAF Regiment, some field guns and some Greek hangers-on under Major Patterson and known as *Patforce*. The Germans were still full of fight and caused casualties when they made a stand at Kozani, but they were in an impossible situation, thousands of miles from a friendly frontier and surrounded on every side by enemies – Greek, Albanian and Yugoslav – who would kill them out of hand and were somewhat reluctant to take prisoners. *Pompforce* kept the Germans on the run until they reached the Yugoslav frontier. The Yugoslavs were awaiting the arrival of the Red Army and wanted no help from the British, so *Pompforce* came to a halt.

Meanwhile, what of Lassen? Lassen was now a major. He had by now acquired three Military Crosses, but he had not learned caution. While Jellicoe and Patterson were busy in the Peleponnese, Lassen was busy harrying the remaining German garrisons in the islands off the coast of Greece, but without much enthusiasm, for the enemy were not offering a great deal of resistance and Lassen, sensing that the war was ending, wanted to get away from this small-scale raiding and take a look at what he would describe to John Lodwick as 'The Big War' – one that was fought with tanks and artillery and large numbers of men.

Having mopped up what little opposition he could find in the northern islands, he acquired a jeep and went ashore at the port of Salonika, the second city of Greece, where he found ELAS forces in control and determined to be as obstructive as possible to this small British force. This was not a wise course of action when dealing with a man like Lassen, as the local ELAS commander soon discovered. Lassen took the man on one side and so terrified him that he fled from the area and was never seen again. Lassen then took direct charge of the ELAS forces and 'suggested' that they should drive the Germans from Salonika. Not being entirely stupid, ELAS took the hint and attacked, successfully driving the Germans from the town.

With that much achieved, Lassen mounted the SBS in two fire engines he had found and drove in triumph into the city, where the red ELAS flags were swiftly replaced by the Union Jack. Lassen and his men killed around fifty

Germans and captured about a thousand before he reported to Jellicoe that he had 'liberated Salonika'. 'It was another superb piece of work,' said Jellicoe later, 'and I am personally convinced that but for Andy the docks of Salonika would have been totally destroyed by the Germans before they pulled out.' Jellicoe told Lassen to round up his fifty-strong squadron, pick up some artillery from the Raiding Support Regiment and remove the German garrisons from Crete.

By this time, November 1944, most of the Greek Islands had been liberated, but Crete, captured by the Germans in 1941, still retained a garrison of some 13,000 men. They were not in good heart, but there were a lot of them and they would fight hard rather than fall into the hands of the vengeful Cretans, whom the Germans had treated very badly. In an effort to delay the inevitable for as long as possible, the Germans had withdrawn to a defensive perimeter around the airfield at Maleme and the town of Chanea, where they were hemmed in by Cretan *andartes* who killed anyone they caught but had yet to carry out any major attacks on the remaining Germans. Lassen landed at Heraklion on 3 December 1944, and set about changing all that.

The Germans were quite relieved to find British troops on the island and suggested that a move in the right direction – towards co-operation and eventual surrender – might be a football match. This Lassen declined to allow, even when the bishop of Chanea offered to be the referee. The Germans were worried that a massacre by the Cretans would follow their surrender, and the situation on the island deteriorated as the ELAS and the right-wing EOK party began to wrestle for control. The SBS tried to keep out of this faction fighting, but a week after they arrived, an SBS officer, Captain Clynes, was shot in an ELAS ambush. A few days later, ELAS rebelled against the Greek Government and the Greek Civil War began, before the invading Germans had even been evicted from Greek soil.

Lassen was recalled from Crete. Patterson's squadron

was involved in the street fighting against ELAS in Athens, which went on until ELAS withdrew from the city at the end of January 1945. It took a full division of British troops to restore order to the Greek capital. Here, the SBS had three killed and twelve wounded, among their highest losses in the war – and from people they had hoped to liberate and whom they regarded as friends.

Such losses were even harder to bear when they came at the end of the war, but they were to continue. The next man to go was Ian Patterson, killed in an air crash at Brindisi. 'Another remarkable man, a great soldier and a terrible loss,' says Jellicoe. Then Jellicoe went, not killed but sent to Haifa on a Staff course. He was replaced by Major David Sutherland, one of the originals from Courtney's No. 1 SBS of 1941.

Lassen was training and reorganising his men for operations on the Italian mainland, while Sutherland's replacement as OC, S Squadron, Captain 'Nobby' Clarke, was preparing to move to the port of Zara on the west coast of Yugoslavia. The Yugoslav Communists had not been able to remove the Germans from the offshore islands in the northern Adriatic, and hoped that the British military would do it for them.

Clarke and fifty SBS men arrived in Zara in early February 1945, when the war in Europe had just three months to run. Yugoslav partisans held the town and, since the streets were filthy and the locals hostile, Clarke swiftly took his men off to the island of Ulyan, which was much more congenial, and set about harassing the enemy from there. His unit had now been augmented by some of the RAF Regiment, a force normally used to guard airfields but which was more than willing to take on any task around and had recently drifted into SBS orbit. The task now was to drive the Germans from the northern islands of the Adriatic, places with jaw-wrenching names like Krk, Pag, Olib and Cherso, and SBS tactics soon brought some useful results.

Stud Stellin took four men to Cherso and shot up the garrison of Italian Fascists, who promptly surrendered.

McGonigal took 21 men to the Villa Puntin on Lussin, found 45 Germans in residence and wiped them out, but the enemy put up a hard fight, killing two SBS men, including Jimmy Lees, a very popular officer, and wounding eight more. A later judgement declared that there were too many men on this raid and they got in each other's way, but the effect on the enemy was dramatic. After this garrison was wiped out, the others, especially those composed of Italian Fascists, became anxious to surrender, provided they could surrender to soldiers of the British Army, who took prisoners – and kept them alive.

On the next raid, against the village of Ossero, which lies by the bridge linking Cherso and Lussin, McGonigal took no less than 38 men. To avoid any confusion in the dark, he broke them into two parties and ordered that they should leave no enemy alive on their approach to the target. The party left Zara in two motorboats and, to revert to the good old days, he sent Sergeant Holmes ahead with a canoe party, tasked to eliminate any sentries.

The first encounter was with a five-man patrol, which the SBS engaged, killing four. The firing alerted the German defenders and a fire-fight developed, the Germans losing nine men killed, the SBS three men wounded. The German garrison of Ossero consisted of eighty well-trained troops and even 35 SBS men could do little against them once surprise was lost. The Germans refused to give up the bridge at Ossero and, though they lost 35 men killed or wounded defending it, they held on all night and at dawn the SBS had to withdraw. David Sutherland declared that these attacks on defended positions were proving counterproductive, and ordered that the SBS should concentrate on attacking road and sea transport, and so starve the Germans into surrender. This proved effective in confining the Germans to their defended localities and in April 1945 a combined force of Royal Marines Commandos, Royal Navy support ships, SBS and the artillery of the Raiding Support Regiment overran Krk, Pag and Rab and obliged their garrisons to surrender.

The European part of the Second World War was almost over, but Sutherland was determined to keep his forces in the field to the end. The next task he took on was driving the Germans from the Istrian peninsula at the head of the Adriatic, especially from the ports of Pola, Fiume and Trieste. SBS attempts to get ashore and get on with this task were inhibited for a while by the battles taking place just offshore between Royal Navy gunboats and German E-boats but eventually, on 12 April 1945, an SBS squadron under McGonigal got ashore. However, they were at once confronted by the local partisans, who intended to seize these places themselves and either absorb them into Yugoslavia or use them as a base for Communist infiltration of Italy. The SBS were subjected to severe provocation and large quantities of insolence by their erstwhile allies but could do little in the face of this intransigence. And so their war in and around the Mediterranean petered out in the early spring of 1945 . . . except for Lassen.

Lassen finally found his way to the 'Big War' in the first week of April 1945. With the end of the war in the Adriatic he and his squadron had gone to join Brigadier Tod's 2nd Commando Brigade – Nos 2 and 9 (Army) Commandos and Nos 40 and 43 (Royal Marines) Commandos – which was spearheading the advance of the Eighth Army up the Italian peninsula towards Venice. Their path lay across the narrow spit of land between a wide but shallow marsh, Lake Commachio, and the sea, a place where the defenders were tenacious and the defences strong.

It was therefore decided that the Commandos should make a waterborne assault across Commachio, and take the German defences from the rear. A Royal Marines corporal, Tom Hunter of 43 Commando, won a VC at Commachio. When the attack was renewed on 9 April 1945, Lassen's SBS squadron was tasked to scout the lake for the advance and then mount a diversion on the northern shore of the lake while the main assault was taking place to the east. Lassen took fifteen men and the party had some difficulty getting ashore, where they were at once engaged by heavy fire from German pillboxes, fire which wounded one man and killed another.

These pillboxes had to be taken and Lassen set out to do just that. He ran forward on his own and knocked out a machine gun with Bren-gun fire. Then he stormed the first pillbox with grenades. He then attacked and silenced another, and then a third and fourth, storming forward with a bag of grenades in one hand and his service revolver in the other. These pillboxes were stepped back in echelon and, when the last one stopped firing and hung a white flag from the weapon slit, Lassen stepped out of cover and advanced to take the surrender.

As Lassen went forward, the white flag was pulled back in and a burst of machine-gun fire cut Lassen down. It did not kill him. He continued to crawl forward, but his men were up with him now, running past to finish the job and knock out the pillbox. They took no prisoners. That done, they returned to Lassen, who told them that he was done for and that they should press on. He died a few minutes later, aged 24. 'Had he lived,' said Jellicoe, 'I think he would have done great things after the war.'

Anders Lassen was awarded a posthumous VC, to go with his three Military Crosses, and there are memorials to him in Copenhagen and elsewhere in Denmark, and at the SBS base at Poole. Few men have done more to earn such distinctions, but he has a finer memorial in the memories of those who served with him in the war, summed up, perhaps, in the words of Pericles, who might have been speaking of rare men like Anders Lassen when he wrote:

> They received, each for his own memory, praise
> that will never die, and with it the grandest
> of all sepulchres; not that in which their
> mortal bones are laid, but a home in the minds
> of men, where their glory remains fresh. . .

14

D-DAY AND AFTER
1944–45

'I am very glad to say that, in spite of the mud, which was often up to our knees, and in spite of other difficulties, we succeeded in clearing the obstacles in the time allotted – with seven and a half minutes to spare.'

Sergeant K Briggs DSM RM

D-Day, 6 June 1944, was the day of decision for many of the Special Force units created during the Second World War. The Commando brigades, the airborne divisions, the vast squadrons of landing craft of every type, ships and boats that had not existed four years before – all these and many more came to justify their existence in 24 hours of violence off the coast of Normandy and in the weeks that followed when the battle of supply was in full swing.

A look at the D-Day operation and Operation *Neptune*, the task of actually getting the troops ashore, reveals how canoe and underwater warfare had developed since those early days in 1940. The overall picture since 1940 is one of constant development, in which new units were created as more tasks became necessary. After the early canoe reconnaissances there was COPP, the Combined Operations Pilotage Parties, examining the beaches and the beach defences by swimming in or using canoes, Chariots or X-craft. The beach obstacles then had to be cleared, so more volunteers were needed to form LCOCU, the Landing Craft Obstruction Clearance Units, which would remove the mines and obstacles placed by the enemy. Then, once the armies had got ashore, they would have to be supplied, a task that would be much easier if the Allies had working ports, so in came the 'P' Parties, to clear the harbours and the quays of mines and booby traps. This entire task, a progression from beach recce to a cleared safe harbour capable of supplying an army, lay in the hands of the underwater soldiers, sailors and marines.

The task of getting the troops ashore and victorious in Normandy was bound to be formidable. The Germans knew that the Allies must land in France sooner or later and the only questions in their minds were when and where. When Field-Marshal Erwin Rommel was appointed German Commander in the West he began his work with a complete study of the coastline defences, from Norway to the Spanish frontier, and was horrified by what he discovered. According to their propaganda, the Germans had constructed a wall – the Atlantic Wall – all down the coast of Europe, a wall which would keep the Allied invaders out and cost them a quantity of lives in the attempt to breach it. Rommel discovered that, except in a few places like the Pas de Calais, the Atlantic Wall barely existed. Being a remarkably energetic officer he therefore set out to create, expand and improve it, concentrating his efforts on the Pas de Calais and the coast of Normandy, the two places which, he calculated, were the most likely for an Allied landing spot.

Rommel intended to stop the invasion on the water line and deny the Allies any opportunity to get ashore and establish a bridgehead. 'Rommel told me,' said Major Hans von Luck of the 125 Panzer Regiment, 21 Panzer Division, 'that if we did not throw the Allies back into the sea in 24 hours it is the beginning of the end.' The first 24 hours, said Rommel, would be decisive – the 'longest day' – and during that day the Allied invaders were to be thrown back into the sea. As an aid to that end he started to draft troops and guns up to the beaches, ordering them to dig in above any likely landing area, and he also began to fortify the beaches on, above and below the water line, with an elaborate system of minefields and anti-invasion defences.

Beams and tree trunks, jutting seaward, were hammered deep into the sand and crowned with mines to impact and explode on landing craft. Some had spikes or steel cutters to rip the assault craft open. Concrete tank obstacles not needed ashore were dragged into the sea to hamper craft beaching and many mines were secured in shallow waters behind the false beaches off many probable landing areas, with tripwires attached to their horns. All manner of obstacles were strewn along the beaches including a new one which became known to the allied planners as 'Element C', which consisted of a heavy steel fence supported by wooden posts on the landward side. Element C was a considerable obstacle, ten feet high by ten feet broad, a heavily mined web of steel weighing more than two tons.

When the dimensions were brought back to the UK a replica of this obstacle was constructed and experiments made on how it could be effectively destroyed, which eventually meant the LCOCU frogmen had to attach no less than 36 small, shaped charges, very precisely, to different parts of the Element, for simultaneous detonation. If this was done, the Element would collapse and the debris would stand no more than two feet off the sea bottom.

This was by no means the only obstacle. There were steel girders welded together like giant steel starfish, wooden ramps to throw the craft on to their sides and a barrier known as 'Belgian Gates', which consisted of concrete dragon's teeth and a metal barrier armed with fused shells. Barbed wire was strewn just under the surface of the water, below the low-water mark, and everywhere there were anti-tank and anti-personnel mines.

Rommel made great use of mines. During 1944, in the four months between the time he took up his appointment and the Allied landing, he laid 4,000,000 mines along the French coast. He had intended to lay 50,000,000 but fortunately, with mines as with everything else he needed, there was a shortage. Nevertheless, he improved the defences considerably and so added to the problems of the Allied planners and the difficulties of the assaulting troops.

Singly or in combination, these obstacles offered a number of probable terrors. They might sink landing craft, throwing their heavily laden passengers out to drown. They might impale the craft and expose them, high and dry, to fire from the shore. They might force the craft away from a safe approach and oblige them to run in directly on to previously prepared minefields and fixed-line machine-gun positions. Above all, they would force the men in the assault craft to get out a long distance offshore and make a long run over the flat, exposed beaches before they could hope to be in among the German defences. The obstacles, in short, aimed to create a killing ground, where the troops coming ashore could be pinned down and massacred by the defenders' guns.

The Allied planners soon came to know about these defences. Frogmen and COPP teams were swimming ashore on to these beaches every night from the end of 1943, examining the entire coast, not just the true landing area, finding the false beaches and testing the sand for soft spots that could bog tanks or guns as they came ashore. They also examined the beach obstacles and took precise measurements back to Britain, where the scientists and engineers worked out how to destroy them. This work went on throughout the bitter winter of 1943/44 and continued until a few weeks before the invasion.

One of the men examining the Normandy beaches was Royal Navy Lieutenant Jim Booth of COPP:

I have told you how we used to operate in the Med, going in by canoe off a conventional submarine. Well, when it came to Normandy that would not work. The Bay of the Seine was too shallow for a big sub to operate successfully, so we had to use midget submarines, X-craft, and two of these, X20 and X23, were allocated to COPP for pre-invasion recce. We could not get our canoes into the X-craft, which were too small, and the X-craft were too slow for a quick nightly dash up to the beaches, so the routine was that a big submarine would tow us across the Channel into the mouth of the bay and then the midget sub would take us to within about 200 yards of the beach and we would swim in from there to do the recce. While we were at work it would submerge and lie on the bottom, surfacing to pick us up after an agreed period of time or after picking up a signal through its periscope.

We recced the whole area, obstacles as well as the ground and gradients, working in teams of two. My CO, Lieutenant Geoff Lyne, surveyed a lot of the obstacles and we did the gradients together with a hand line, while the Royal Engineers people took sand and beach samples, looking for quicksand or mud that would bog the tanks. All this was done well before D-Day.

You didn't have to be a very good swimmer incidentally, though it probably helped, but I was just 23 at the time and very fit. It was a good job and we didn't have many casualties – they wanted us back with the information and took good care to recover us.

While COPP were at work on the British landing beaches, this sort of activity was also going on off Omaha and Utah, the two American landing beaches, as Matthew Kaye of the Scouts and Raiders recalls:

During the Big War I was a Scout and Raider, and beach recon was one of our prime functions. My particular unit, Group One, was commanded by Lieutenant Phil Bucklew, who was recalled to service for the Korean War and then organised the cream of all covert groups, the US Navy SEALS. The UDT boys, Underwater Demolition Teams, claim Bucklew and the

SEALS as theirs but he was first and last a Scout and Raider. Anyway, Bucklew scouted the Normandy beaches in the weeks before the invasion the same as your COPP boys did. He anticipated that some sceptics would not believe our information and the story goes that he once came in with a bucket of Normandy sand and dumped it on the desk of a British intelligence officer. Maybe. Anyway, your COPP guys were just as capable.

COPP and the US Scouts and Raiders did not only survey the true landing areas. Indeed, for security reasons they did not know which the true areas were, and were sent to survey enemy defences all along the French coast, so that, should anyone be captured or their activities detected, it would not reveal where the Allies were actually going to go ashore. Once the Allied planners had full information about the beach defences, plans and equipment could be prepared to counter or eliminate them.

The first task was to plot all the natural and physical obstacles, like mud, quicksand and especially the false beaches, on charts. False beaches are sandbars, a hundred or so yards offshore, where the sea shallows to a few feet. A landing craft would grind on to the sandbar and the cox'n, thinking that he could go no further, would open the bow doors, drop the ramp and order, 'Out Troops!' The infantry or Commandos would then swarm out and start to wade ashore, only to discover that a deep channel, far too deep to wade, lay between them and the actual beach. If a machine gun began to play on them at this point, these men were doomed and if the landing craft had withdrawn they were stuck. Beach recce was necessary to avoid all that.

The quicksand and mud was more of a danger to tanks and guns than to infantry. If possible, such natural hazards were avoided, but if this could not be done then the loading schedule on the landing craft was altered so that a specially adapted tank, one of the 79th Armoured Division 'Funnies' – called a 'Bobbin' – went ashore first.

Bobbin tanks could lay a carpet over the patch of mud or quicksand and were followed by 'flail' tanks, to beat a path through the minefields, and 'petard' tanks, mounting a heavy gun to blast a hole in the sea wall. Using the Funnies enabled the British to breach the Atlantic Wall with comparative ease – the Americans did not use the Funnies and paid for it with heavy casualties on Omaha beach – but none of this would have been possible without prior beach recce by COPP.

The Funnies could usually deal with obstacles above the water line but on or below it the task of destroying the beach obstacles was the task of LCOCU – frogmen, trained in demolition, and equipped with ready-prepared explosives and a detailed knowledge of where to attach these charges to the different kinds of obstacle. This was not a simple task; put the charge in the wrong place and the obstacle would either remain undamaged or simply become an equally awkward mass of metal.

Moreover, the sheer scale of the Normandy operation, along fifty miles of enemy-held coast, meant that scores of men had to be recruited into LCOCU and trained in diving and demolition techniques in the months before D-Day. In the end, over a hundred LCOCUs were formed for D-Day, and the rush to train and equip them threw a great strain on the available facilities. The LCOCUs were trained at a special base at Appledore in North Devon, close to the long beaches at Woolacombe, which stood in for those on the Normandy coast during the endless day and night exercises before the invasion. In all, between January and the end of May 1944, the LCOCU trainees at Appledore put in more than 20,000 dives and used many tons of explosives.

By 1944, underwater training, techniques and equipment had improved considerably since the early days in Gibraltar when Crabb and his men dived in swimming trunks and DSEA equipment. A proper frogman suit with hood and facepiece was now available, protection which enabled the men to stay in the water for long periods and see what they were doing. The men had swim-fins, or flippers, which enabled them to swim about easily, and at some speed, underwater. The breathing sets, which used a mixture of oxygen and nitrogen, were also much safer, and although the task of destroying obstacles a few hundred yards off the beach under sniper, machine-gun and shell fire could not be described as easy, it was made a good deal less difficult thanks to the work done – and the risks taken – by those early pioneering frogmen.

There was another new hazard facing these underwater warriors. In 1943, when examining some of the booty captured in North Africa, British scientists had discovered a collection of explosive devices in a warehouse in Bizerta, mines of various types which had clearly been designed for sowing in North African harbours and left behind to prevent these harbours being rapidly exploited to supply the Allied advance. The essence of the D-Day landing was a rapid advance inland and an equally rapid build-up of forces ashore, two projects that depended entirely on acquiring the facilities of ports with the least possible delay. Now it appeared that any port captured would have been immobilised by mines and demolition – so, what to do?

One answer was for the invaders to take a port with them, so two artificial harbours, the Mulberries, were towed across the Channel and assembled off Utah beach and at Arromanches, where the remains of the caissons can be seen to this day. The other solution was to train teams of frogmen in mine clearance. These men, the P Parties, were based in a shore establishment, a 'stone frigate' as the Navy call them, with the appropriate name of HMS *Firework* and they were on hand when the armies embarked for D-Day.

All this work, with its attendant risks and not a few tragedies, came to fruition on D-Day when ten LCOCU teams – four Royal Navy and six Royal Marine – were sent in to clear the British and Canadian beaches for the landing of the Allied armies. They did their work in the hours before H-Hour, the moment of assault, 0730 hours on 6 June, when the water stood at half-tide on the flood and the bow ramps fell to let the tanks and infantry go ashore.

These underwater warriors made a great contribution to the success of D-Day, both by prior reconnaissance and then by clearing obstacles during the invasion. First there were the men of COPP and the Scouts and Raiders, who swam ashore in freezing seas, night after night, to prowl mined beaches and bring vital information back to the planners. On the basis of that information the LCOCU boys went in to do their stuff, and although the casualties were small, just two men killed and ten wounded, the risks they took were considerable, not least because, in spite of all the preparation, matters did not go entirely as planned.

The landing was fixed for half-tide on the flood, which was calculated to offer the best option of a short run up the beach and enough water to get the landing craft close inshore. Since the Channel tides flow in from the Atlantic in the west this meant that the men went ashore at different times, the Americans in the west landing up to an hour before the British landed on Sword beach fifty miles to the east. As in other invasions, COPP marked the beaches to direct the assault craft, sending two X-craft, X20 and X23, to act as markers for the landing craft heading for Sword. These craft sailed for Normandy on 2 June and were to lie off the beaches until the morning of 5 June, surfacing to shine marker lights out to sea as the assault craft swept in. Jim Booth of COPP recounts what happened:

I was on X23, a midget sub that now lies outside the Submarine Museum in Gosport, Hampshire, the only survivor of all the X-craft. Anyway, there were buoys to lead the invasion shipping into the bay of the Seine, but with so many ships about it was thought a little extra help would not go amiss. Our beach was Sword, one of the British beaches just west of Ouistreham. We were towed across the Channel as usual by a big submarine, sailed to our position submerged on 3 June and lay on the bottom all day and the next, ready to come up and put out a beacon on the night of the 4th/5th. When we finally came up the first thing we got was a message that the invasion had been put back for 24 hours and so down we went again. We came up again on the morning of the 6th, put out the beacon and sailed out of the bay on the surface, with hundreds of landing craft and ships heading past us, the troops cheering and waving. It was something I will never forget.

These X-craft were the first vessels off the Normandy coast on D-Day, and the first troops to go ashore were those in the LCOCU teams, just 120 in all, in twelve-man units, one officer and eleven men, tasked to clear a way through the obstacles for the craft now surging past X23. None of these men were professional divers, and most of them had had just a few months' training in diving and demolitions before they went in to the beaches.

The LCOCU teams crossed the Channel in LSIs (Landing Ship, Infantry), small unstable craft which, according to one LCOCU member, 'would roll on wet grass'. Just beyond artillery range the teams transferred into small craft and went in to the beaches, rolling out of their craft before the obstacles and swimming in to start work. They were already under direct rifle and machine-gun fire and suffered from the effect of concussion as shells from attackers and defenders detonated in the water around them.

To reduce the effect of these detonations the men wore kapok-lined jackets, which kept them alive but did not fully cushion the blow. Many men were concussed, or otherwise injured by shellfire, but the work went on regardless. The teams first worked to clear gaps though the outer obstacles, and then went in closer, to clear obstacles on the beach itself. All this work was done during the preliminary bombardment, at dawn or shortly afterwards, and long before the actual hour of the assault, which meant that the German defenders could concentrate all their attention and firepower on the frogmen working offshore.

The LCOCU men did not clear all the obstacles from every beach. It would have taken a fleet of frogmen to do that and they did not have either the time or the manpower. They did make the invasion possible, and completed the task begun by their colleagues in COPP many months before; thanks to their efforts many craft got ashore that would otherwise have become hung up offshore or been destroyed on the mines or the obstacles. Once the troops were firmly established on the beaches, the LCOCU turned to other tasks, attaching hooks underwater to winch trucks and tanks ashore, clearing mines, removing booby traps and unloading stores. They did sterling work and at the end of the day had 10 per cent casualties, two killed and ten wounded.

Having torn a breach in the Atlantic Wall, the next task for these parties was in the harbours along the Normandy coast, where the 'P' Parties (Pilotage Parties), Nos 1571, 1572, 1573 and 1574, took up the work of mine clearing. Every port was heavily mined and booby-trapped and the underwater mines had to be cleared before the port was usable. The 'P' Parties – frogmen – became known as human minesweepers, tasked to crawl about on the bottom of harbours, day and night, among deep mud and other filth, feeling for mines and booby traps, removing detonators with their bare hands and making the mines and booby traps safe.

'I don't think the thought of dying bothered me half as much as the thought of being mutilated, blinded or something like that. It did not do to think about what might happen or you could not have done the job,' says one former diver. 'In fact, the worst part was approaching a device or a mine, not actually working on it. If it went up when you were sitting on it you had had it and would not know anything about it . . . but getting up to it was really hard on the nerves, half expecting it to go up in your face – not that you could often see them, but the thought was always there . . . and we never got any counselling later, like they do today.'

Being blown to bits was a distinct possibility. Many of the mines left behind by the retreating Germans were fitted with delayed-action fuses, and exploded up to a month after the Germans had left. There were acoustic mines, clock fuses, magnetic mines and all manner of ad hoc booby traps to cope with, and in Cherbourg the divers discovered the 'K' mine or 'Katy', weighing nearly a ton, which was anchored to the bottom of the harbour by a concrete block from which a thin floating line trailed up to the surface. If this line snagged on a ship or caught on a propeller the line would tighten and the mine would explode. But, one by one, all the ports, Cherbourg, Ouistreham, Le Havre, Boulogne, Calais and the rest, were cleared as the Allied armies pushed north into Belgium.

Antwerp, which fell into Allied hands in September, is a very large port with twenty miles of quays and wharves, all of which had been left behind well furnished with mines, including 36 fused depth charges attached to the pilings of the E-boat pens. Working conditions were terrible, with the divers having to work up to their waists or necks in mud or, as on one occasion, with the mud over the divers' heads. Added to the 'normal' risks, Antwerp was being attacked by German V1 rockets – buzz bombs – and, strangely enough in view of the daily hazards the men were meeting underwater, it was a V1 rocket that caused the first 'P' Party casualty, killing Able Seaman Brunskell, not in the harbour on duty, but while he was ashore, in a cinema.

This work went on until the end of the war, and after it, until all the rivers, coasts and ports of Europe were safe. The work these men did has been quantified by Messrs Waldron and Gleeson in their book, *The Frogmen*:

They spent more than six hundred working days underwater. They searched a total area of twenty million square feet and travelled more than one thousand three hundred miles underwater. A hundred and fifty mines, fifty teller mines and one hundred and twenty assorted charges were dealt with, including one V2 rocket.

These are telling statistics but they omit the conditions under which these men worked; in freezing water, in mud and slime, in pitch darkness, and alone. The Second World War employed many heroes, but very few endured as much as these men did in the course of their daily work.

With the armies ashore in France and advancing rapidly towards the frontiers of Germany, the task of many of these amphibious units had been accomplished, at least as far as the European and Mediterranean theatres of war were concerned. There remained the Japanese, and before the war in Europe ended the underwater warriors were heading there, to apply their skills and weaponry against a new and formidable enemy.

15

CANOES AND X-CRAFT IN THE FAR EAST 1945

'I offered to go out and release the starboard charge but Maginnis said it was his job and he would do it. So out he went with a bloody great spanner and the next two minutes were the most anxious minutes of my life.'

Lieutenant Ian Fraser VC, XE3, Singapore

The war in Europe ended on 8 May 1945 but VE Day was not the end of the Second World War, which still had some months to run. The Japanese still fought on in the Far East and Burma and were to carry on doing so until the atom bombs dropped on Hiroshima and Nagasaki brought their dreams of Asian domination to a shattering conclusion. There were still some bloody battles ahead before the Second World War ended, and the end of hostilities in Europe enabled more underwater warriors to head east and take up the war against the Japanese.

Not everyone was keen to do this. Many men felt that, having driven Italy out of the war and defeated Nazi Germany, they had already, in the phrase of the time, 'done their bit', and it was time for someone else to have a go. As far as the frogmen and canoeists were concerned, operating in the Far East presented a number of difficulties, not least that the distances were vast and the enemy well deployed. Chariot operations had already ended, even in the European theatre, and frogmen teams were being kept fully employed clearing up the war-torn harbours and sweeping mines from rivers and estuaries. The amphibious and underwater war in the Far East would be fought by canoeists and X-craft, but they too faced some snags, for underwater warfare in the Far East offered a mixture of advantage and disadvantage. The advantage was warmer water, the disadvantage was sharks.

Sharks are not as dangerous as they are alleged to be, but any sensible diver keeps a wary eye out for a creature that is often twice his size, a skilled and voracious hunter, and in his natural element. Warm water is not the only habitat for sharks, which are found in all the world's seas. US Navy SEAL swimmers operating off California from their Coronado base have had to cope with questing great white sharks, which inhabit the Californian waters in great numbers in search of seals. In the 1960s, a Royal Marines SBS man parachuting into the sea off Singapore saw a tiger shark circling below him and had to quell its eagerness to eat him by dropping his reserve parachute into its gaping mouth. Sharks were also on hand when Lieutenant Paddy Ashdown of the SBS was diving off the coast of Malaya:

When I was in the SBS in the Far East we used to go on training dives at a place called Pulau Tioman, off the east coast. The water was clear and the sea bed beautiful but the area was a breeding ground for sharks. They were everywhere, none of them very big at about six feet, but there is something absolutely terrifying about rounding rocks underwater and seeing a shark . . . you in your clumsy diving apparatus and suit, and this thing eyeing you with such sleek power and speed; in short, the sight of a shark, however large or small, always makes the heart beat a little faster.

The danger from sharks is not great, but it is real. Thanks to a series of documentary films and a great deal of research, more is now known about sharks than was common knowledge fifty or sixty years ago when all sharks were widely regarded as man-eaters. Divers now concede that the most dangerous place to be in shark-infested waters is on the surface, for divers are rarely attacked when underwater. The places to avoid are polluted, unclear waters, especially after dark and when there is blood in the water, but sharks can be attracted by noise or confusion and are usually lurking about somewhere in tropical waters, especially around reefs. Troops wading ashore on Japanese-held atolls were wary of shark attack and the theory that the sharks would be driven away by the previous naval gunfire and the explosion of shells in the water does not seem to hold up. Film of the assault on Iwo Jima in 1945 clearly shows a large tiger shark questing about close to the beach, even as the assault went in.

Though the thought of shark attack – and the attention of barracuda, octopus and other dangerous denizens of the deep – was never far from their minds, no diver was attacked by a shark during operations in the Far East during the Second World War and, although many sharks were seen, none seemed eager to try conclusions with a Second World War frogman. Survivors from torpedoed ships and the crews of shot-down aircraft, on the other hand, were often attacked; more than half the crew of the USS *Indianapolis* were taken by sharks after the cruiser was torpedoed off Guam in July 1945.

The divers found that a far more common ailment, and one that was potentially crippling, was the sores caused by cuts and abrasions from coral, which were slow to heal and often ate the flesh away down to the bone. From the point of view of comfort, the best diving rig was often a pair of shorts, provided the skin was blackened to escape the attention of sharks, but in practice the men found that their normal diving dress, while uncomfortable on board ship or submarine in tropical climes, offered the best protection against coral cuts and sores. There was also another problem, at least to begin with, for when the X-craft and their crews arrived in the Far East in 1945 the US Navy would not let them operate.

The SBS spearhead in the Far East was provided by Major Godfrey Courtney and the men of Z SBS, who arrived in Ceylon (now Sri Lanka) in January 1944, where they were under the direction of Lord Louis Mountbatten's South-East Asia Command (SEAC). They were to work with Force 136, the Far East equivalent of SOE, in harassing the Japanese.

At the time, Z SBS consisted of nine men led by Major Godfrey Courtney and Captain E J Sally Lunn. Four more men joined later but this was still a very small force and it was soon brought under the control of a new organisation, the Small Operations Group (SOG), which was established on 12 June 1944, under Royal Marines control. The CO of this group was Colonel H T Tollemache RM and the second-in-command was Lieutenant Colonel Blondie Hasler RM.

The SOG included four COPP parties, the Army SBS groups under Courtney, some Royal Marines Commandos, Detachment 385, another Royal Marines raiding unit and four Sea Reconnaissance units whose task was to go ashore on paddleboards, a form of surfboard, leaving their parent submarine many miles offshore, and using miniature paddles to propel themselves in to the beach. The idea was to drop SRU paddlers up to twenty miles offshore, and this may be why the SRUs saw very little action. The SOG soon split into various component parts, with some men, including Major Godfrey Courtney, going to Australia to operate with submarine flotillas there, while others were detached to Burma for operations in the Arakan. After the formation of SOG, the fortunes of the SBS can be followed quite clearly.

The prime task of Z SBS was to land agents and stores in Malaya, where they would train and supply the men of the mainly Chinese Malayan Peoples Anti-Japanese Army (MPAJA), which Force 136 were actively supporting. This task was not without risk and a number of landing operations were ambushed by the Japanese, but they went on without ceasing until the end of the war.

Godfrey Courtney had taken part of Z SBS to

Fremantle in Australia to work with the Australian Services Reconnaissance Department (SRD), the Australian equivalent of SOE, and tasked to carry out limpet mine and sabotage attacks in Japanese-held territory. Some of these attacks were carried out from American submarines and in the course of one operation, in April 1945, an Australian canoe team were picked up by the Japanese who then tried to lure their parent submarine inshore. Though this failed, the submarine was detected and subjected to a severe depth-charge attack. After that, US submarines were not allowed to take part in SBS operations and, since they were big, long-range submarines ideal for operations in the Pacific, their withdrawal restricted the area open to attack. It also stopped the move of the SRD to the US base in Subic Bay and, as a result, all SBS and SRD activity was switched to Mountbatten's South-East Asia Command.

The first operation there was launched from Australia on 21 September 1944, when HMS/M *Telemachus* took a party to Malaya, tasked to land and set up a radio station in Jahore, the State just across the causeway from Singapore. The voyage passed uneventfully and the submarine surfaced off the coast of Jahore on 5 October. The idea was that the entire party and half the stores would be ferried ashore on the first night and the rest of the stores on the second night, after which the ferry party, whose main task was to help the shore party get established, would return to *Telemachus*. The first part went according to plan and the submarine dived after just an hour and a half on the surface, ready to return on the following night.

However, when the submarine surfaced on 6 October, the area was found to be humming with enemy activity, including patrol boats and aircraft. The submarine waited for a signal from the shore, dodging patrol craft and aircraft, but eventually the captain decided that the shore party had been caught or compromised and went on his way. The ferry party, which had been supposed to stay ashore for 24 hours, were not evacuated for another four months; fortunately, they had been wise enough to take their weapons and extra stores ashore and were able to play their part in the subsequent operation, though the commander of the landing party, Major Davis, was killed when the Japanese located and stormed their camp in January 1945.

Meanwhile, another part of the SBS, A and B Groups from the UK, commanded by Major Mike Kealy, had arrived in India and joined the Royal Marines SOG in Ceylon. C Group SBS arrived later and the three groups spent some time training with new types of canoe, some fitted with outriggers; another, the Mark VI canoe, was fitted with outboard motors and Vickers K machine guns. Those SBS who had not qualified as parachutists in Britain did a parachute course at Rawalpindi, while the A Group, now fully trained, left for Burma, for service in the Arakan, mainly with the 3rd Commando Brigade which was carrying out raids and landing operations to harass the gradually retreating Japanese.

The SBS were to carry out pre-landing recces of both the beaches and the Japanese defences, beginning with a look at Ramree Island in October 1944. This was to have been carried out by three canoes, but when the unit commander, Major Holden-White, and Corporal Merryweather made it to the beach they found themselves alone. Making their way along the beach they found the other two crews and plenty of evidence that Ramree Island had strong if unmanned defences. The party withdrew without loss after a Japanese patrol had found their canoes but failed to remove or destroy them.

Three weeks later Holden-White was asked if his men could rescue a Royal Marines corporal who had got left behind after a raid by 42 Commando on Elizabeth Island. Major Kealy elected to lead this one and the party patrolled the island for some hours before concluding that the Marine was either dead or captured; in fact he turned up after the war, barely alive in a Rangoon jail. Meanwhile, 3 Commando Brigade had worked out a cunning plan for an attack on Ramree Island. The idea for this attack was that the SBS would again recce the defences and, if these were unoccupied, a troop of No. 5 Commando would come ashore and lay booby traps and anti-personnel mines. That done they would then create the effect of an imminent landing. The hope was that the Japs would then rush to man their defences, step on the mines, run into the booby traps . . . and blow themselves to pieces.

All went well until the SBS were actually ashore. Then, just as they started to move up the beach there was a small bang overhead, and a large parachute flare lit up the landing area, catching some SBS canoes still just off the beach. Chaos then reigned and the SBS had to beat a hasty retreat. The Japanese were clearly on the alert for just such an event and proceeded to illuminate the coast with fires and flares. The canoes paddled out to sea without loss and finally met up with the MLs carrying the disgruntled men of 5 Commando. After a short conference, it was decided that something had to be done and the craft then cruised off the beach, hosing the Japanese defences with Lewis-gun, Bofors-gun and three-inch-mortar fire. The Japanese replied to this with machine guns and rifles and after an hour of this, honour satisfied, the SBS and the Commandos withdrew out to sea.

John Ferguson of 5 Commando remembers this raid:

At this time we trained by embarking in LCAs (Landing Craft, Assault) about 0200 hours every day and getting into a position offshore just behind the point where twelve-foot-high breakers broke and thundered in to the beach. We then had to jump in and be carried ashore in the waves, kit and all; how no one was drowned I will never know, but we took it to be part of our normal training. Not so, however.

A few weeks later we embarked in two MTBs and went to the tip of Tefnek where, to my delight, we met a party of SBS. The Japs had erected bamboo watchtowers right down the coast and six of them were in our area. These SBS had found them to be guarded by about a company of Japs, and our job was to dispose of both towers and Japanese. The SBS went ashore in folboats and we were to follow up in some spare craft. We also had a Carley float loaded with pyrotechnics, to distract the defenders if need be. Anyway, we set off at about 0200 hours, as per rehearsal, aiming for a break in the surf. The advance party of SBS got ashore, but the Japs were there in strength and on the alert, and it got a bit hectic. We decided to call it off as we could not have got anywhere near the towers with the Japs on the alert, so it was back to the MTBs, where we launched the Carley float to tickle them up, and we set off at speed, opening up on the Japanese as we passed with everything we had, and they of course replied. An exciting if abortive raid.

Similar SBS raids or recces went in every couple of weeks from then on, sometimes with the support of Commando units from 3 Commando Brigade, sometimes alone. These raids brought back some useful information, but not all of it was put to good use. The landing of 5 Commando at Myebon in January 1945 might well have been a disaster, for the beach survey carried out by the SBS and reported back to GHQ was ignored by the planners. According to the SBS report, 'before firm ground can be reached, a wide stretch of mud covered with a foot of water will have to be traversed'. This report, and some aerial photographs, were studied by the planners at GHQ who decided to ignore this advice and land the men on a falling tide, with an ever-widening patch of deep mud to cross. Let John Ferguson of 5 Commando recount what happened:

For our landing at Myebon, the LCAs took us to within two hundred yards of the beach and dropped the ramps. As we got out, the water came up to our chests, but the bottom half was three feet of mud, thick slime, terrible stuff. It took hours, not minutes, *hours* for some men to get ashore for, as the tide fell, the distance they had to wade through the mud increased and they got to the beach exhausted, many without their boots. Our landing should have been supported by Sherman tanks of the 19th Lancers but they could not land here either, and had to be put ashore further up the coast. Fortunately, the Japanese did not show up, though we lost some men to mines on the beach.

While the A Group were making themselves useful to 3 Commando Brigade in the Arakan, the B and C Groups, under the command of Major D H Sidders, were operating on the west coast of Malaya, making raids on the island of Sumatra in co-operation with the 4th Submarine Flotilla. Their work began in early September 1944, with Operation *Spratt Baker*, when an eight-man party under Major Sidders sailed in the submarine HMS/M *Trenchant*, to destroy a railway bridge over a river in North Sumatra. This task was not accomplished easily and it took two attempts before the party finally destroyed the bridge.

The party arrived off the coast of Sumatra on 10 September. On the following night the submarine surfaced at about 1900 hours and the canoes were passed out on to the casing and left there while the submarine started to move inshore and the raiders got into their equipment and primed their explosive charges. At 2030 hours they boarded their canoes and at 2040 hours they left the submarine, paddling in arrowhead formation towards the shore. They had to be back on board by 0200 hours so they had no time to spare, but on landing on the beach at 2230 hours they found they were in the wrong place. The idea was to find the mouth of the river and walk in along the bank, but they could not find it.

Eventually, they went back to sea and paddled up and down the coast, looking for the river mouth. This was soon located but, on passing through the surf, Major Sidders was swept away. It was nearly midnight before he was located and the party could proceed. Then came the next snag; the banks were choked with undergrowth and mangrove trees and progress was either very slow or virtually impossible. At 0100 hours, furious with the lack of progress, they made their way back to their canoes and, at 0300 hours, rejoined the submarine, shamefaced but quite determined to try again on the following night.

This raid was to be matched by another just up the coast by SBS men sent in from HMS/M *Terrapin*. When Sidders's group heard that *Terrapin*'s SBS men had not managed to get ashore either, and the enemy was therefore still unaware that raiders were about, the attack on the bridge was on again for the following night, 12 September. This time matters went much better; after getting ashore at 2200 hours the raiders made their way through fields to the railway line and followed that to the bridge, the only alarm coming when one heavily loaded man failed to notice a stream and fell, with a tremendous splash, into the water. Mining and wiring the bridge took two full hours and it was not until well after 0200 that the work was completed. Then, setting the fuses for a one-and-a-half-hour delay, they set off back to the beach. By 0300 hours they were out at sea and at 0335 they heard the gratifying sound of an explosion. They looked back to see the sky lit up by the flash and they heard a long rumble as the bridge collapsed into the river.

For a while they were elated, but elation was slowly replaced by worry – they could not locate the submarine and it began to get light. The captain had agreed to surface at dawn if they were not back, provided they were at least five miles offshore, so the crews paddled hard out to sea, partly to make the rendezvous and partly because the Japanese would be looking for them and were not likely to be too gentle to any saboteur who fell into their rarely gentle clutches. Then, just as the hills behind were becoming visible, someone said, 'There she is,' and the bow and conning tower of *HMS/M Trenchant* came surging out of the sea. The men were picked up at 0500 hours and, five minutes later, *Trenchant* dived. For this attack, Major Sidders was awarded the Military Cross and Sergeant Williams the MM.

The SBS continued raiding until the end of the war, harassing the Japanese along the coast and down the rivers, especially the Irrawaddy. These were the main Japanese lines of retreat and the SBS ambushed them night after night, lying up in anchored canoes and raking any Japanese craft that passed by with Vickers K machine-gun fire and showers of grenades. They continued to do this until the war ended on 15 August 1945. The unit was disbanded at the end of October, after which the men made themselves useful, or scarce, around nice billets in Ceylon until the time came for demobilisation and their trip back to Blighty.

The British SBS were not alone in making canoe raids on the Japanese and this account of Far East operations cannot end without the tales of two operations mounted by a combined British and Australian canoe unit against Japanese shipping in Singapore harbour. The first of these, Operation *Jaywick* in September 1943, was a great success. The second, Operation *Rimau*, a year later, was a total disaster, but one which illustrates the very real risks taken by behind-the-line raiders in the Far East.

The commander of *Jaywick* and *Rimau* was an officer of the Gordon Highlanders, Major Ivan Lyon. He had been in Singapore before the Japanese takeover and had succeeded in escaping after the surrender, first to Ceylon and then to Australia where he was employed as an advisor and instructor with SRD. Lyon was determined to return to Singapore and he convinced the authorities that a raid on the port was possible, and that a large number of Japanese ships could be sunk in the process. Since the Japanese were then carrying all before them in South-East Asia and had been threatening the frontiers of India, this idea had obvious appeal and Lyon was permitted to work out a viable plan.

The first problem was to get to Singapore, which lies 1,500 miles from the north coast of Australia, across seas and past islands then occupied by the Japanese. A submarine was the obvious answer but Lyon had another idea. He intended to get into Singapore using a captured

Japanese fishing boat, which he had brought to Australia and renamed the *Krait*. The *Krait* was barely seaworthy and her engine was unreliable, but Lyon proceeded to assemble his crew. He eventually found seventeen volunteers, some British, some Australian, and put them through a period of intense training at the Flinders Naval Base. The training lasted five months and included escape and evasion, survival, the use of a range of small arms and canoe raiding with the use of limpets. By the time this training ended, the *Jaywick* party had shrunk to fourteen.

Lyon's plan was to take the *Krait* right into Singapore harbour and then use the canoes for night attacks on the assembled shipping. From the fourteen who completed the course, six, including two reserves, were selected to canoe in to the actual attack with Lyon and his second-in-command, Lieutenant D M Davidson RNVR, with the rest coming along to crew the *Krait*. The party left Sydney and so began the first leg of their voyage, round the coast to northern Australia.

It is rarely a bad thing if things go awry in the early stages of a Special Force operation, and a great deal went wrong with the *Krait* on the voyage to the Torres Strait. She arrived at the jumping-off point in the Exmouth Gulf in a perilous state of repair and needed a new engine and propeller before she could proceed. These were found and, on 2 September 1943, the *Krait* sailed for Singapore.

The voyage to Singapore took three weeks, through the Lombok Straits, past Bali and the other islands of Indonesia. The *Krait* flew the Japanese flag and the men stripped to the waist, dyed their skin, and wore sarongs, hoping to pass for Indonesians, if not for Japanese. The idea now was to drop off the three canoe teams on Durian Island, thirty miles from Singapore, and paddle in from there while the *Krait* sheltered somewhere on the coast of Sumatra. The canoeists would paddle over to rejoin her after the raid. During the voyage this plan changed and it was decided that, after dropping the men off on Durian Island, the *Krait* would sail south and wait off Borneo. Then the drop-off point was changed to Pandjang Island.

The raiders were indeed dropped off there, and the *Krait* headed off towards Borneo. This was on 19 September, and on the following night the raiders started paddling towards Singapore, covering some ten miles before beaching for the day on Bulat Island. They spent the next night in a mangrove swamp being consumed by mosquitoes and on the next night, 23 September, they reached Dongas Island, from where the shipping in Singapore harbour was in plain sight – just eight miles away.

The original plan was to attack on the night of 26/27 September, but that was still three nights away and the temptation to attack at once was too great. They decided to attack at once, on the night of 24 September, and might have done so, but they were defeated by the strong tide and offshore currents. After five hours' paddling they gave up the struggle and went back to Dongas which, they now decided, was too far from the target to serve as the final position for the attack. Therefore, on the night of 25 September, they paddled halfway and landed on Subor Island. With time running out, and only four days left to rejoin the *Krait*, the attack went in on the following night, 26/27 September. It was aimed at all the anchorages with one canoe attacking the shipping in Keppel Harbour, another going in to Examination Anchorage and the last attacking shipping in the offshore roads opposite Pulau Bukum. It was decided that after the attack they should head at once for the rendezvous with *Krait*, with Davidson, in the best canoe, tasked to get there first and tell the *Krait* to wait if need be, at least until the night of 1 October.

Davidson and his no. 2, A B Falls, found no shipping in Keppel harbour but attached limpets to three ships in the roads. They completed their task by just after midnight and powered their way out to sea. Three hours later they heard the first explosion and from the number that followed they realised that the other raiders had also succeeded in placing their limpets. In all, the *Jaywick* raiders sank seven ships. Now they had to get away, with the Japanese on full alert and combing the islands and offshore waters in search of the attackers. However, the Japanese also suspected sabotage by local resistance groups and carried out a great number of executions and reprisals among the local Chinese population.

Davidson and Falls reached Batam Island, six miles from Singapore, by dawn. They hid their canoes and lay up during the day. The other two canoes had also got away, laying up on Dongas Island. They all pressed on for the next three nights, finally risking a daytime paddle in the hope of rejoining *Krait* on 1 October. When they got to the rendezvous off Pompong, *Krait* was not there.

The men then realised that they were in the wrong place and must make the right rendezvous by 3 October when *Krait* was due to make one last effort to pick them up. The men paddled to their new RV on 2 October and on the following day, just after dark, *Krait* reappeared and picked them up. *Krait* returned to Australia on 19 October, after a round trip of over 5,000 miles and having spent 33 days behind the Japanese lines. *Jaywick* was a highly successful attack, all the raiders returned and, thus encouraged, Lyon planned a return match in November 1944 – Operation *Rimau*.

This time the raiders would use submarines, HMS/M *Porpoise* to take them in and HMS/M *Tantalus* to bring them out. This was to be a much larger raid, employing over thirty men and a variety of craft including folboats and motor submersible canoes, or MSRs, craft popularly known as SBs (Sleeping Beauties) which were as yet unproven on operations. They were to prove useless.

The plan for *Rimau* was audacious, but too complicated. It required the *Porpoise* to sail up close to Singapore and then stop a Chinese trading junk, which the raiders would then take over for the next leg into Singapore harbour. They would then use the junk as their base for the canoe and MSR attack. No suitable vessel presented itself and they finally settled for a Malay *prahu*, which had no engine. This vessel, with the raiders embarked, was challenged by a Japanese patrol vessel outside Singapore and the raiders were forced to abandon it, and the MSRs, and make their escape in canoes. What happened after that is obscure and has only come to light gradually over the years since the end of the Second World War. From the moment the *Rimau* party left the *Porpoise*, none of them were seen alive again.

It appears that only hours before the raiders were due to put in their attack they were surprised on the island of Kasu, close to Singapore, by a boatload of Indonesians who reported their presence to the Japanese. All but seven raiders then left Kasu and paddled back to Merapas Island, while the raiders, using folboats and led by Ian Lyon, went into Singapore harbour and attached limpets to three ships. That done, they paddled back to the Riouw Straits and were surprised and attacked on 16 October by the Japanese. Four men were killed, one captured and two escaped to join the rest of their party on Merapas Island. The *Rimau* party stayed on Merapas until 4 November, when a party of Japanese soldiers landed and started to search the island. Fearing detection, the *Rimau* party engaged the enemy, killing the Japanese commander.

The Japanese withdrew, sent for reinforcements and attacked again next day. At least one *Rimau* raider was killed. The Japanese now mounted a major search of the surrounding islands, killing six of the *Rimau* raiders and capturing the survivors. Four men made an epic escape bid, paddling for over a thousand miles through the Indonesian islands to Romang Island, less than 500 miles from Australia. One man was murdered by the locals and another was killed by a shark and then the last canoe pair, Willersdorf and Pace, were picked up by the Japanese and sent to Singapore.

What happened then is rather better known. One of the *Rimau* raiders died in captivity, probably from wounds. The remainder, though clearly military personnel, were tried by a Japanese court martial and beheaded on a plot outside Changi in July 1945, barely a month before the ending of the war. The *Rimau* party was totally wiped out: ten were beheaded, one died in captivity, and six were killed in clashes with the enemy. As with the *Frankton* raiders three years before, their execution was a war crime – it was nothing short of murder. The Japanese, for all their protestations, were well aware of that fact, and these criminals made great efforts to conceal what they had done before they surrendered to the Allied armies.

The final underwater operation in the Far East was rather more successful. X-craft had been sent to the Far East in late 1944 and straightaway ran into the same opposition that had faced the Australian and British canoe raiders – the Americans did not want them there. The Pacific theatre had been an American lake since the Battle of Midway in 1942 and part from US Navy UDT teams, which had surveyed and cleared beaches ahead of the US Marines, the US Navy had made very little use of Special Forces. They had no time for small units or the notion of underwater attacks against Japanese merchant shipping or naval units by frogmen or X-craft.

Their main experience of small submarines had been when Japanese midget submarines attempted to attack Pearl Harbour in 1941, and the failure of that attempt convinced Admiral King, the head of the US Navy, that the British X-craft would be equally ineffective. The US commander in the Pacific, Admiral Nimitz, felt much the same way and refused to let the X-craft flotilla deploy for action.

However, the commander of the six-strong X-craft submarine flotilla was Captain 'Tiny' Fell, a man not easily discouraged. He flew from Australia to the US base at Subic Bay in the newly reconquered Philippines and had a long talk with the admiral commanding the US Submarine Fleet, James Fife. Fife quickly grasped that the X-craft were real submarines, that could go into places barred to larger craft and were therefore ideal for harbour raids. Captain Fell eventually discovered that the Americans were anxious to cut the submarine telephone cables connecting the Japanese bases in Hong Kong and Singapore.

This task seemed the ideal way to demonstrate the

capabilities of the X-craft and in early August 1945 the XE4 successfully located and cut the Singapore cable. Before that however, her sister craft XE3 had made an even more convincing demonstration of X-craft capability by entering Singapore harbour and sinking the Japanese cruiser *Takao,* an exploit for which two of her crew – Lieutenant Ian Fraser RNR and the diver, Leading Seaman Maginnis – were both awarded a very well-deserved Victoria Cross.

Operation *Struggle* began on 30 July 1945 when the XE3 slipped her moorings with the towing submarine, HMS/M *Stygian,* which had brought her up from Darwin on the north coast of Australia. During the tow, as in long-distance operations in the North Sea, the X-craft had been manned by a passage crew. The attack crew took over on the night of 30 July and set course for Singapore harbour, where they were due to put in an attack on the following day.

The *Takao* was a heavy cruiser mounting eight-inch guns and, since the British were in the process of launching Operation *Zipper,* the seaborne invasion of Malaya, it was considered desirable to sink or damage the *Takao* before she had any chance of attacking the troop transports or adding her heavy guns to those defending Singapore. The Second World War only had six weeks to run when XE3 ran into Singapore harbour, and *Zipper* never took place, but the crew of XE3 did not know that; they did know that if they were seen they would certainly be depth charged, and if they were captured they would probably be tortured and beheaded. Even at this late stage in the war the Japanese were routinely beheading shot-down aircraft crews, captured seamen and, in particular, any Special Force soldiers, like the *Rimau* canoeists, who fell into their hands.

To keep on schedule, XE3 made most of the journey up to Singapore on the surface, with Fraser picking his way carefully into the Singapore roads using landmarks and such buoys as were still in place. Singapore was a busy harbour and it was necessary to alter course several times to avoid enemy ships and patrol craft. Just before dawn on 31 July they were almost seen and forced to crash dive in shallow water, so shallow that the X-craft struck the bottom with considerable force. The craft then rose to a depth of some thirty feet and maintained that depth through several sharp course corrections until mid-morning when they passed under the harbour boom. It was just before 1300 hours when Fraser sighted the top masts of the *Takao* through the periscope.

The attackers were faced by a number of snags. Firstly, it was broad daylight and the harbour was buzzing with activity. Taking a quick look round after one snatched glimpse of the *Takao*, Fraser was alarmed to see the full lens of the periscope filled with the legs and boots of some Japanese seamen on a boat just thirty yards away, but, by some miracle, the Japanese failed to see the periscope jutting out of the water. Fraser made a careful approach to the *Takao*, lining up on the warship's forward turret and making as little use of the periscope as possible. As they drew closer it became apparent that the *Takao* was in very shallow water, too shallow, it seemed, for the X-craft to get underneath her and drop the casing charges. The bottom was shelving steadily to less than twenty feet of clear water and it is yet another miracle that they were not seen as they crept closer and closer until, with a definite clang, the bow of the X-craft struck the side of the enemy cruiser – in fifteen feet of water, about as much as there is in the deep end of an Olympic swimming pool.

Lieutenant Fraser did not lack nerve or professional skill. He now needed to get the XE3 at least parallel with the *Takao* in order to drop the main side charge effectively, but it transpired that the bow of the X-craft was caught under the hull of the cruiser and they could not move. It took a quarter of an hour of manoeuvring before she came free; this activity must have created disturbance on the surface, easily seen by any Japanese seaman looking over the side, but again XE3 was lucky.

Somewhat shaken, the crew took the X-craft out and, having caught their breath while sitting on the bottom, they came in again for a second attempt. The decision this time was to aim for the *Takao*'s engine room, and in mid-afternoon they were finally jammed in position under the cruiser. Fraser had not gone to all this trouble for nothing, and as well as the two hull charges he was also anxious to attack with limpet mines. This required the diver, Leading Seaman Maginnis, to exit the submarine through the Wet and Dry compartment and do the work on the cruiser's bottom. Even getting out was not easy, for the *Takao* had settled on top of the X-craft and there was so little distance between the hulls that the hatch could not be fully opened. Fortunately, Maginnis was a slender man and he managed to wriggle through the gap.

When he finally got out on the pressure hull it was well after 1500 hours, and here he found yet another snag. The *Takao* had not been in dry dock for some time and the bottom of her hull was a forest of weed and barnacles. Before any of the mines could be attached it would be necessary to hack and scrape all this growth away and clear a number of patches on the hull, right down to the bare metal, before the magnets on the limpet mines would grip. This took a full hour and Maginnis returned to the X-craft with hardly any air left in his tank and in a state of exhaustion. When he was back on board and the X-craft was ready to move, Fraser slipped the hull charges – and found that the starboard one would not budge. They tried and tried, again and again, to work it free, but it was hanging by a bolt and they could not clear it. This meant another job for Leading Seaman Maginnis.

Fraser knew that Maginnis had already done enough and suggested that he – Fraser – who had had diving training, should go out this time and clear the charge, but Maginnis insisted that it was his job and that he would do it. Half an hour after he had re-entered the X-craft Maginnis went out again, armed with an assortment of spanners, and after a few minutes of cursing and banging he managed to loosen the bolt and the charge dropped the few remaining feet to the floor of the harbour. They had now placed the main charges and the limpets; if they all went up, the *Takao* was finished, and all they had to do now was get away.

Engines were reversed and the X-craft slowly crept away into deeper water and set course for the Straits of Jahore and safety. They had been in an enemy harbour for nine hours and the air on the submarine was getting ever more foul. They also had difficulty in keeping their depth in patches of fresh water and actually broke surface when close to the boom, but finally, at 2100 hours, they were clear and able to surface, taking in great gulps of fresh air as the diesels powered them out to sea and back to their rendezvous with the *Stygian*. The charges under the *Takao* all went off, taking the bottom out of the ship, which was still lying on the bottom of Singapore harbour when British troops entered the city, unopposed, six weeks later.

And so, with this last successful operation – the destruction of an enemy cruiser in a well-defended harbour – the story of underwater and SBS warfare in the Second World War can be brought to a close. The six years of that war were the proving ground for all manner of raiders, above and under the waves. At no little cost in lives, these small units had played a major part in the Allied victory. Now they were to be disbanded and to a large extent forgotten, but their hard-won skills were too good to be set completely aside and before long many were to be revived and restored to their new custodians, the SBS units of the Royal Marines.

16

THE SBS IN THE POST-
WAR WORLD
1945–91

'The days of "private armies" are finished.'

The Globe and Laurel
Journal of the Royal Marines, 1947

Lord Louis Mountbatten's proposal that the Royal
Marines should retain three Commando units was both
the salvation of many wartime skills and the basis of the
modern SBS – the Special Boat Service. If the Royal
Marines were to become the repository of Britain's
amphibious skills, which, at least in theory, had been the
prime purpose of the Corps since the time it was created
in 1664 and a role pursued with even greater tenacity in
the present century, then skill in Commando tactics,
assault-craft handling and seaborne raids must be retained
and kept in good order.

This decision also meant that some form of SBS unit
was going to be necessary to handle the problems of beach
recce and obstacle clearance, which, even on a peacetime
landing exercise, could cause problems to the assault
landing craft or loss of life among the troops going ashore.
COPP and LCOCU might go, but their skills had to be
retained; the SBS was the unit chosen as the depository
for these techniques which became Royal Marine tasks at

the end of the Second World War, and have remained with the Corps ever since.

The first task after VJ Day was to pull all the relevant amphibious units together and have a sort-out, deciding what functions and equipment should be deployed to the new body, which assembled at Appledore in Devon, the wartime COPP base, at the end of 1945. Many of the HO ranks and reservists had already returned to civilian life, and the regular officers to their normal employment in the Army, Navy or Royal Marines. Tug Wilson, that pioneer canoe raider, returned from captivity and went back to the Royal Artillery, and most of the other Second World War veterans did the same; the war was over, and the time had come to get back to real soldiering.

No more than fifty men finally assembled at Appledore, mostly Marines who had served in COPP, in Courtney's SBS or the RMBPD, which was now commanded by Lieutenant Peter Davis DSC, an officer who had worked with irregular troops and Commando units in the islands of the Adriatic. 'Pug' Davis was to become the leader, and later the father figure of the modern SBS, though the entire force was under the command of Lieutenant Colonel Blondie Hasler. 'Pug' Davis transferred to a regular commission at the end of 1945, and spent most of his subsequent career in the SBS.

Hasler's first task was to draw up a blueprint for his new force – then languishing under the title of the Combined Operations Beach and Boat Section (COBBS) and he proposed that, rather than the diversity of tasks being allocated to a diversity of units, as in the recent war, COBBS should absorb the RM Boom Patrol Detachment and all the necessary amphibious functions should be contained in a single, well-trained force under Royal Marines command.

These skills were, broadly, beach recce, seaborne raids and sabotage. The Chariots had gone out of fashion and the X-craft had already been consigned to the breaker's yard, though one was retained for experimental purposes and was later consigned to the Submarine Museum at

Gosport, but the canoe, the scuba breathing set and the parachute all offered ways in which small units could penetrate the enemy defences along the coastline or in harbours.

Hasler thought in broad terms; his men would first of all be trained Commandos, skilled with a range of infantry weapons. They would be good swimmers, 'comfortable in the water', accustomed to using scuba equipment, handling small boats, working with the Royal Navy, especially with the submarine flotillas, and trained in escape and evasion, demolition, sabotage, night movement and parachuting, this last not merely on to land, but also into the sea . . . and at night. These were, and remain, the basic skills of the SC3 but others have been added over the years as the role of the Royal Marines has expanded. Modern SBS men are at home in the jungle and in the Arctic, and can use skis with the same facility as they use canoes.

'One point that has to be made,' says one former SBS officer, 'is that the SBS story is a constantly evolving one. Not only have tasks and equipment changed and advanced considerably: the attitude and quality of the men have changed also. My generation of SBS operators, working in the 1960s and 1970s, was quite different from Pug's, as the present generation is from mine. There have been constant improvements in fitness, intelligence, technical skills and professional attitude. I find it very refreshing to find a part of Britain that I can honestly say is getting better and about which I do not have to complain that it is not what it was like in my day.'

Hasler's proposals were accepted, and in August 1947 the new unit, just six Royal Marine officers, 25 NCOs and Marines and six naval ratings, arrived at the Royal Marines Barracks at Eastney, a bastion of the 'Sea Marines', to start training in their new role. The Corps at large was dubious about the entire Commando concept. The Royal Navy still had many large ships and it was felt by a number of the Royal Marines powers-that-be that the right rig and place for a Royal Marine was in best blues and white gear, guarding the keyboard on a battleship, not 'playing pongos' in a green beret, let alone poncing about in canoes. Fortunately for the good name and continued survival of the Royal Corps, these antique opinions were soon overcome and the modern Corps emerged from this time warp during the 1950s.

COBBS settled down to its new existence; training began in earnest and it attracted an adequate number of volunteers from the Corps. The trained men were soon being deployed in suitable tasks and in 1947, when 40 Commando were in Palestine in the final days of the British Mandate, the unit was joined by three COBBS divers under the command of Sergeant 'Sticks' Dodds, a former Royal Marines drummer, and tasked with searching for and removing limpet mines from British ships in Haifa, which had been placed by Israeli Irgun terrorists. Then COBBS had had yet another name change and became the Small Raids Wing (SRW) of the Amphibious School at Eastney, a place that was largely devoted to training landing-craft crews.

SRW training was directed only at trained Marines who had volunteered for this work and had passed stringent medical, swimming and aptitude tests. The medical included such tests as a heart examination after doing twenty standing jumps on and off the seat of a chair, and part of the swimming test included picking up a dozen metal balls from the deep end of a swimming pool in the course of one dive. Those accepted then went on the basic Swimmer Canoeist course for their SC3 qualification, a course which lasted some six months and covered scuba diving, canoeing, navigation, night work, escape and evasion, a parachute course at RAF Abingdon and a survival course.

However, apart from periodic deployment to places like Palestine, the SRW was mainly employed as part of the Corps' post-war recruiting drive, attending demonstrations and Navy Days to demonstrate either parachute skills or the mysteries of the frogman's craft. They also suffered losses, not least when four members of the SRW were drowned when the submarine *Affray* was lost in the Channel.

Then, in 1949, when Lieutenant Colonel 'Titch' Houghton – who had taken part in the 1942 Dieppe Raid and commanded 40 Commando in Palestine – was in charge of the Amphibious School, it was finally decided that the SRW should not merely be a training unit for special skills – it should be the base for an operational unit. Colonel Houghton was therefore ordered to form such a unit, to be entitled No. 1 SBS, for 'Special Boat Section', a name suggested by 'Pug' Davis. Just why the Corps decided to form an operational unit in 1950, after five years without one, is still a matter of speculation, but the renewed interest in special warfare, and the re-forming of the SAS in Malaya, may well have had something to do with it.

The final organisation was a Special Boat Company, comprising a Headquarters and five operational sections – later raised to six. No. 1 SBS was based at Eastney, 2 and 3 SBS were based in Germany and 4 and 5 SBS were units of the Royal Marines Forces Volunteer Reserve, later the RMR. The strength of the SBS was around sixty, all trained to at least SC3 standard, with higher qualifications for the officers and senior NCOs. There was then a small tiff between the Commandant General, Royal Marines, and the CO of the newly formed 21 SAS, a London territorial unit. The SAS officer complained that the name 'SBS' properly belonged to the SAS as the wartime SBS had been, at least for a time, part of the SAS and had worn the same cap badge and beret. The matter was settled amicably and the Royal Marines won.

The 3rd Commando Brigade was then in Malaya, which was in the grip of a communist-inspired guerilla war, and a number of SBS-trained ranks were sent to the Brigade, where their reconnaissance skills soon proved very useful on jungle patrols, though SBS sections were never used as separate units. No. 1 SBS remained in Eastney, but a second twelve-man SBS unit under Peter Davis was frequently deployed for recce operations on and along the Rhine as part of the Royal Navy Rhine Squadron. Then in 1950 the Korean War provided the Royal Marines and the SBS with the chance to show what they could do. This began in the autumn when General Douglas MacArthur, the American general commanding UN forces in Korea, decided to outflank the communist advance by landing the 1st Marine Division, United States Marine Corps, behind the enemy lines at Inchon.

Inchon was a major port, in a bay subject to forty-foot tides, so a prior recce seemed advisable. Since US UDT teams were not available and the USMC did not have a beach recce facility at this time, the task was delegated to a small part of Royal Marines from the British Far East Fleet under the command of Captain E G D Pounds, and therefore known as *Poundforce*. This volunteer force embarked on a British frigate, HMS *Whitesands Bay*, and went ashore at Inchon in small boats to recce the landing. Although they were detected and fired upon, one of the boats returning full of bullet holes, they delivered a promising report and the USMC landing went without a hitch.

Meanwhile, back in the UK, the Corps had been asked to supply the 1st Marine Division USMC with a reconnaissance and raiding force. This unit, a 200- later 300-strong Commando force, was raised at Stonehouse Barracks, Plymouth, by Lieutenant Colonel David Drysdale, and as 41(Independent) Commando Royal Marines it was to gain a US Presidential Unit Citation and a great reputation during the fighting in Korea. A number of the men in this unit were SBS-trained and, after converting to US weapons at the Marine Corps base at Camp McGill in Japan, they joined other 41 men from S Troop and the C and D rifle troops of 41 Commando. They then joined a US submarine, the USS *Perch*, which had had her torpedo tubes removed and converted to carry up to 110 raiders, and two US Assault Personnel destroyers, the USS *Bass* and the USS *Wantuck*, for a series of raids on the railroads that ran down the Korean coast. The SBS did not feature in Korea as a unit but 41

Commando contained many SBS men, including Sticks Dodds, Mac Hine MM and Kenneth 'Mick' Byrne.

On the first raid, anti-tank mines were laid under the railway track and a train destroyed, though one Marine was killed before the force withdrew. The Commandos then carried out two further raids, in early October, before withdrawing to join the 1st Marine Division for the epic march to and from the Chosin Reservoir. Then, in the spring of 1951, part of the unit – 'Charlie Force' under Captain F R D Pearce RM – was despatched to Yodo Island, sixty miles behind the North Korean lines, from where a number of raids in small boats and canoes were made on North Korean-held islands. More of 41 came up later; SBS-style canoe operations became common, and their area of operations was gradually extended.

B Troop took over Modo Island on 9 August and SBS observers from 41 directed naval gunfire from US destroyers on to targets on the mainland. At the end of August canoe patrols were made against Hodo Pando on the mainland in which two men, Lieutenant Harwood and Sergeant Barnes, were killed in a clash with a North Korean patrol. In some of these raids the British Marines were joined by men of the US UDT teams, now operating in Korean waters, and a number of canoe raids were made against various points on the North Korean coast. In Operation *Swan Song*, the unit's last attack in December 1951, two SBS men in a canoe, Lieutenant Walter and Sticks Dodds, made a successful attack on enemy shipping in the harbour at Changguok Hang. Sticks Dodds received the DSM for his part in these operations and Lieutenant Walter the DSC. During their fifteen months in Korea the unit had carried out eighteen raids on the enemy coast and taken part in the Chosin battle; they also convinced the USMC that they were not, as one US Marine put it, 'The only troops fighting this goddam war.' Thirty-one men of 41 Commando were killed or died of wounds during their time in Korea, two of them from the SBS, and the unit was finally disbanded in Plymouth in February 1952.

There were now five SBS units, three regular and two in the RMFVR. The City of London unit of the RMFVR included Marine Ned Sparks, Blondie Hasler's bo. 2 on the *Frankton* operation, now a London busman, who for many years laid the London Transport wreath at the Cenotaph on Remembrance Sunday. The SBS were seen as an integral part of the Royal Marines and represented the corps with great success on the annual 124-mile Devizes-to-Westminster canoe race, an exhausting event held each Easter and fraught with various hazards.

This race suffered from an absence of water on long sections of the canal course, which forced the participants to pick up their canoes and run. The 'Great Swan of Newbury', a large and ferocious bird that lurked in the lock cut, guarding her nest, would set about any canoeists foolish enough to paddle in, leaping on to the back of a canoe and beating the no. 2 about the head with her wings. This could be alarming and many canoes were overturned, but the Great Swan was only one of several local terrors. The next hazard was the steep, water-chute tunnel under Newbury mill, a short cut back to the canal but very narrow and endowed with a metal pipe which ran right across the tunnel halfway down. To avoid the pipe it was necessary to lean back hard in the canoe and those who did not know this – or had not been tipped off by the opposition – were often knocked unconscious and emerged at the bottom of the shaft with large bumps on their foreheads.

Men were sucked through lock sluices and spent days in terrible weather plugging on to the Thames and London. However, the SBS were soon putting up formidable times of well under twenty hours for the entire run and they became recognised – as they still are – as the crew to beat, though operational requirements have curtailed SBS participation in recent years. During the 1950s and 1960s the SBS dominated the Devizes-to-Westminster. Gillie Howe entered the race ten times and was in the winning crew five times. Other winners at that time were Tom Shenton, Stuart Syrad, David Mitchell,

Ted Tandy, Pinky White and Keith Aston. Tom Shenton and A K Alan Williams later canoed for Britain in the Olympic Games. Alan 'Ram' Seeger MC entered the race five times and came second five times.

The Devizes-to-Westminster was good training, a chance to test skills in planning and endurance, but there were also a number of clandestine operations abroad. In May 1952, an SBS party under Lieutenant H B Emslie MC flew to Tobruk and embarked on the submarine HMS/M *Teredo,* for a secret visit to the Egyptian port of Alexandria, where, or so it is supposed, they were to rescue King Farouk from the clutches of his ever-more mutinous soldiers. The SBS were to carry out the recce after which two British destroyers would go in and get the King and then transport him to safety in the Suez Canal Zone or Malta. It all sounds a little far-fetched, and it all went gloriously wrong.

No one was properly briefed and, when the submarine surfaced off Alexandria and the two SBS-manned canoes paddled into the harbour, no one was sure of what they were doing. Since Alexandria had been a British naval base until quite recently, it is hard to understand what an SBS recce hoped to achieve. One canoe, with Lieutenant Emslie and his no. 2, returned at dawn, but the second one returned without its swimmer, Sergeant Lofty Moorhouse. The submarine could not hang about offshore in daylight and when it reached the alternative rendezvous they found an Egyptian frigate on patrol and aircraft circling busily overhead. Meanwhile, Sergeant Moorhouse had been picked up by the Egyptian Navy, who found him outside the harbour, hanging on a buoy and telling some highly unlikely tale about having fallen off a fishing boat.

Egypt was then in the delicate process of divesting herself of British control and no one wanted any trouble, so the Egyptians found Sergeant Moorhouse a pair of trousers, took him to the Canal Zone and handed him back. A month later Colonel Nasser seized control of Egypt; King Farouk went into exile and, four years later, the British launched the notorious Suez operation of November 1956 to retake the Canal, an operation which, though a military success, was a political disaster.

Another, rather earlier, political disaster, though on a much smaller scale, was the *Ordzhonkidze* incident of April 1956, the last operational dive of that distinguished Second World War pioneer and frogman hero, Lieutenant Commander Buster Crabb. Like many good, brave men, Crabb found it very difficult to settle down in peace time – 'too bloody dull' being their usual explanation. He had tried finding an occupation that could utilise his diving skills and got involved in various Intelligence operations in Europe, but without achieving very much. He was also getting on a bit for underwater work and was 46, very unfit and very out of practice when, in April 1956, the two Russian Premiers, Kruschev and Bulganin, made an official visit to Britain, arriving at the Portsmouth Naval Base in a brand-new, *Sverdlov*-class cruiser, the *Ordzhon-kidze*.

At the end of the 1990s, after the recent collapse of the Soviet Empire, it is hard to recapture the depth of distrust that existed between the Soviet Union and the West in the 1950s, in the middle of the Cold War. Naval Intelligence believed, probably correctly, that the Russian politicians had decided to arrive in a cruiser and dock at Portsmouth, rather than flying in to Northholt or Heathrow, so that they could intimidate the British with this new and powerful class of warship – and the crew could do a spot of spying. British Naval Intelligence badly wanted to have a look at the bottom of the *Ordzhonkidze*, inspect any Asdic dome that the ship was equipped with and take a look at the propellers, a task that would, and certainly should, have fallen within the remit of the SBS.

The snag was the question of 'deniability'. The Soviets were both notoriously touchy and had the unfortunate knack of successfully inflating any incident that put the Western powers in a bad light. It would not be good if a British Marine frogman was caught close to the ship, or even seen swimming about under it . . . but if a civilian like Crabb were caught, this could be put down to private enterprise or simple curiosity – no one would believe it, of course, but faces could be saved. Besides, Buster Crabb knew the bottom hulls of ships better than any man alive and, if there was anything interesting under the *Ordzhonkidze,* he would swiftly spot it. Naval Intelligence duly approached Crabb and offered him a good sum to carry out this underwater inspection and, as Crabb needed the money, he agreed.

This was a dangerous assignment. Russian security around the ship was very tight and the possibility that they were also deploying underwater devices or frogmen to fend off just such a reconnaissance is highly probable. Crabb knew this, but was not deterred and on the afternoon of 17 April he checked into the Sally Port Hotel in old Portsmouth Two days later he left the hotel to carry out his mission. He was never seen alive again and his body, or part of it, was not found until a year later when it washed up in Langstone harbour, twelve miles away, still in its wet suit.

No one knows what happened to Commander Crabb. The best theory is that he drowned or suffered a heart attack, or fell victim to Oxygen Pete, but he was a very experienced diver and the notion that he was attacked and killed by Soviet frogmen remains a possibility. In any event, he disappeared. After his belongings were removed by some means from the Sally Port Hotel, the press became interested, probably because some of them had been tipped off about the operation by Soviet sympathisers in the Intelligence services. Commander Crabb was reported missing by the Admiralty on 29 April, the statement adding that he had been lost 'while carrying out a test dive', but by that time the fat was well and truly in the fire.

The matter was raised in the House of Commons and became the subject of furious exchanges between the Prime Minister, Anthony Eden, and the Leader of the Opposition, Hugh Gaitskill, who accused the Prime Minister of a 'grave blunder'. The Soviet Government now had their opening and delivered a formal protest, adding that a frogman *had* been spotted on 19 April, swimming between the *Ordzhonkidze* and one of her anchored escort destroyers. The Russian leaders then accused the British Government of spying and demanded an apology.

Meanwhile, Portsmouth harbour was being scoured for Crabb's body and when it could not be found the press began to speculate that he had been captured, taken back to Moscow and tortured in the Lubyianka prison by the KGB. Well, perhaps, but there is not evidence for that allegation. It would not have been impossible to take Crabb away and later return his body by submarine, but there is no evidence to support that theory either. Crabb was buried in Portsmouth Cathedral in 1957 and a large number of his former divers attended the funeral.

Britain's *annus horribilis* of 1956 concluded with Operation *Musketeer*, the Suez landings of 1956, when France and Britain attempted to retake the Canal Zone, which Colonel Nasser, with Russian backing and tacit American support, had nationalised in July. This was an airborne and amphibious operation, involving 3 Para and 3 Commando Brigade, which until Nasser seized the Canal were otherwise engaged fighting EOKA terrorists in Cyprus.

The SBS team tasked for *Musketeer* was No. 1 SBS, then based at the newly opened Amphibious Warfare Centre, Royal Marines, at Poole in Dorset. No. 1 SBS flew to Malta, where they were briefed for an operation in Alexandria with the job of destroying the anti-invasion boom the Egyptians had strung across the entrance to the harbour. The actual assault was made at Port Said, at the northern end of the Suez Canal, but it was widely believed that the Anglo-French forces would land at Alexandria and be reinforced there by the 10th Armoured Division, then based in Libya, which would join them for a drive on Cairo. Since the Anglo-French force had no intention of attacking Alexandria, this attempt on the boom was cancelled and No. 1 SBS returned to Poole.

The next SBS unit to get involved in *Musketeer* was No. 6 SBS, based in Malta with the 3rd Commando Brigade. This SBS unit was tasked to recce the Egyptian coast west of Port Said, but this task was cancelled when it was decided that the Commando Brigade should land on the beaches at Port Said itself, with a parachute drop by 3 Para to spearhead the attack and a helicopter assault by 45 Commando to back them up. No. 6 SBS sailed from Malta with the brigade and made their way ashore on 6 November, but the action was called off at the end of the day, after US and UN intervention, and Britain's humiliation was complete.

The Suez debacle did not end Britain's involvement in the Middle or Near East. During the latter half of the 1950s there was a small anti-guerilla campaign in Cyprus against the EOKA terrorists, who were hoping first to drive out the British and then attach Cyprus to Greece, a move viewed with horror by the large Turkish minority. This campaign ended in 1960 when the island was granted independence as a republic, but this happy state did not last. The Greeks continued to harass the Turks; eventually the Turkish Army invaded from the mainland and today, more than thirty years after the British left Cyprus, it remains partitioned. Here again the SBS involvement at unit level was small and mainly restricted to beach surveys, locating points where arms might be brought ashore for the EOKA terrorists, but many SBS corporals and sergeants served with the Commando units, where their well-honed reconnaissance skills were highly valued.

In the 1960s the Royal Marines Commandos and the SBS were engaged in two further campaigns, in the Crown Colony of Aden in the Arabian Gulf, where 45 Commando was committed to fighting in the Radfan mountains, and in the streets of Aden Town. An SBS officer takes up their story at this point:

When I joined the SBS in 1959 they were not really operations-oriented. Their only permitted purpose was to keep on top of their basic skills but the likelihood of their being able to put them into practice was far from certain. While SC ranks in Commando units were involved in operations, the SBS in formed sub-units seldom were. Our role was very much linked to amphibious warfare – as indeed were the Commandos – but while it was deemed OK to use the Commandos in Korea or as infantry battalions in imperial policing tasks, there seemed to be a reluctance to use the SBS in a similar war.

6 SBS were in Malta in the 1960s, with a detachment in Bahrain, and 2 SBS were in Singapore, and a small HQ and Training section was based at Poole, as was 1 SBS. The OC was 'Pug' Davies, and Hamish Emslie was the training officer. At this time we began to make contact with the SAS and several of our officers – Ram Seegar was one of the first – went on an SAS Combat Survival course, which in those days was for officers only.

This course combined escape and evasion with resistance to interrogation and was a new and controversial discipline. It was a good course, very realistic and some of the lessons learned there were soon being pushed at Poole . . . so, in quite a small way, the SBS began to play a part in covert warfare.

The SBS then became involved in Borneo, in the long campaign against Indonesian military incursions during what came to be known as the Borneo Confrontation. This began in 1961, when Indonesia advanced a claim to Sarawak, Sabah and Brunei, three territories in the north of the island of Borneo – or Kalimantan as the Indonesians call it – which on gaining independence from Britain were about to join the Malaysian Federation. The Indonesians wanted to incorporate them into Kalimantan and sent strong forces across the border to coerce the inhabitants into agreement. These incursions were met head on by Gurkhas, Royal Marines from 40 and 42 Commandos and the men of various British country regiments. This was a jungle war, fought by small parties in very difficult terrain, and soon came to involve reconnaissance parties of the SAS and the SBS.

Another SBS officer takes up the story:

When Confrontation started there was a resident SBS section, 2 SBS in Singapore under Major David Mitchell and 1 SBS under Seeger was in the UK. 1 SBS was moved in great secrecy from the UK to Singapore, where Seeger went to 40 Commando as a company commander, and Chris Roberts took over 1 SBS, the two units being under the command of David Mitchell. The SBS then got a proper role, involving waterborne reconnaissance by raiding craft and canoe around the Indonesian islands. The SAS were involved with the indigenous Border Scouts and cross-border reconnaissance. There is one outstanding story of two SBS swimmers who were not picked up as planned at the RV and, rather than swimming back to shore and risk compromising the operation, they swam out to sea, reasoning that the recovery craft would eventually find them. Luckily it did.

The SBS did well in the Borneo Confrontation. Ram Seeger got an MC for attacking an Indonesian jungle camp and then was part of the team setting up the Malaysian Special Forces. Gillie Howe got an MM and Gillie, Pinky White and Ted Tandy all did well serving as 40 Commando's combat tracker team.

The two SBS units assembled in Singapore were despatched in small parties to undertake long-range recce and river-patrol tasks with the Commando units in the field. Borneo is both mountainous and well supplied with both swamp and jungle. The easiest way to get about is down the numerous fast-flowing rivers on which canoes and ridged assault boats could operate if in skilled hands. The jungle is not for everyone, as this SBS account reveals:

You asked about jungle soldiering. Well, I very much enjoyed the jungle. It is excessive and overpowering and I prefer other kinds of wilderness, but it is very satisfying to operate in. If you are efficient and well organised and follow good procedures you will fare well. If you are not, and don't, you won't! The jungle is made for small-unit patrolling. Because of the closeness of the vegetation you have to move in single file for close control, and this is obviously easier with a four-man patrol than with a company of eighty men, the number that could be taken across the border when we were hitting the Indonesian bases.

You are also very safe in the jungle providing you keep off tracks (obvious ambush sites), keep quiet, no talking or hacking at the vegetation, and keep moving. You are always in danger if you stop to 'basha-up' early or leave late the next day, for an enemy on your trail can catch up and hit you when you are relaxed or preoccupied with packing up or getting under way. Movement by night in the jungle is virtually impossible, at least without torches – I have tried it, but it was too black and I got nowhere.

Helicopters give useful support, but finding suitable and secure sites is not easy. In Borneo we would use helicopters to move between our front-line bases but patrol out from these on foot. We seldom went out for more than a week, firstly because it wasn't necessary as you can get to most parts of your area of responsibility in that time and also because carrying more than a week's food supply made your load too heavy. Essential survival items, map, compass, pills, emergency food, went in your pockets; water and ammunition and other essential gear on your belt and the rest in your pack. Your pocket gear always stayed on your person as did, whenever possible, your belt kit – and if you took the belt off you kept it within arm's reach. I remember being told of an SAS patrol that got caught in a fire fight and split up. One man ended up on his own without his pack or belt and with nothing in his pockets and had great difficulty getting back over the border to safety. His efforts were hailed as very gallant and determined, which may be so, but I felt he had also been very careless and inefficient.

The Borneo Confrontation ended Britain's role as an 'Imperial Policeman', and when it was over the SBS, like the SAS, had to find new roles and fresh fields for endeavour. These came in areas which are increasingly shrouded in mystery: the fight against the IRA in Northern Ireland and against terrorists generally, wherever they can be found. The SBS had also to put up a stiff fight for operational employment with the powers that be in the Admiralty. Counterterrorism has been absorbing an increasing amount of attention in the SAS and the Royal Marines since the 1950s, usually during anti-terrorist campaigns in the old Empire or as part of that military task usually known as 'giving aid to the civil power'. Apart from Northern Ireland, this kind of activity has largely come to an end and been replaced by an increasing emphasis on counterterrorism.

Special Force units are increasingly reluctant to talk about their counterterrorist role, training or operations. It is claimed, rightly or wrongly, by some of their senior officers, that if the terrorist opposition know too much about Special Force methods, say from studying the mass of books on Special Force operations currently on the market, they will be able to calculate the response to one of their outrages and cause casualties to the Special Force troops tasked to deal with them.

Well, maybe. Since terrorism rarely achieves anything worthwhile, one might doubt if any terrorist is that intelligent, but since, again rightly or wrongly, Special Force units, in the UK, are the bodies tasked with handling terrorist attacks, it would be as well to give this claim the benefit of the doubt. That said, Britain is a democracy, free speech is at least part of what democracy; is all about and, within reason, the taxpayer has a right to know what the people he is paying are up to.

Apart from the police, Special Branch and the Intelligence agencies, Britain has two anti-terrorist forces, the Special Air Service Regiment and the Special Boat Service, Royal Marines. Both of these units come under the command of the director, Special Forces, who is usually a senior Army officer. Their anti-terrorist roles come under two broad headings, clandestine and covert. These words are often used interchangeably but their meanings are different. Clandestine means being unnoticed by the enemy – perhaps by relying on darkness or natural cover for concealment – a well-honed SBS skill and essential for surveillance operations. The second – covert – means being noticed by the enemy but not being recognised as hostile, and some SBS operations, in Northern Ireland or on the liner *QE2*, fall into this category.

One of the most bizarre incidents in the SBS's post-war career began in New York on 17 May 1972, when an unidentified caller rang in to say that bombs had been planted on board the liner *QE2*, then in mid-Atlantic with a full complement of passengers, and would go off with *Titanic*-style results unless the caller received a ransom of $350,000 – which, even in 1972, was a fairly trifling sum.

This threat had to be taken seriously and, though a discreet and detailed search by the crew of the ship revealed nothing, it was decided that a search and bomb-disposal team, drawn from the SBS and SAS, along with Captain Robert Williams of the Royal Army Ordnance Corps bomb-disposal unit, should parachute into the Atlantic, 1,500 miles west of England, board the liner and carry out a professional search. Captain Williams had never parachuted before but the others, Sergeant Oliver from the SAS and two SBS men, Lieutenant Richard Clifford and Corporal Tom Jones, were experienced parachutists. While Cunard continued to negotiate with the 'terrorist', or more correctly the blackmailer, plans went ahead for the drop.

An RAF Hercules took the team to mid-Atlantic, located the *QE2*, and dropped the men in a tight group close to the ship, under the bemused eyes of the passengers. A lifeboat picked the men out of the water; the ship was searched from stem to stern and nothing dangerous was found. No more was heard of the ransom demand and the bomb-disposal team had a wonderful time for the rest of the voyage to Southampton, entertained royally by passengers and crew alike.

This was not the last time the SBS became involved with the *QE2*. Some time later it was decided that, in view of a threatened incident, a team of SBS should again be placed on the liner. This operation was leaked to the press, perhaps in the hope that the publicity itself would act as a deterrent. The third incident came when a large group of Jewish passengers chartered the liner for a cruise to Israel and the SBS were again asked to provide security. This operation was successful and not without its lighter moments, as the following account reveals:

> After the previous incident, we decided to insert our men in three parties of which only one would be obvious. Three men therefore went on board as part of the normal security staff, but looking suitably military. The next three went on as part of the ship's entertainment team, and they may have been spotted fairly quickly, perhaps because they were not gay. The last team were three officers who went on board as passengers, accompanied by their wives – and had a high old time out and back, all at Cunard's expense – but they would have been on the spot and ready to go if anyone had turned nasty.

The SBS has remained a part of the Royal Marines and enjoys a major role, like beach recce, in Commando-landing operations. However, since the end of the 1960s, counterterrorism in its various forms has taken up a large amount of training and a certain amount of operational time. Broadly speaking, the SAS look after land-based terrorism, and the SBS take care of matters at sea or on board ship – which would include a ship tied up to a dock and the North Sea oil rigs. In this respect, the SBS support unit is Commachio Troop, Royal Marines, a special unit tasked with protecting the hundred-plus oil rigs in the North Sea and nuclear material and plants in the UK.

This process, and several more connected with Northern Ireland, began in 1970, when, with the end of the Borneo Confrontation and the withdrawal from Suez, the SBS sections were all withdrawn to Poole. By this time, notably during Confrontation, the SBS had started to work with the SAS and with overseas units like the Australian and New Zealand SAS.

The SBS sections at Poole were mustered into a new SB Company under the command of Major Stuart Syrad MC, with Captain Ram Seegar as operations officer. The SBS then began to break away from their traditional role as a unit dedicated to tasks within the remit of the corps, taking a path which would make them one of the few units placed directly under NATO command and then, as today, under the command of the director, Special Forces, rather than under the commandant general, Royal Marines.

Northern Ireland was then at its bloody worst and, in an effort to get better intelligence about IRA activity, a secret unit, the MRF (Military Reaction Force) was formed in the Province, a unit that later became rather better known as the 14th Intelligence Company. The men in this force were drawn from units then serving in Northern Ireland, and this included four SBS men who had been on attachment to 40 Commando. SBS men, mature and self-confident, are ideal for such covert work and a steady supply of men went from Poole for service with these units, where they did extremely well. The movement to expand SBS activities into clandestine spheres had started but almost immediately the SB Company hit another problem.

In the mid-1970s the North Sea oil boom was at its height and high wages were on offer for any trained diver seeking employment. As a result, the SBS began to lose many of its best NCOs. 'What I wanted out of life,' one told the author, 'was either excitement or money. I'd trade money for a good exciting time, but other than Northern Ireland there was not much on, and the oil companies were offering a fortune, so . . .'

The SBS lost a lot of good men to the oil companies and had to resist pressure from on high to reduce standards in order to keep the numbers up. The answer was to provide the men with more realistic training and an actual, active role. During the rest of the decade, the SBS became ever more closely involved with the SAS, took on a number of covert or clandestine roles in Northern Ireland, and added Arctic warfare training to their impressive list of maritime skills, by working in Norway with 45 Commando. The SBS also raised a reaction team to deal with maritime hijacks, like the *Achille Lauro* affair in the Mediterranean, and for seizing North Sea oil rigs. Then in 1982 came the Falkands War.

The Falkands War took Britain and most of the world outside Argentina by surprise. Landing without warning on 1 April, Argentine forces quickly overran the islands and, though the Royal Marines of Naval Party 8901, which garrisoned the islands and the outpost of South Georgia, put up a stout resistance, it was all over within a day and the Argentines settled down to enjoy their new conquest – the renamed *Islas Malvinas*. A month later the British struck back, and within two months the Argentine forces on the Falkland Islands had been comprehensively defeated.

The reconquest of the Falkland Islands began with Operation *Paraquat*, a preliminary attack on the Argentine troops in the dependency of South Georgia. This was handled by M Company of 42 Commando under Major Guy Sheridan, D Squadron 22 SAS under Major Cedric Delves, and 2 SBS from Poole. This force joined HMS *Endurance* on 12 April, eleven days after the Argentine invasion, and *Endurance*, accompanied by the destroyer HMS *Antrim*, the frigate HMS *Plymouth* and the RFA tanker *Tidespring*, closed the coast of South Georgia.

The plan was to put the SBS ashore first, to recce the port at Grytviken, after which M Company and the SAS would mount an assault. The SAS then decided that they wanted to be lifted by helicopter to the Fortuna glacier, from where they would recce other settlements on the island. From that moment on, matters started to go awry, not least because of the weather. The SAS team, established on the blizzard-swept glacier, had to be withdrawn; two precious helicopters were lost in the process and it is a miracle that no one was killed or the defenders alerted.

Meanwhile, some of the SBS had got ashore at Hound Bay by helicopter but then the weather closed in and their support ship, HMS *Endurance*, had to withdraw. Attempts to put the rest of the SBS ashore in inflatables succeeded and, with the entire team ashore, they split into three patrols and set out on the recce. Little was achieved, for the weather was terrible and after three chilly days ashore the men were extracted by helicopter.

On 25 April, the weather having moderated, Major Sheridan, the Force commander, tried again. An SBS recce team was flown in from HMS *Antrim* and on its way back to the ship the helicopter attacked an Argentine submarine, the *Santa Fée*, which it caught on the surface and damaged with rockets. The *Santa Fée* limped back to Grytviken, and it was decided to follow up this success with an immediate assault. The problem now was that the main force, M Company, 42 Commando, was on *Tidespring*, and not immediately available. Sheridan therefore mustered all the men he could find, SBS, SAS and ten Royal Marines from the detachment on HMS *Antrim*, put them ashore by helicopter close to Grytviken – and overran the Argentine position without a shot being fired. Round One to the Royal Marines, and a great fillip to morale in the Task Force now approaching San Carlos Water, the landing area in the Falkland Islands.

The biggest worry for the Force commanders on Operation *Corporate*, the retaking of the Falkland Islands, was a shortage of air support. With two small carriers available, they had exactly eighteen Harrier jets to protect the Task Force and provide air support to the troops ashore. The Argentines had their entire airforce, equipped with Mirage and Dagger fighter bombers, Exocet missiles and ground-attack Pucara fighters equipped with fragmentation bombs and napalm. Most of these were based on the Argentine mainland and had 400 miles of sea to cross on the way to the islands, but there were some aircraft, including Pucaras, on the airfield at Stanley, the island capital, and on Pebble Island, off the coast of West Falkland. Eliminating these aircraft was one of the preliminary tasks for the Special Force units now descending on the Falklands, and the aircraft on Pebble Island were wiped out in an SAS raid.

The number of Special Force units on the Falkands was now increasing as 2 SBS and 3 SBS embarked on HMS *Hermes* and 6 SBS were on the submarine HMS/M *Conqueror*, which later sank the Argentine cruiser *General Belgrano*. What the SBS were doing on *Conqueror* remains a mystery, but there is speculation that they were landed in Argentina to recce the coastal airfields and give the Task Force early warning of impending Argentine air strikes.

Beach recce on the Falkland Islands was less essential, for that task had been executed some years previously by Major Euan Southby-Tailyour RM. During his time in command of the Falklands garrison, Southby-Tailyour had made a careful study of all the Falkland beaches that could be used to land an invading force, and his carefully marked maps and charts were an invaluable aid to the Landing Force cmmander, Brigadier Julian Thompson of 3 Commando Brigade. There remained the matter of locating and estimating the strength of the Argentine defenders on or near these beaches, especially around San Carlos. This task was deputed to the SBS, who sent parties ashore to see where the Argentines were, and what they were up to.

The task was carried out successfully and without much difficulty after several two-man teams were inserted at Ajax Bay, Johnson Hill and in San Carlos, though poor weather made life uncomfortable and two SBS corporals caused a certain amount of anxiety when they became separated from their patrol. The two men in question stayed under cover, carried on with their tasks, and were picked up, safe and well if somewhat dishevelled, after a full week ashore. The Landing Force were now approaching the islands and the main task for the SBS was to eliminate the Argentine position on Fanning Head at the entrance to San Carlos Water, a position which commanded the landing area. This position was shelled by HMS *Antrim* and, when the SBS were in position, Captain Rod Bell RM, who spoke Spanish, summoned the defenders to surrender. They refused and were attacked with machine-gun and mortar fire before the assault went in. 'We gave them every chance to surrender, but they wouldn't and after that, well, it was a duck shoot,' said a Royal Marine officer later. A dozen Argentine soldiers were killed and the rest taken prisoner.

While the two landing brigades, 3rd Commando and 5 Airborne, were advancing on Stanley, the SBS were retained on board the Fleet for anti-shipping operations from helicopters, the role of Brigade Patrol Company being filled by the Royal Marines Mountain and Arctic Warfare Cadre, which had a full course complement almost trained when the Argentines invaded the islands, and used the war as the final exercise. A party of 2 SBS did land on the Argentine fishing vessel *Narwhal*, operating inside the Security Zone around the islands. On the last night of the war, when 2 Para were taking Wireless Ridge, the SBS and the SAS launched a joint operation in Stanley harbour, which they attempted to enter in rigid raiding craft. On the way in, the craft were illuminated by lights from the Argentine hospital ship *Bahia Paraiso* and swept with fire from all sides of the harbour. By some chance – and the presence of the hospital ship may have helped – this fire was inaccurate and only three men were slightly wounded before the party were able to withdraw into the darkness. So the war ended, successfully both for the British Government and the military and navel units that took part in it. It would be eight years before such an opportunity arose again.

The Gulf War of 1990–91 did not provide Special Forces with many opportunities for action, though it produced several best-selling books including *Bravo Two Zero*, about an SAS patrol. General Schwartzkopf, the American commander of the UN Forces in the Gulf, was not an admirer of Special Forces, having observed them without much favour in Vietnam. 'Weirdos and snake eaters, who get into trouble and expect other people to get them out of it' is allegedly one of his comments. This view may have changed slightly after the SBS took on the task of severing some of the Iraqi High Command's communication cables.

Without secure, reliable communications, command cannot function and these cables linked Saddam Hussein's various headquarters in Iraq with his forward troops in Kuwait City. He also had wireless and satellite communication, but these land cables were secure from interference and vital to his strategy. An SBS team of 36 men flew into Iraq by helicopter on the night of 22 January 1991, landed thirty miles west of Baghdad, located the buried cables, dug down and cut them along a fifty-metre stretch and then placed explosives and booby traps in position before withdrawing. The entire operation took less than two hours; the party withdrew without loss; and a piece of cable, decorated with ribbons, was presented to General Schwartzkopf, 'With the compliments of the Royal Marines'. At the end of the Gulf War, when the Iraqis had been driven from Kuwait City, the SBS were among the first Coalition troops to return, flying in by helicopter and roping down on to the roof of the British Embassy. After that, their task completed, the SBS returned to Poole and took up whatever task awaited them.

A new task for the SBS is action in support of the Customs and Excise officers tackling the drugs trade. British Customs and Excise officers are not armed and there is no provision for weapons on their seagoing cutters, yet, increasingly, the drug smugglers are carrying arms and seem prepared to use them.

'As a result,' says one Customs and Excise officer, 'we have started to call on the SBS whenever we think it likely that the gang we are going to intercept, who are often on large craft far out in the Atlantic – and carrying cargo worth millions if they can get it ashore – are going to make a fight of it. I have to say that the sudden arrival of a heavily armed section of SBS Marines in their hard-hitting gear certainly makes the druggies think again. So far, we have not had much real trouble, but the way things are going it cannot be too long before we actually see gun fights on the high seas . . . and, if, or rather when, that happens, it will be a great comfort to have the SBS on our side.'

A curtain must now fall across the SBS. This book has traced their actions from the beaches of Rhodes via a hundred other beaches and a great deal of dangerous coastal waters, all the way from the warm Mediterranean to the freezing waters of Norway and the South Atlantic. It has shown how a dozen varied skills have been mustered into the armoury of one small Royal Marine unit. It has covered the activities of a dozen varied units and a few hundred brave and resourceful men, for the SBS has never been large, and it is not likely that it will ever get any larger than it is today, when fewer than 200 Royal Marines wear the SC badge on their sleeves.

Skill and cunning rather than brute force and ignorance have always been the watchwords of the SBS, and so they must remain, as we move from those sunny, freewheeling and difficult days of the Second World War into the dark and doubtful tasks that will await the SBS in the next century.

SELECT BIBLIOGRAPHY

Courtney, G B lieutenant-Colonel, *SBS in World War Two: the Special Boat Section of the Army Commandos*, Hale, 1983.

Kofod-Hansen, Mogens, *'Andy': A Portrait of Major Anders Lassen*, ??.

Langley, Mike, *Anders Lassen VC MC of the SAS*, Grafton Books, 1990.

Lassen, Suzanne, *Anders Lassen VC*, Frederick Muller, 1965.

Lodwick, John, *The Filibusters: The Story of the Special Boat Service*, Methuen, 1947.

Lucas-Phillips, C E Major General, *Cockleshell Heroes*, Pan Books, 1957.

Neillands, Robin, *The Raiders: The Army Commandos, 1940–1943*, Weidenfeld and Nicolson, 1989.

Neillands, Robin, *By Sea and Land: The Royal Marines Commandos, 1942–1982*, Weidenfeld and Nicolson, 1987.

Neillands, Robin, *In the Combat Zone: The Story of Special Forces*, Weidenfeld and Nicolson, 1997.

De Norman, Roderick and Neillands, Robin, *D-Day, 1944: Voices from Normandy*, Weidenfeld and Nicolson, 1993.

Parker, John, *SBS: The Inside Story of the Special Boat Service*. Headline, 1997.

Pitt, Barrie, *Special Boat Squadron: The Story of the SBS in the Mediterranean*, Century Publishing, 1983.

Royal Marines Historical Society, *41 Independent Commando, RM, Korea, 1950–52*, Copenhagen, 1955.

Seligman, Adrian, *War in the Islands*, Allan Sutton, 1996.

Thompson, Julian, Major General, *War Behind Enemy Lines*, Sidgwick and Jackson and the Imperial War Museum, 1998.

Waldron, Tom and Gleeson, James, *The Frogmen: The Story of Wartime Underwater Operations*, Pan Books, 1954.

Warner, Philip, *The Special Boat Squadron*, Sphere Books, 1983.